CISTERCIAN STUDIES SERIES: NUMBER ONE HUNDRED-THREE

D0901696

TOWARD AN INTEGRATED HUMANITY:
THOMAS MERTON'S JOURNEY

CISTERCIAN STUDIES SERIES: NUMBER ONE HUNDRED-THREE

TOWARD AN INTEGRATED HUMANITY:
THOMAS MERTON'S JOURNEY

Edited by
M. Basil Pennington, ocso

CISTERCIAN PUBLICATIONS
KALAMAZOO, MICHIGAN
1988

Available in Britain and Europe from
A. R. Mowbray & Co. Ltd.
St Thomas House Becket Street
Oxford OX1 1SJ

Available elsewhere (including Canada) from

Cistercian Publications
WMU Station
Kalamazoo, Michigan 49008

The work of Cistercian Publications is made possible in part by support from Western Michigan University to the Institute of Cistercian Studies.

Library of Congress Cataloging-in-Publication Data:

Toward an integrated humanity.

  (Cistercian studies series; no. 103)
  1. Merton, Thomas, 1915–1968. I. Pennington, M.
Basil. II. Series.
BX4705.M542T69   1987   271'.125'024   87–15870
ISBN 0–87907–403–5 (cased)
ISBN 0–87907–603–8 (perfect)

Typeset by Solaris Press
Printed and bound in the United States of America.

Contents

Introduction

When an idealistic young man, Thomas Merton or any other, enters a monastery he 'leaves the world behind'. And all too soon he discovers that in the gate with him has snuck the biggest problem he had had 'out in the world' — himself, with a memory well stored and ready to play reruns. The first paper in this collection, and indeed in one way or another all the papers in this collection, look at how Merton dealt with this problem and its many ramifications as he pursued his ideal.

Merton was a man of extraordinary genius with a background that enabled him to develop that genius in many extraordinary ways. When he set his heart on becoming a Cistercian he applied his genius to that task. As the Second Vatican Council would later counsel, one of the steps on the way to becoming a good Cistercian is to get in touch with the spirit and aims of the founders of the Order. In a way that would be impossible for most aspirants, Merton spent many long hours during his first years in the monastery with the Cistercian Fathers in their writings. At that time these

1

Fathers were available for the most part only in the intimidating volumes complied by P. J. Migne: small print, large tomes, all in Latin.

Young Frater Louis, as Merton was then called, came to love these Fathers and their Latin, He tried hard in later years to get his choir novices, who supposedly had the necessary Latin background, to delve into the richness that lay hidden in the Fathers' writings. He was remarkably successful in some cases. Yet he did admit the need to make the Fathers' thought available in translation if more than a chosen few were to be exposed to it. He did a certain amount of translating himself in those early days, and later encouraged others, including myself.

It was out of a shared vision, responding to an admitted need, that we obtained the sponsorship of the American abbots to begin Cistercian Publications in 1968. Its primary purpose was to publish the Cistercian Fathers in English, although other useful studies were also to be published. Father Louis offered one of his own manuscripts: *The Climate of Monastic Prayer.* This was an expansion of an essay he had written some years earlier. It included some material from an earlier unpublished manuscript, and in its later sections some very deep sharing of Merton's own prayer experience, cast in the impersonal mode in accord with his usual reticence in regard to his own prayer life.

Before that volume, our first, was published, Father Louis completed his journey. In fact, the last card I received from him, which arrived on the same day as the terrible news from Bangkok, was about the galleys for that book. The publications project went on, receiving continuing inspiration and, I am sure, heavenly benediction from our departed brother.

In order to encourage competent scholars outside the Order to contribute to our undertaking, I invited a dozen 'Cistercian-ologists' to a meeting at Spencer Abbey in September 1969. We ended up with about twenty-five participants—and many more wanting to come. One of the participants, Dr John Sommerfeldt, offered to host the next conference at Western Michigan University, in conjunction with their annual International Medieval Studies Congress. Thus began the annual Cistercian Studies Conferences at Kalamazoo.

In part because of the conjunction with the Medieval Conference, but also in part because of the emphasis of our publishing project on the writings of our twelfth-century Cistercian Fathers, most of the papers offered at these annual conferences have dealt with the Cistercian fact as it existed in those formative times. The conferences have been rich inter-disciplinary events bringing together scholars from the fields of theology, liturgy, history, philosophy, art, music, linguistics and others. Effort has been put forth to make the rich Cistercian heritage more actual by celebrations of liturgy, prayer workshops and presentations on Cistercian life today. Over the years a few papers have been offered concerning the renewal taking place among contemporary Cistercians. In 1985 I attempted to organize a Merton session, with little success. I gave the only Merton paper that year, but it was one of the best attended sessions at our conference. It encouraged me to make a greater effort toward the 1986 conference.

Such was the response this time that we decided to have a related but relatively independent Merton Conference, concurrant with the regular Cistercian Studies Conference. The plan provided space for the contributors, each a well-known Merton scholar in his own right, to interact and contribute to each others' scholarly pursuits. Presentations were offered, open to the general public, and drew sizeable crowds. The conference opened with a sung Latin mass—Merton loved the Latin and continued to use it most of the time in his last years. There was also a workshop to introduce that simple form of contemplative prayer fostered by Father Louis, Centering Prayer.

This volume brings together most of the papers which were presented at the conference and some others which were offered by scholars invited to the confernece. In the appendix there is a brief presentation of Centering Prayer drawn from the workshop.

There is a remarkable complementarity among the papers which meld together to present a well-rounded presentation of Merton's multi-faceted journey toward the realization of his ever cherished ideal. I will not endeavor to summarize them here, or even offer a synthesis, but perhaps offer a single guiding thought.

Father Louis was an existentialist in the best sense of the word. For him, what was important was what is — not thoughts or ideas, but reality experienced. He came into a real experience of God, of his relation with God, and of the absolute centrality of this relationship. In that experience he resolved to let go of all to be to God. Yet some consciousness of his oneness with all others — this Gospel truth is too clearly stated to be ignored — confronted him. He struggled with this until the breakthrough on the corner of Fourth and Walnut. (One of the many things that must keep Tom laughing in heaven is the sight of fervent Merton pilgrims wandering down Fourth in search of the famous corner — and their eventual shock when they discover it is now Fourth and Mohammed Ali! How he must love that!) With this Louisville experience came the freedom and the necessity to be to all. Still struggle — now because of the institution within which he lived and the formation it sought to impose, one that does not flow from a deeper contemplative insight, from a powerful grasp of reality.

I think it is necessary to see all Thomas Merton wrote before and after this experience in the light of the absence or presence of it. Obviously, it is not a question of an absolute black and white. What broke forth in a hymn of thanksgiving that day was always there within and, in subtle and not so subtle ways, had its impact on the man, monk and writer. Before that day he knew by faith and concept the reality of his solidarity — as do most of us. After that experience he had to struggle continually against the weight of his previous formation in the Cistercian Trappists. But a very profound shift in consciousness had taken place and it radically effected the course of his development and orientation.

The reality of his solidarity with every other man, woman, and child on this planet meant that he could in no way attempt to be to God without his fellow humans. As long as any one of them was held back by unfreedoms that chained, such as those most blatantly present in racial prejudice expressed in segregation, he had to anguish over them and, in accord with his vocation as a monk and writer, he had to pray and speak out for the conversion which would bring freedom.

Merton came to know, in the way that only profound enlightened experience can teach, that he could never again seek to close out anyone in the world and seek to be to God without them. We are all in this together. There is but one humanity to the Father in Christ. There is no other way to be truly to God. There is no other way to be. All attempts at being without God and without every other human person are illusion.

The journey to full human integration is what life is all about for Thomas Merton, for any monk or nun, for any Christian, for any human being. We have in Thomas Merton, monk, Christian, man, a marvelously inspiring guide and companion for the journey, just because he was so truly human, so deeply Christian, and so much the monk—the man for every man and woman.

Victor A. Kramer

Literary Patterns in The Sign of Jonas: Tension Between Monk and Man of Letters

THOMAS MERTON'S JOURNAL *The Sign of Jonas* is a record of his growing awareness of what it means to be a monk, yet beyond that the text suggests what it means to be so while also a writer. Merton's journal records various attempts to minimize an awareness of his incipient vocation as a man of letters, but finally the journal becomes a documentation of that very awareness. This early journal, then, might be described as the history of a man of letters *malgré lui*. Merton apparently chose the title *The Sign of Jonas* because for him it signified a generation which did not understand God, while it also was a sign of resurrection, especially the power of Christ's resurrection for Christians. This sign also has a special application for monks who have heard the call to obey God, and specifically for Merton who found the years 1949–1952 especially difficult in terms of his vocation. Having spent a decade at Gethsemani; penned books which brought him recognition as an artist; and then finding himself ordained in 1949, yet unsure of how he would best fulfill a vocation which seemed to demand some combination of roles as monk and writer, Merton recorded in his 'journal' an answer for himself, but also paradoxically for his readers.

Another Merton book, written just before *Jonas*, is Merton's history of the Cistercians, the final section of which, 'Paradisus Claustralis', is a meditation about Cistercian common life. There Merton celebrates the life he personally felt to be intoxicating. That history, *The Waters of Siloe*, was finished just as Merton started *Jonas*. At that time, for him, monastic life seemed to be intoxicating, a life wherein love of God and others demanded self-effacement, but a life where such love brought peace unknown in other circumstances. Thus while *The Waters of Siloe* provides a sometimes romantic overview of the history and development of the Trappists, it is as well Merton's personal meditation on some of the mysteries of the contemplative life. *Siloe* also shares characteristics with other books which Merton wrote during this early period and helps us to understand why for him a monastic life made good sense. Yet for someone with a mind and heart as active as Merton such an historical method could only reveal one facet of his interests. His own inner struggles, questions about what it meant for *him* to be a monk were to be recorded in another manner. The journal *The Sign of Jonas* offers evidence of this and is perhaps the best way to understand Merton as a writer during the years immediately after *Seven Storey Mountain* was written. His title suggests the fundamental paradox which he felt about a developing career as writer and contemplative, and the writing reflects many personal doubts, questions, and investigations. In the published journal we also clearly see many of his doubts about how best he could write. The subject matter for *The Sign of Jonas*, therefore, might be described as a short history in the life of one Cistercian. It is a personal history about the difficulties and pleasures of being a writer.

In *Jonas*, dated from December of 1946 to July of 1952, Merton provides a specific record of his development as a monk, as priest *and* writer. The book is deceptively simple in appearance, but just as with *The Seven Storey Mountain*, upon examination it proves to be carefully orchestrated. The journal entries document Merton's success as a monk and show him examining issues (literary, personal, contemporary) which he finds of value in his developing spiritual life. Just like Jonas in the belly of the whale, he saw his life formed by divine providence. In this journal his job became one of organizing journal entries which were faithful to that experience, but also a book which dramatized God's providence and the mystery of that encounter with God — rather than just a particular writer-monk's actions, thoughts, and meditations.

Basic to the literary structure here is the tension which makes the writer so unhappy (as he travels toward his 'destiny in the belly of paradox') but which also allows him to produce a beautifully contrived journal. The book is arranged in six parts and also includes prologue and epilogue. In this essay I trace some of the basic literary patterns of paradox which contribute to the success of this book.

In the prologue, 'Journey to Nineveh' Merton examines the paradox, not just of his life, but of the fact that his journal records 'a rare and unusual moment in the history of one particular monastery'.[1] What he realizes is that the phenomenon of extreme change at Gethsemani was something which suddenly occurred 'without anybody's foreseeing it and without anyone making any logical attempt to control it' (p. 5). The six major units of text, arranged chronologically, are Merton's confession (and *apologia*) about how he had contrived to seek control over his life during these years, while gradually he was able to conclude that the secret both for being a successful writer, as well as a good monk, was acceptance of one's place within a particular monastery. Thus, Merton's use of his own experience (like Thoreau in *Walden* who sees such a necessity because he happens to know himself best, but also like Henry Adams whose third-person narrator envisions himself as symbol for all who have lived through similar difficulties) allows the writer to demonstrate archetypal events.

The journal *Jonas* includes eight parts. Its six major divisions are united by the prologue and epilogue. Part One begins exactly five years after Merton had come to the Abbey — toward the end of the period of simple vows, and as he 'was making up his mind to take solemn vows and stay in the monastery for good'. Subsequent sections are about steps taken toward ordination, and his first years as a priest. Merton also records facts about his personal loneliness and spiritual aridity experienced in 1949 and 1950. The final major portion of the journal covers a longer time period than any of the others. In that concluding division Merton explains how he found a new kind of spiritual peace during the Christmas season of 1950. His excerpts from the remaining eighteen months, or so, reflect a new found peace.

The Sign of Jonas is cumulatively a demonstration that internal observation and celebration of mystery can be built upon the simplest most ordinary kinds of circumstances; obliquely it is a demonstration that it is possible to be a man of letters even while swallowed in the belly of the whale. But the real question for Father Louis was what kind of writing to do? Merton is literally in the process of dying unto a new life, but part of that very process is in his writing, while part of the fun remains in telling about it. By giving birth unto words, the old self dies; at one point he writes:

> It is sometime in June. At a rough guess, I think it is June 13 which may or may not be the feast of Saint Anthony of Padua. In any case every day is the same for me because I have become very different from what I used to be. The man who began this journal is dead, just as the man who finished *The Seven Storey Mountain* when this journal began was also dead, and what is more the man who was the central figure in *The Seven Storey Mountain* was dead over and over. And now that all these men are dead, it is sufficient for me to say so on paper and I think I will have ended up by forgetting them. (p. 328)

In the prologue to his book Merton set the scene for his dying through words by insisting that these journal entries are his ideas:

> I have attempted to convey something of a monk's spiritual life and of his thoughts, not in the language of speculation but in terms of personal experience. This is always a little hazardous because it means leaving the sure, plain path of

an accepted terminology and traveling in byways of poetry
and intuition. (p.8)

His journal succeeds as a work of art precisely because he allows
the reader to glimpse the difficulties which *he* experienced; tension is usually apparent, but Merton does not linger with par-
ticulars which were disturbing. Above all, what this monk-writer
has to learn is that he must accept appointed tasks as they are
given. Ultimately the reader comes to perceive that maybe this
writer could never fully understand why he was asked, under the
special circumstances of life at Gethsemani, to be a writer. *The
Sign of Jonas* is especially valuable therefore, because, in addition to being a record of Merton's activities during the years of
preparation for the priesthood and just after, it also treats
(sometimes indirectly) the question of literary vocation.

In the six major parts we would, perhaps, at first expect Merton to be concerned mostly with matters of spiritual conse-
quence. What he cumulatively demonstrates is that the tension
caused by his desire to write, and also requests by his Abbot
Frederic that he write often seemed problematic. However, he
learned that there is 'nothing to prevent a monk from praying
even while he writes a book' (p. 15).

Merton's frequent questions about what it means to be a
writer are crucial; and ultimately *Jonas* becomes a record of his
working out an accomodation with the vocation of writer. We
recall, that at first Merton thought that it might have been ad-
vantageous had he not been asked to write, but *Jonas*
demonstrates that he fast came to the realization that his earlier
'lamentations' about an obligatory writing job had been foolish.
Many entries indicate that he earlier believed that he needed to
cease writing for he felt he could be a better contemplative
without the distractions of preparing books for the press. Yet he
had been told by his superiors to go on writing and he eventually
understood that he was 'to go on trying to learn to write under
the strange conditions imposed by Cistercian life'. It is also clear
from these journal entries that he also remained ambitious about
being a good writer. Thus he indicates he was dissatisfied with a

recently completed book about Mother Berkmans because it seemed too verbose and throughout *Jonas* it is quite clear that Merton admires other writers. Without a doubt he too wants to write well. Perhaps the fact that he included such references within this published journal indicates that he felt he had not attained the level of artistic proficiency he desired. References to T. S. Elliot, Rilke, and Dylan Thomas are typical of his self-criticism. He qualifies by adding:

> I am not talking about grammar and syntax, but about having something to say and saying it in sentences that are not half dead. Saint Paul and Saint Ignatius Martyr did not bother about grammar but they certainly knew how to write.
>
> Imperfection is the penalty of rushing into print.

What he implies is that he needs to find ways to be more concerned about good writing while less concerned about a public and literary production. He knows, as he puts it just a few pages later, 'the chief thing that has struck me today is that I still have my fingers too much in the running of my own life'. He then notes he should remember many souls are dependent upon his writing. What the writing might bring the writer should, he realizes, remain secondary.

Merton uses a journal format as a way of showing that he has finally found his vocation as contemplative, without ceasing to be concerned about his responsibilities as writer. The result is a book which documents how he found his way toward God through the writing. In his introduction to the first major section, 'Solemn Profession', he notes 'There is nothing to prevent a monk from praying, even while he writes a book'. However he adds, "This discovery did not come to me until I finally resigned myself to being a writer, and found out that the job had one big compensation: it brought me solitude." His job as a writer in this book became to show how he *gradually* came to such a realization. Throughout the journal he holds the reader's suspense. Thus early, 'February 10, Lent', he writes

> I went and talked over the whole business of my vocation again with Father Abbot and he assured me once again, patiently,

that everything was quite all right and that this was where I belonged. In my bones I know that he is quite right and that I am a fool. And yet, on the surface, everything seems to be all wrong. As usual, I am making too much fuss about it. (p. 26)

As a strategy for the way a reader will be drawn into this book, such expression of doubt works well. Merton will hold our subsequent attention through other reports of the *apparent* dilemma of being a writer-contemplative. Thus on March 8, he notes:

I continue writing this journal under obedience to Dom Gildas, in spite of my personal disinclination to go on with it. It is sufficient to have the matter decided by a director. If it is tedious to keep a journal, it is still more tedious to keep wondering whether or not I ought to give the thing up. I do not know whether it will give glory to God: but my writing of it has been disinfected by obedience. I need no longer apologize either to God or to myself for keeping a journal. (p. 27)

But as we move with him, to, and through the text which moves toward solemn profession, the mood changes. By April 1st while the Abbot General is visiting, Merton can assure us that

Dom Dominique said, first of all, that he was very pleased with my writing, although he did not understand the poems. He told me emphatically — in fact it was the most emphatic thing he said, and the only thing that seemed like an official pronouncement, an *ex cathedra* fulmination — that it was good and even necessary for me to go on writing. He said specialists were needed in the Order — writers, liturgists, canonists, theologians. If I had been trained in a certain profession, I should make use of my training. In any case, he concluded, it was a matter of obedience. (p. 35)

But, of course, this is what concerned him most. He did not want to be a 'specialist' working in what seemed like a factory which would turn out monastic literature. And a month later, more doubts. Perhaps he is writing too much:

Today I got two new jobs. Father Abbot gave me the notes that Father Alberic was working on, for the revised edition of his history of the Order. Then I am to write a new postulant's guide. That means I now have no less than twelve jobs in various stages of completion. . . . (p. 45)

And there were still more temptations:

I have also been thinking of a Spanish-English edition of the *Dark Night of the Soul,* with a preface and commentary. Somewhere I have a few notes I scraped together for a life of Father Joseph Cassant. And on top of all that Reverend Father speaks of a new critical Latin edition of Saint Bernard for 1953. That last one is definitely beyond me. (p. 46)

In October of 1947, he reports he has not yet resolved his dilemma. Reading other monks who have suggestions to make only makes it more difficult to know what he might do:

When I first looked into the pages of 'The Dedicated Life and Poetry' by Patrice de la Tour du Pin and saw so many words like 'solitude' and 'virginity,' I became extremely interested. But on reading it more carefully it began to depress me a little. Clever and obscure language in a context that I do not quite grasp — all the traditional formulas of the contemplative life transplanted into a garden of flowers that are no longer any fun for me . . . I am living on the inside of a wall where such metaphors have ceased to make an impression. Dedication, for us, is not romance, it is routine.
    Yet perhaps if I paid more attention to Patrice de la Tour du Pin I might discover something quite the way he does. (p. 70)

Merton seems to realize that he needs a method of his own, something other than routine. It is not an accident that this opening section ends with a consideration of Cistercian architecture, and question of style:

How shall we build a beautiful monastery according to the style of some past age and according to the rules of a dead tradition? Thus we make the problem not only infinitely complicated but we make it, in fact, unsolvable. Because a dead style is dead. And the reason why it is dead is that the motives and the circumstances that once gave it life have ceased to exist. (p. 56)

We remember Merton wrote the same thing about his life. What we will witness in *The Sign of Jonas* is the literal building of a personal style — as the more predictable and conventional elements are eliminated.

In subsequent sections (Part two is the 'Death of an Abbot', but also the time of admitted self-satisfaction with being 'an author' after *The Seven Storey Mountain* was published) Merton structures observations around the tension of his love of God and (while he has a hard time admitting it) his pleasure in realizing he *is* 'an author'. It does not seem an accident that this part of the book begins with allusions both to T. S. Eliot and St. John of the Cross. In the second major section, 'Death of an Abbot', its arrangement is such that discussion of writing is minimized; yet the ending is especially interesting for Merton continues to wonder if his writing has any value at all:

Sooner or later the world must burn, and all things in it — all the books, the cloister together with the brothel, Fra Angelico together with the Lucky Strike ads which I haven't seen for seven years because I don't remember seeing one in Louisville. Sooner or later it will all be consumed by fire and nobody will be left. . . .
And here I sit writing a diary. (p. 122)

Nevertheless he repeats himself:

. . . sooner or later the world must burn — and *The Seven Storey Mountain* and *Figures for an Apocalypse.*

And Merton, the journal writer, can write about what he is thinking day by day:

And I have several times thought how at the last Day I am likely to be one of the ten most abjectly humiliated sinners in the history of the world, but it will be my joy, and it will fill me with love, and I will fly like an arrow to take a back seat very far in the back where the last shall be first. . . .

Now it is a toss-up whether I should ask Reverend Father to give me another and fatter book to fill with *Journal,* for we have been talking about my writing less. In fact, I have begun to tell him all about my temptations to become a Carthusian and he says he doesn't see why things can't be fixed up right here. (p. 123)

Merton leaves the reader hanging — in suspense. (Of course, we know he will ask for more blank pages, and we will be allowed to keep on reading.)

In Parts three, four and five difficulties about writing are one of the motifs which unite Merton's journal. It is ironic that through writing he deals with the problems of writing; yet in retrospect, how could it be otherwise with visits by Evelyn Waugh, and letters from Robert Giroux, and James Laughlin and projects, projects, projects? Reading Kenneth Patchen; talking to Naomi Burton; analyzing a passage from Rilke — all these things are indications both that Merton could not deny he got his fuel from contact with things and persons literary, yet he also had to ask questions about how his own method as a writer worked. How for example, could Rilke insist that 'to people who do not know me, I cannot possibly write,' Merton wonders? 'Is this last sentence true of me? No! I write for a hundred thousand people who do not know me', says Merton. More significantly, he immediately adds 'but I am not writing for them'. This is the real paradox of a book which is first for the writer but also for a public. The journal entries of *The Sign of Jonas* are often extremely private, yet Merton also admits he realizes they will most likely be published.

In the third section, called 'Major Orders', Merton gives more glimpses of a monk at work — the fun of writing, but also the difficulties he is experiencing:

Yesterday when I had to do a prefatory note for *The Waters of Siloe,* it went like a breeze. I had six pages done in an hour and a half, and time to spare to write to Bob Giroux before the end of work. And besides that I had taken time out to read a long letter from Laughlin and another from Sister Thérèse.

I had been thinking of tearing up *The Cloud and the Fire* for a long time. I haven't done that, exactly, but I have simply stuffed it into an envelope, plans and all, and reconsidered what it was I was supposed to start.

About *The Cloud and the Fire* — I have in mind something that needs ot be done some day: the dogmatic essentials of mystical theology, based on tradition, and delivered in the context and atmosphere of Scripture and the liturgy. In other words a mystical theology that is not a mere catalogue of 'experiences' . . . and this is what I seem to be incapable of writing at the moment. (p. 160–161)

Of course, ironically, what he could write was this very record or writing down what he could not. His real job is to make all this interesting enough to keep readers reading. What can one do when one of the facts to be faced is that systematic theology is *not* easy?

I wonder how many plans I have made for this book, *The School of the Spirit*? Perhaps six — including the ones I made for it when it was called *The Cloud and the Fire.* So I sit at the typewriter with my fingers all wound up in a cat's cradle of strings, overwhelmed with the sense of my own stupidity, and surrounded by not one but a multitude of literary dilemmas. (p. 178)

As Merton documents his steps toward ordination in subsequent parts of the book, he emphasizes the idea that perhaps he must try to be more systematic in his study of theology; yet (ironically) the more he studies, the more he comes also to realize that he will have to do whatever he does *alone.* Maybe that is why he overwhelms us (and himself as a potential scholar) with the facts of what must be studied:

Fillion, a Scripture scholar whom I am appointed to read, encourages young priests to study Hebrew, Greek, Aramaic, Itala, Arabic, Syriac, Assyrian, Ethiopian, Coptic, Armenian, Persian, Slavonic, Gothic, and the three main Egyptian dialects, namely Sahidic (spoken at Thebes), Fayoumic (spoken at the oasis of Fayoum), and Memphitic (spoken at Memphis) etc. . . . . When you have mastered all this you will be able to elucidate the ivy passage in Jonas, for instance, and you will come to the conclusion that Jonas in Nineveh sat under a castor oil plant (ivy) and became attached to its shade.

On the whole, I think Saint Teresa's interpretation of Jonas's ivy is more interesting, and she didn't know one word of Egyptian either. (pp. 219–220)

Fillion the scholar seems to be having an effect on Merton just the opposite from what one might expect; thus:

The Abbé Fillion has written a book that is in some ways strange. However, it is very good — especially for someone like myself — to read, under obedience, a book that I would not otherwise have touched with a ten-foot pole. And now although I still think some of his notions are funny, I have conceived a real affection for Fillion. . . .

This paradigm for the monk-writer insists that a monk-scholar must intimately know the geography of the Holy Land, and Merton finally quips:

Since I have a vow of stability, geography has more or less ceased to interest me — except when I think we are going to start a new foundation somewhere.

Which is to say his real interest is not abstract geography, but his inner experience, and to get to that contemplative awareness one must first confront one's doubts, fears, and questions. What is documented, is that to be a true solitary is *not* to be separated from others. Just the opposite; solitude brings union. But this writer first has to learn that he will probably never be a writer who produces systematic abstract tracts. Instead, he will lead others precisely by recording his own experiences in the desert, or in the belly of the whale.

In the final section we see the writer moving more toward an acceptance of his role as writer while also serving as master of scholastics, and still more importantly being a monk in a particular place. Yet even then Merton was reading (p. 305); making poetic observations about a Negro with his junk wagon in Louisville (p. 308); working on the manuscript of *Bread in the Wilderness* (p. 313); recalling Thoreau (p. 316) and the memories of that same junk wagon (p. 317); noting Gertrude Stein (p. 320). All these things conspire to give him material for his journal. All these thing are gifts. All are to be enjoyed, and that means writing.

The final section, entitled 'The Sign of Jonas', deals explicitly with Merton's realization that his 'new desert' is compassion.

> What is my new desert? The name of it is *compassion*. There is no wilderness so terrible, so beautiful, so arid and so fruitful as the wilderness of compassion. It is the only desert that shall truly flourish like the lily. It shall become a pool. (p.334)

Usually as the journal progresses, Merton records the fact that he knows that it will be through personal experience that he will refine his abilities as a writer; his job will be to accent *his* quiet.

The passage about Jonas and the whale prepares us for the ending of the book; it pulls many of the themes together. Merton is writing about himself and for others.

> It is the whale we cherish. Jonas swims abandoned in the heart of the sea. But it is the whale that must die. Jonas is immortal. If we do not remember to distinguish between them, and if we prefer the whale and do not take Jonas out of the ocean, the inevitable will come to pass. The whale and the prophet will soon come around and meet again in their wanderings, and once again the whale will swallow the prophet. Life will be swallowed again in death and its last state will be worse than the first.

We must get Jonas out of the whale and the whale must die at a time when Jonas is in the clear, busy with his orisons, clothed and in his right mind, free, holy and walking on the shore. Such is the meaning of the desire for death that comes in the sane night, the peace that finds us for a moment in clarity, walking by the light of the stars, raised to God's connatural shore, dryshod in the heavenly country, in a rare moment of intelligence. (p. 341)

There are many levels of concern in *Jonas,* and Merton indicates that particular writers focus on different levels of reality; one of the most important facts of *The Sign of Jonas* is how it reveals this writer sorting out various possibilities. Sometimes this is implicit (by the materials included) and sometimes it is explicit.

The epilogue, 'Fire Watch, July 4, 1952', a long prose-poem, which grows naturally out of the preceding sections — which more and more stress the need to accept what one is given with all its particularity — is Merton's celebration of the beauty of night watch duty. It is appropriate that the end of the preceding section, six, is Merton's report of going to Louisville to become a U. S. citizen. The Independence Day song which follows is a celebration through which now as priest (yet also as an unseen man of letters always gaining more material) he can breathe life into a poem which documents the mystery of God's presence in the middle of a strange place on a hot July night. Merton walks about the place of his God-given and paradoxical literary entrapment. This place is both the ironic source of Merton's inspiration, and the documentation of the mystery of finding oneself in darkness. This is a process which Merton also gradually realized could never be completed.

Jonas ultimately focuses on what Merton calls his second level, the depth of darkness which he says is apparent when one closes one's eyes to troubles apparent on the surface. This is especially true of the conclusion of the book, 'Fire Watch, July 4, 1952', an excellent example of Merton's focus.

This concluding meditation is a lyrical description of the writer's actual movements as a night watchman when he moves

from place to place within the monastery, yet on another level it
is metaphor for Merton's vocation, and acceptance of that vocation. As we move with him through the various physical levels of
the monastery, and finally to the spire (and his awareness of the
transcendent) we come to understand that it is only through a
familiarity with this world that anyone can move toward the
transcendent. For this writer, then, the human element is *always*
there. He stresses the fact that for him God is not easily found in
abstruse theology, or by scholarly methods, but through simple
living:

> Around one corner is a hole in the wall with a vat where they
> stew fruit. Under this vat Dom Frederic told me to burn all the
> letters that were in the pigeonholes of the rooms where he had
> been Prior. Around another corner is an old furnace where I
> burned the rest of the papers from the same room. . . .
>
> Then suddenly, after the old brooding catacomb, you hit
> something dizzy and new: the kitchen, painted by the brother
> novices, each wall in a different color. Some of the monks com-
> plained of the different colored walls, but a watchman has no
> opinions. There is tile under the shining vats and Scripture
> close to the ceiling: 'Little children, love one another!' (p. 351)

This tour through the monastery is Merton's metaphorical answer
to many of the questions which he has raised throughout the entire text. All of a sudden everything seems to be falling into
place — not that it is explained; rather its mystery can now be accepted. One learns to live in the present, and one stops thinking
about the past. And as the tour proceeds it becomes clearer and
clearer that while many questions will never be answered, one accepts one's place right now:

> With my feet on the floor I waxed when I was a
> postulant, I ask these useless questions. With my hand on
> the key by the door to the tribune, where I first heard the
> monks chanting the psalms, I do not wait for an answer,
> because I have begun to realize You never answer when I
> expect.

The third room of the library is called hell. It is divided up by wallboard partitions into four small sections full of condemned books. The partitions are hung with American flags and pictures of Dom Edmond Obrecht. I thread my way through this unbelievable maze to the second room of the library, where the retreatants used to sit and mop their brows and listen to sermons. (p. 358)

Questions arrive, assume their actuality, and also disappear. In this hour I shall cease to ask them, and silence shall be my answer. (p. 361)

As the writer continues, he speaks to his God, with whom paradoxically he knows there can be no complete dialogue:

The marriage of souls in concepts is mostly an illusion. Thoughts which travel outward bring back reports of You from outward things: but a dialogue with You, uttered through the world, always ends by being a dialogue with my own reflection in the stream of time. With You there is no dialogue unless You choose a mountain and circle it with cloud and print Your words in fire upon the mind of Moses. What was delivered to Moses on tables of stone, as the fruit of lightning and thunder, is now more thoroughly born in our own souls as quietly as the breath of our own being.

The hand lies open. The heart is dumb. The soul that held my substance together, like a hard gem in the hollow of my own power, will one day totally give in.

Although I see the stars, I no longer pretend to know them. Although I have walked in those woods, how can I claim to love them? One by one I shall forget the names of individual things. (p. 361)

We ask, as Merton does: is one of the basic points stressed in *Jonas* that real unity with God comes only through contact with the world, and with others; is it only through such contact that one is saved? I believe Merton is coming to such a conclusion. In a passage toward the very end of this text he muses about the prayers of those who are in the world, and his relationship to them as a writer:

I am beginning to believe that perhaps the only, or at least
the quickest way, I shall become a saint is by virtue of the
desires of many good people in America that I should
become one. Last night I dreamt I was telling several other
monks, 'I shall be a saint,' and they did not seem to question me. Furthermore, I believed it myself. If I do become
one — (I shall) — it will be because of the prayers of other
people who, though they are better than I am, still want me
to pray for them. Perhaps I am called upon to objectify the
truth that America, for all its evil, is innocent and somehow
ignorantly holy. (p. 323)

It is ironic that Merton should have such a dream because in fact he is
literally saved by his readers. In a way his journal, done in obedience — and not contemplative prayer or systematic theology
— became his objectification of the truth that America is innocent
and holy.

As Merton later developed as a writer, the simplicity of levels of
depth, an illusion of life separated into strands, became ever more
unsatisfying for him. As the literary career progressed, he assumed
the responsibility of drawing more and more connections between
the quiet of his monastery and the troubled surface of the world
which at this particular time he chose to ignore. (What immediately
sets a journal of more than a decade later, *Conjectures of a Guilty
Bystander,* apart from *The Sign of Jonas* is its systematic concern with
contemporary problems. In *Conjectures,* Merton makes connections
between what he observes in his reading, thinking, and prayer, with
the contemporary world. That is still another story.)

The Sign of Jonas is, perhaps, most importantly Merton's journal of his acceptance of a dual vocation. It is the record of someone
gradually coming to the realization that not only had he not been in
control of his life as he moved through Gethsemani, but ironically he
would never be in control of such a deep mystery. His job as a writer
was to accept what God asked him to do; and what that meant for
him was that he finally wrote about the difficulty of writing and admitted he was not different than many other writers who first have to
deal with themselves.

When we study the early books of Merton, it is as if there are two completely different facets to Father Louis. One is that man of "projects" who will write sucessful books, usually restrospective ones, such as *The Seven Storey Mountain* and *The Waters of Siloe,* or theoretical ones like *The Ascent to Truth.* The other facet is that much more private and imaginative Merton who will continue to look, question, and wonder—more often than not about himself. Such is the Merton who evolves in *The Sign of Jonas.* This does not mean that he is writing about himself as a personality; it means paradoxically that he has to learn to efface himself—at least in some ways—by writing about himself. In so doing he became a man of letters despite himself.

Georgia State University
Atlanta, Georgia

NOTE—Literary Patterns in *The Sign of Jonas*

[1]*The Sign of Jonas* (New York: Harcourt Brace. 1953) p. 3. All subsequent references are noted parenthetically.

Thomas P. McDonnell

Why Evelyn Waugh Worried About Merton's Prose

T HE NOVELIST EVELYN WAUGH was such a complete master of English prose, perhaps its most accomplished practitioner in our century, that he could well have worried about anyone's prose style, let alone that of a Trappist monk writing from a monastery in the knobbed hills of eastern Kentucky. Still the late Thomas Merton was good enough at writing such reams of acceptable American prose as to have stacked up a formidable shelf of spiritual writing before he was through—and, as everyone knows, somewhat before his time, at 53, by accidental death in Bangkok. The fact remains, however, that the great English novelist was worrying about Merton's prose style long before that tragic and untoward occurrence.

It was Evelyn Waugh himself who prepared the British edition of *The Seven Storey Mountain* (1948) for publication by Hollis & Carter under the title *Elected Silence*—a phrase taken from the first line of Gerard Manley Hopkins' 'The Habit of Perfection'. The first serious biography of the monk, Monica

25

Furlong's *Merton* (1980), consistently refers to Waugh's version as an abridged edition of *The Seven Storey Mountain;* but it is not an abridged edition and was not prepared as such by Waugh, at least not in the sense that an abridgement is a deliberate shortening of text for both editorial and marketing reasons. One abridges *War and Peace,* for example, but not *A Farewell to Arms.* Waugh happened simply to be better at his job than were the American editors—or editor—of Merton's unexpectedly popular first prose work. In short, Waugh's preoccupation with style was something that did not in turn preoccupy Merton's American editor to any discernible extent.

There is cogent evidence to support this contention in the entry for August 28, 1948, from *The Diaries of Evelyn Waugh:*[1] 'Tom Burns gave me the enthralling task of cutting the redundancies and solecisms out of Tom Merton's *Seven Storey Mountain.* This took a week and resulted in what should be a fine thin volume'. The second sentence, of course, is obviously in Waugh's ironic mode. So it was a case of Waugh's conscientious editing on behalf of English prose that resulted in the so-called abridgement and not any planned intent to amend the sacred text itself. Since the British edition is generally unavailable in this country, one cannot readily estimate whether Waugh's 'fine thin volume' is an improvement over the original manuscript. It may be improved English, no doubt, but not necessarily better Merton.

Moreover, it is almost shocking to have to say that Thomas Merton was not that slovenly a writer, not by any account, but he did not have the finesse or the elegance that Waugh could master in any given sentence or paragraph through any number of pages. By elegance, however, one should not take to mean an indulgence of mere ornamentation for its own sake. Elegance is simply a subtle and uniquely recognizable cadence of the mind that is intellectually satisfying and even delightful in itself. The formation of Evelyn Waugh's prose style seems as natural and unforced as dew condensed from the morning air, fresh and incandescent on a well-groomed English lawn. He was clearly a master of the language and therefore anybody's tutor in that regard.

It is important to understand Evelyn Waugh if we are to gain anything at all from his attitude on the prose of Thomas Merton. Waugh had a very penetrating type of mind. For example, in his great war trilogy and masterpiece, *Sword of Honour* (1961), he had a perception of World War II that no other novelist, major or minor, has yet managed to handle with equal adroitness or with anywhere near his degree of awareness concerning the political realities at stake. He had also the type of mind that provoked in him a well-oiled capacity to write some of the most amusing letters in the language. Again, it is important to remember that Waugh was dealing with the young monk from a clearly superior attitude. His mind was as lively as Merton's, surely, and much more fastidious.

Curiously enough, Waugh seldom faulted writers in public whom he hastened to correct in the privacy of the letters. He once wrote to fellow-novelist Graham Greene to say that in the just published *The End of the Affair* (1951), Greene had used the word 'cornice' when he clearly meant 'buttress', and the correction was duly noted in a subsequent edition. He advised the American novelist of manners, Louis Auchincloss, on the misuse of the word 'mutual,' describing it as a tricky term that is 'best left alone if you aren't happy about its precise meaning'. He was also compelled to remind his favorite and liveliest correspondent, the British novelist Nancy Mitford, that 'nobody' and 'each' take singular verb forms. And even though Waugh considered himself 'a bully and a scold' in these matters, he also presumed that writers themselves must somehow care about the craft they had chosen to practice in public.

So when it came to the prose of the monk Thomas Merton, the English master did not hold back or show any hint of the deference he usually extended to the various religious of his acquaintance. Waugh recognized in Merton's second book of prose, *The Waters of Siloe* (1949), the flaws he had already corrected in *The Seven Storey Mountain*. Published in Great Britain under the title *The Waters of Silence,* Waugh had recommended changes of structure which, again, the American editor or editors should have initiated on their own. In a letter to Merton, Waugh asked: 'And in the non-narrative passages, do you not think that you tend to be diffuse, saying the same thing more than once? I noted this in *The Seven Storey Mountain* and the fault persists.'[2] In an irony that Waugh could not have fully appreciated, he added that Merton's writing was based on 'pattern-bombing instead of precision bombing'. The Trappist monk, of course, was a well-publicized peace activist.

As if that were not enough, in the same letter Waugh went on to compound the offending rhetoric — 'You scatter a lot of missiles all around the target instead of concentrating on a single direct hit' — and suggested that the monastery's tailor and bootmaker would not have wasted materials that way. 'Words are our materials', he advised Merton, and any waste of them only encourages vice in one's readers: 'They will not trouble to study a sentence for its proper meaning if they have learned to expect much the same thing to be said again later on.' Hostile critics, he added, are always lurking in the background waiting for signs of the author's deterioration. Merton accepted these and other criticisms most graciously: 'I have no difficulty', he wrote back to Waugh, 'in accepting you as the delegate of the Holy Ghost in this matter.'

It is a curious but understandable aspect of Waugh's letters that he was often kinder (if that is the word) in his one-on-one exchanges with a given correspondent than he was in writing about that same person as a subject for discussion with a corresponding third party. For example, Waugh confessed to his friend and confidant, Katharine Asquith, that he had just about despaired of editing *The Waters of Siloe* to any presentable advantage. He said that he found the book so fraught with defects that he questioned whether Merton had actually known what he was doing when he wrote it. He even concluded that Merton's time might have been better spent at work in the fields with the other monks than sitting at a typewriter producing 'two or three books a year for the rest of his life'.

The charge against Merton for his diffusion of materials is, in large part, justified. It is in fact justified against almost any prolific writer. In that exquisite and, regrettably, only volume of his memoirs, *A Little Learning*,[3] Waugh himself writes as a lead sentence in one paragraph, 'I was no success as a speaker', followed some fourteen lines later in the immediately succeeding paragraph by, 'Nor had I any oratorical gifts'. Surely, this too is 'saying the same thing more than once', as Waugh had held against Merton. The spectre of diffusion haunts the especially gifted writer who also produces in quantity.

Another of Waugh's criticisms of Merton's prose style was that the American monk sometimes wrote literary English and then just as easily lapsed into slang. This, however, will not bother anyone familiar with H. L. Mencken's observations of the differences between literary English and American usage. The offense is in the mixture of the two modes, as when the British often mistake good American usage for expendable slang.

In that sense, then, and without too much damage to his reputation as a writer, it may be said that Thomas Merton was a sometimes careless craftsman who relied on some of the more usable and wordy gimmicks of the trade. He frequently said, for example, 'in order to' when a simple 'to' might have done just as well. But these are merely the thumb prints that any strong or individualistic writer is bound to leave on the page. What remains important is that Merton early found his own voice after the almost Hemingway-like opening paragraphs of *The Seven Storey Mountain;* and though that first popular work would be too easily discredited by Merton himself (and still is by some of his self-styled advocates), it contains just about everything that he would later extend into the more spiritually sophisticated volumes of his middle and last periods. In a similar way, his early poetry now and then fell into bad imitations of T. S. Eliot just as his last efforts took on some on the pretentions of the bad anti-poets writing today.

In the end, why did Evelyn Waugh fret so much about the prose of Thomas Merton? I think that he recognized in Merton not only a very talented Cistercian monk in the New World but also a spokesman for moral stability in the post-christian world at large. But Waugh himself had mistakenly presumed that an apparent spiritual awakening in the United States was a prefiguration of what the Church itself might soon become throughout the world. His own dourest predictions had not foreseen the actual degree of the Church's degeneration in the United States and elsewhere, which is to say, of course, western Europe. Today, perhaps, he would have been cheered only by the efforts of Pope John Paul II to restore the primacy of the papacy, to preserve the integrity of its teachings, and to suggesat at least the possible restoration of the liturgy in due time.

Therefore, for Evelyn Waugh, writing was a thoroughly moral act of the most sustained commitment possible, whether in the writing of common or exalted things, and he believed that the writer should never approach the performance of one's duty in an off-handed manner. This is the chief quality in Waugh that has been clearly recognized by the cynic V. S. Pritchett, on the one hand, and by the realist Paul Fussell, on the other. To this end Waugh developed a direct but elegant style which would be universally recognized as his own unique voice. No one in our century has combined the literacy of elegance with an economy of style in quite the same way that Waugh had managed to do. Hemingway wrote with great and original economy, but with practically no sense of elegance.

The monk Thomas Merton had meanwhile developed a plain but often impassioned and very direct style without the subtleties and more refined cadences of English prose at its best. He shared with Evelyn Waugh, however, a sense of the moral duty that is involved when one attempts to deal with true and everlasting subjects. For it is in dealing with such matters as these that the morality of style itself becomes a kind of saving grace.

Stoughton, Massachusetts

NOTES — Why Evelyn Waugh Worried

1. Davie, Michael, ed., *The Diaries of Evelyn Waugh* (Boston: Little, Brown, 1976).

2. Waugh, Evelyn, *The Letters of Evelyn Waugh* (New York: Ticknor and Fields, 1980).

3. Waugh, Evelyn, *A Little Learning* (Boston: Little, Brown, 1964).

M. Basil Pennington

The Spiritual Father:
Father Louis' Theory and Practice

LREADY IN HIS EARLIEST writings Thomas Merton
affirmed the value and importance of spiritual direction. In the patronizing piety of *The Seven Storey
Mountain* which he later rightly disowned he disavowed the
value of the teaching he received in the Protestant church
because it was not made actual by spiritual direction.[1] More accurate perhaps was his awareness that it was a lack of direction
that left his first year as a Catholic one filled with confusion and a
certain amount of moral back-sliding.[2]

In May, 1951 Father Louis (as he was called in the
monastery) became spiritual father of the scholastics and began
to speak of 'my children'.[3] This seems all the more incongruous as
be brings out in the same passages that these young professed
monks are going through the same experiences the thirty-six-
year-old Merton went through just five years earlier.[4] But at this
point in his development he was to some extent a product of the
pre-Vatican Church which had recently admitted him and not

yet the prophet of a renewed Church. It was a paternalistic Church within which spiritual direction tended to be maternalistic. Yet one of his scholastics has assured me this was more a matter of language than of attitude. He did not seem paternalistic in the sense of making one dependent; he made decided demands on his 'sons'. He was free and aimed at freedom. At the same time if one of the young monks had a real problem he found a most sympathetic and patient father. All of this would certainly be affirmed later in the things Father Louis would say about spiritual direction in an article published in *Sponsa Regis*[5] and then republished in *Spiritual Direction and Meditation.*[6]

Before looking at this more formal treatment of the matter there is a good bit to be gleaned from passages in *The Sign of Jonas,* where Merton speaks of his relationship with his 'children.' Merton comes out of a tradition where the role of the spiritual father is, when the tradition is liveliest and fullest, held in high esteem. The Cistercians were founded to live Benedict of Nursia's *Rule for Monasteries* to the full. The Strict Observance or Trappists to which he belonged sought with very varying degrees of success to maintain the spirit of the Cistercian founders. Saint Benedict placed at the head of his monastery an *abba,* abbot, who was to be a Christlike spiritual father to his monks.[7] If the monastery was large he would appoint deans to assist him in this task.[8] For the novices he provides a wise old man who knows how to win souls.[9] Again wise old monks are to help him in caring for the troublesome and recalcitrant.[10]

When Dom James Fox, who had been his abbot for twenty years, was about to retire Father Louis made it very clear that he was not open to being elected abbot and assuming the role of spiritual father of that large monastic family. But this was an older and wiser Merton who had moved towards the eremitical life and who had in fact exercised an extensive spiritual paternity at Gethsemani, even to the extent of being the abbot's confessor.[11] In 1951 he was very happy to be appointed spiritual father of the scholastics or young professed monks. And in 1955 he was eager to move on to be father of the novices, an office he held for ten years.[12] Thus he held within his community the two offices under abbot which most implied the service of spiritual paternity.

But let us return to Merton in the early 50s and *The Sign of Jonas.* In his various reflections on his new role Father Louis gives us some insight into the elements he saw within the role of spiritual paternity.

First of all, the spiritual father is a listener, he provides space, he is open and lets people reveal themselves. Merton as spiritual father of the scholastics continued to spend many hours in his work room, but now in addition to writing (he wrote *No Man Is an Island* during this period) and translating (in his early years he had been put to translating a number of Cistercian documents and hagiographies) he listened and learned. He came to reverence these young men: 'The more I get to know my scholastics the more reverence I have for their individuality. . .'[13] It is very important for a spiritual director to realize this, that each is a unique individual. What worked well for the father might not be the answer for the son. 'This is to me both a confusion and an education — to see that they can mostly get along quite well without what I used to think I needed. . . .'[14]

The listening of the spiritual father is not a passive thing, it is very active. Merton expresses it beautifully: 'I have looked into their hearts. . . .'[15] And he adds immediately another important aspect of this role, one which the concept of spiritual father, with its implied loving, responsible relationship, seems to evoke more than that of spiritual director: '. . . and taken up their burdens upon me'.[16] The spiritual father, in accepting this service knows that his love must be such that as the disciples' openness discloses sufferings, wounds, and needs, they become his sufferings, wounds, and needs. I can remember one of the great spiritual fathers on Mount Athos telling me that he considered his most important service as spiritual father is to stand before the icon of Christ and mystically visit his sons in the night.

Merton, in questioning the effectiveness of his service, brings out what he saw to be the goals of spiritual direction: 'I do not know if they have discovered anything new or if they are able to love God more, or if I have helped them find themselves, which is to say to lose themselves.'[17] Merton was convinced of the teaching role of the spiritual father: 'I constantly preach to them from the encyclicals that they must know theology.'[18] He himself though was in a learning mode: 'I have discovered that after all what they most need is not conferences on mysticism but more light about the ordinary virtues whether they be faith or prudence, charity or temperance, hope or justice or fortitude. And above all what they need and what they desire is to penetrate the Mystery of Christ and to know him in his Gospels and in the whole Bible.'[19] What is most important in Merton's growing understanding is the insight he expresses in the Prologue to *The Sign of Jonas:* 'I found in writing *The Ascent to Truth* that technical language, though it is universal and certain and accepted by theologians, does not reach the average man and does not convey what is most personal and vital in religious experience.'[20] Thus he shifted his focus from talking about dogmas in themselves and rather tried to bring out 'their reprecussions in the life of the soul in which they begin to find concrete realization.'[21] This is the kind of theology, of learning, he as a spiritual father wanted to bring to his sons, and for two purposes: to enable them to love God more—the obvious first purpose of everything—and to help them find their true selves.

Merton would later explore this notion of 'self' very extensively, challenged and enlightened by psychology, the behavorial sciences, and the spirituality of the East. As the young Merton penned these lines I doubt if he had any inkling of what was to come. In spiritual direction we do seek to help one to discover the true self, the image of God so one with him whom it images, the child of God baptized into an inconceivable oneness with the very Son of God. As Merton here states, the discovery of this true self is at the same time the lose of the false self, the self we in our folly have created to distinguish ourselves from God and from our fellows, the self that requires defensiveness and begets competition, envy, jealousy, and fear.

Merton, who was a man of quick and deep perception, knew right from the start that 'the one who is going to be most formed by the new scholarsticate [at the time Father Louis was appointed, this was a new structure for the rapidly growing Gethsemani community, one called into being by their canonical visitor, Dom

Louis le Pennuen] is the Master of Scholastics.'[22] It is something in the ordinary providence of God that when he uses us for others it is his intent that we be the greater beneficiaries. Christ came and died 'for us and for our salvation' but rightly he receives the greater glory out of being our savior. God can use us as unwilling and unprofiting instruments for the benefit of others. But if we enter lovingly into his plan we will benefit by all that he gives to others through us and more besides.

Since *The Sign of Jonas* is a personal journal it is not surprising that we hear more of what Merton himself got out of his ministry than of the ministry itself. But this is important to hear. The candidness of some of these passages is what is most touching and attractive in Merton's journaling. 'Their [his 'children's'] calmness will finally silence all that remains of my own turbulence. . . . They refresh me with their simplicity. . . . I make resolutions to speak less wildly, to say fewer of the things that surprise myself and them.'[23] He found a ministry a stimulus to live more faithfully: 'I am obliged to live the Rule in order to talk about it.'[24] In his ministry he accepted his failures: 'I have not always seen clearly and I have not carried their burdens too well and I have stumbled around a lot and on many days we have gone around in circles and fallen into ditches because the blind was leading the blind.'[25] He saw his temptations in a positive light, 'to learn how to help all the other ones who would be one way or another tempted.'[26] He was confronted by his limitations: 'On all sides I am confronted by questions I cannot answer, because the time for answering them has not yet come. Between the silence of God and the silence of my own soul stands the silence of the souls entrusted to me. Immersed in these three silences, I realize that the questions I ask myself about them are perhaps no more than a surmise. . . .'[27] But in all this Father Louis found fulfillment, and most surprisingly for him and for us, he found fulfillment, at least for a time, of his greatest desire, the desire for solitude:

> All this experience replaced my theories of solitude. I do not need a hermitage, because I have found one where I least expected it. It was when I knew my brothers less well that

my thoughts were more involved in them. Now that I know
them better, I can see something of the depths of solitude
which are in every human person, but which most men do
not know how to lay open either to themselves, or to others
or to God.[28]

And again: 'I know what I have discovered: that the kind of work
I once feared because I thought it would interfere with "solitude"
is in fact the only path to solitude.'[29] But he adds: 'One must be
in some sense a hermit before the care of souls can serve to lead
one further into the desert'.[30]

Let us leave Merton for the moment, in his content, and
turn to his first *ex professo* treatment on spiritual direction. As I
have said this first appeared in a periodical for religious women
and later was incorporated in a greatly expanded form in a little
book published by the same publisher, Liturgical Press, Collegeville, Minnesota. The article was written for the Christian,
especially the religious, seeking direction rather than for the
director, although Merton hoped by it to encourage the average
priest to venture some direction in the administration of the
sacrament of reconciliation.[31] This ties in with his later note that
direction is not necessary for all; those who do not have a special
vocation or mission in the Church should be able to get enough
'direction' in the course of ordinary Christian life with its family
and community interaction and the sacraments.[32]

Merton makes it clear why he undertook to write on spiritual
direction; he wants to dispel over-rigid and stereotypical ideas.[33]
He is here as everywhere in his later years a champion of freedom,
full humaness, and personal responsibility. When he comes to
speak of the necessity of spiritual direction he maintains it is absolutely necessary for young religious. The reason he gives surprises: to safeguard them against deformation.[34] Merton shows
himself the true son of Author of the *Apologia*[35] when he
unleashes his ironical pen against authoritarian rigidity:

> It assumes as a basic axiom of the spiritual life that every
> soul needs to be humiliated, frustrated and beaten down;
> that all spontaneous aspirations are suspect by the very fact

that they are spontaneous; that everything individual is to
be cut away, and that the soul is to be reduced to a state of
absolute, machine-like conformity with others in the same
fantastic predicament. Result: a procession of robot 'victim
souls' moving jerkily from exercise to exercise in the
spiritual life, secretly hating the whole business and praying
for an early death, meanwhile 'offering it up' so that the
whole may not be lost.[36]

In the preface Merton gives his description of a spiritual director:

a trusted friend who, in an atmosphere of sympathetic
understanding, helps and strengthens us in our groping efforts to correspond with the grace of the Holy Spirit, who
alone is the true Director in the fullest sense of the word.

Later in the work he underlines this subordination to the Holy
Spirit:

His direction is, in reality, nothing more than a way of
leading us to see and obey our real Director—the Holy
Spirit, hidden in the depths of our souls.[37]

In the body of the book Merton gives another less descriptive definition:

A spiritual director is, then, one who helps another to
recognize and to follow the inspirations of grace in his life,
in order to arrive at the end to which God is leading him.[38]

But extensive descriptions are offered:

The director is one who knows and sympathizes, who
understands circumstances, who is not in a hurry, who is patiently and humbly waiting for indications of God's action
in the soul. He is concerned . . . with the whole life of the
soul. He is not interested merely in our actions. He is much
more interested in the basic attitudes of our souls, our in-
most aspirations, our way of meeting difficulties, our mode
of responding to good and evil.[39]

The third section of Merton's essay is entitled 'How to Profit by Direction'. In it he notes three elements: gratitude, balanced expectations — look for kindly support, not freedom from all problems or wish fulfillment; look for wise advice, not all the answers — and a simple and sincere manifestation of conscience. The last he considers so central he devotes another, longer section to it. He emphasizes it is not the same as confession of sins. 'What we need to do is bring the director into contact with our real self, as best we can, and not fear to let him see what is false in our false self.'[40] This may not involve anything sinful but it may be much more humiliating and difficult to reveal than our sins. Indeed, as Merton notes, sometimes it is more difficult to reveal the good aspirations that the Lord is inspiring in the depths of our being. 'We must learn to say what we really mean in the depths of our souls, not what we think we are expected to say, not what somebody else has just said.'[41]

There is a very direct reciprocity between the qualities of the director and the responsibilities of the directee.

In this treatise Merton does distinguish in some way between the spiritual director and a spiritual father. In the opening paragraphs of the work he notes that Christian spiritual direction had its origins with the spiritual fathers in the desert. Then he goes on to say:

> It must not be forgotten that the spiritual director in primitive times was much more than the present name implies. He was a spiritual father who 'begot' the perfect life in the soul of his disciple by his instruction first of all, but also by his prayer, his sanctity and his example. He was to the young monk a kind of 'sacrament' of the Lord's presence in the ecclesial community.[42]

I am sure that Merton would not want this to be seen as a real distinction. It is a realistic recognition that the relationship between director and directee cannot always be as intimate — 'The neophyte lives in the same cell with him, day and night, and did what he saw his father doing'.[43] — but every good Christian spiritual director will strive to move in the direction of being a true spiritual father (or mother).

Merton notes that spiritual direction is not counseling nor psychotherapy.[44] He warns against amateur attempts at the latter.[45] The director should know when to refer someone to a professional therapist. His direction is spiritual, integrating spiritual principles that have been revealed, and aiming at a fullness of life that is beyond even a fully human integration.

After forty pages of sometimes rather intricate, and always very rich consideration, Merton wisely concludes by warning us not to make too much of all this. If spiritual direction for us is largely experienced as a quietly deepening friendship with a special openness and grounding, we shouldn't look for trouble or problems but rather realize that the steadiness of this special friendship is perhaps one of the big reasons why things are generally progressing peacefully for us.

Merton's article was published in June of 1959, the book came out early the next year. In this latter year Merton began a course for the priests of his monastery entitled 'An Introduction to Christian Mysticism (From the Apostolic Fathers to the Council of Trent)'. He 'published' the lectures in a mimeograph book in August of the following year, 1961.[46] The lectures included Various Approaches to Mystical Theology, Mystical Theology in Saint John's Gospel, The Most Relevant New Testament Texts, Martyrs and Gnostics, Divinization and Mysticism, Evagrius Ponticus, Contemplation and the Cosmos, The Dionysian Tradition, Western Mysticism, Fourteenth-Century Mysticism, and Spanish Mysticism. The last forty-five of the hundred and seventy pages are two lectures on 'The Spiritual Direction of Contemplatives'. Indeed the whole course is geared toward this, as Merton says in his Foreword: 'The lectures were intended primarily for monastic priests . . . who sought background and contact with sources that would enable them to be of benefit to their brethren in spiritual direction. . . '. The title is a bit deceptive. The first conference, the longer of the two, is really dedicated to direction in general. The second conference is on the 'mystical crisis' and devoted wholly to the example and teaching of St Teresa of Avila (four pages) and St John of the Cross (twelve pages). His material is difficult to read not only because it is presented in somewhat schematic form giving Merton's insightful content without his rich poetic prose, but also because it is almost rigidly scholastic. His first conference is almost a scholastic *quaetio:* seven arguments against spiritual direction, some arguments from the magisterium in favor of it (the *Sed contra*), and then the *corpus.* Here he presents the two extremes: the 'strict, technical and "modern view"', emphasizing institutional authority, guidance, and formation according to a particular school of spirituality, and the 'broad and pre-technical way', emphasizing authority from spiritual experience and sometimes charism, exercised in a fluid and informal relationship. Then he espouses the monastic view which incorporates in a balanced way elements from the two extremes — though certainly leaning toward the latter.

The emphasis on freedom and responsibility again stands out. A director should never be imposed. When one is chosen he has no jurisdiction, no right to obedience. His authority is spiritual, it should call forth a complete docility — an ability to learn what is to be prudently applied to one's life. Learning, humility, prudence, and charity are more important in a director than holiness and experience, though these, too, are very desirable qualities.

Again and in more detail and with greater precision Merton emphasizes the difference between spiritual direction which 'is the art of leading souls to their proper perfection according to their personal vocation and their place in the Church',[47] and counselling, psychotherapy, and psychoanalysis. He then goes on to develop extensively the use the director can profitably make of psychology in preparing persons for direction and in avoiding many obstacles. He addresses himself to some of the significant crises where this is especially true: adolescent, vocational, post-ordination let-down, full-development reintegration. His insight and advice are excellent.

In the section of this study where Merton surveys the history of spiritual direction we get a further hint of the evolution of a

broader vision. He situates the Christian history in the broader
world context. He passes over 'the very interesting and important
topic of direction in Yoga and in Buddhism' for these had not yet
captivated his interest as they soon would, but he does explore
extensively the master-disciple relationship in classical philosophical schools. In the next few years his horizons would expand as
is evidenced in the 1967 volume, *Mystics and Zen Masters*.[48]

But first his expansion and deepening would come through
his increasing study of the spiritual fathers of the Christian East.
Keith Egan in his very interesting and informative series of taped
talks, *Solitude and Community. The Paradox of Life and Prayer,*
speaks at length of Thomas Merton in his third talk, 'The Desert.
Place of Discovery'. In it he notes:

> He began to read the literature that came out of the desert,
> the Christian desert of the fourth century. And one of the
> most important books he wrote is his shortest and that is
> *The Wisdom of the Desert*. . . . The study that lies behind
> the writing of this little book was transforming and changed
> Merton's life forever.[49]

About the same time that Father Louis was giving his lectures on spritual direction to his fellow monks he put together
this little collection of the sayings of the Fathers of the Desert.
These he first published in the rather exclusive edition prepared
by his friend Victor Hammer.[50] However, they soon came out in
the popular edition mentioned by Egan.[51] In the twenty-two-
page introductory essay Merton never uses the term 'spiritual
direction' and says relatively little of the relationship between the
spiritual fathers or elders and their disciples. This is significant
for this is the quiet, ever-present context of the whole.
Statements in the essay are important indicating the evolution
and thrust of Merton's thought which would profoundly affect
his approach to spiritual direction.

> The society they sought was one where all men were truly
> equal, where the only authority under God was the charismatic

authority of wisdom, experience and love. . . . What the
Fathers sought most of all was their own true self, in
Christ.[52] He could not retain the slightest identification
with his superficial, transient, self-constructed self. He had
to lose himself in the inner, hidden reality of a self that was
transcendent, mysterious, half-known, and lost in Christ.[53]
They sought a way to God that was uncharted and freely
chosen, not inherited from others who had mapped it out
beforehand. . . . There was nothing to which they had to
'conform' excpet the secret, hidden, inscrutable will of God
which might differ very notably from one cell to another![54]

    We see a new terminology coming into Merton's vocabulary
here:

The 'rest' which these men sought was simply that sanity
and poise of a being that no longer has to look at itself
because it is carried by the perfection of freedom that is in
it. And carried where? Wherever Love itself, or the Divine
Spirit, sees fit to go. Rest, then, was a kind of simple
nowhereness and no-mindedness that had lost all preoccupation with a false or limited 'self'. At peace in the possession of a sublime 'nothing' the spirit laid hold, in secret,
upon the 'all' — without trying to know what it possessed.[55]

This terminology did not come from the *Verba seniorum*. A clue
to its origins comes on the next page: 'In many respects, therefore,
these Desert Fathers had much in common with Indian Yogis and
with Zen Buddhist monks of China and Japan.'[56] The opening to
the East through the Christian East was underway.

    Among the essays published in 1967 in *Mystics and Zen
Masters* there is a Preface Merton wrote for Sergius Bolshakoff's
study of the *Russion Mystics*.[57] As this book's publication was
delayed, Merton published his work as an essay under the title
'Russian Mystics.' In this he has a very significant statement on
spiritual direction which indicates the simplicity to which his own
notions on this subject had attained:

The purpose of *Starchestvo* [the daily manifestation of one's thoughts to one's spiritual father] is, then, not so much to make use of daily spiritual direction in order to inculcate a special method of prayer, but rather to keep the heart of the disciple open to love, to prevent it from hardening in self-centered concern (whether moral, spiritual or ascetical). All the worst sins are denials and rejections of love, refusals to love. The chief aim of the starets is first to teach his disciple not to sin against love, then to encourage and assist his growth in love until he becomes a saint. This total surrender to the power of love was the sole basis of their spiritual authority. . . .[58]

In spite of the title of this volume, there is little formal consideration in it of the relationship of the Zen Master and his disciple. It is rather conveyed in a multitude of stories and sayings, scattered through the essays, which remind one constantly of the stories and sayings of the Desert Fathers. Merton notes that Zen monks (like Eastern Christian monks) 'seek out a particular monastery more because of a *Roshi,* or "venerable teacher", who is found there, than for the sake of the community or the rule'.[59] The one description of the master-disciple relation he does draw is not particularly attractive, to say the least, and does not readily offer much insight into the whole rather paradoxical relationship that does exist.[60] Merton, himself, is at pains to state that it really cannot be understood or appreciated out of the context of a full understanding of Zen.[61] This relationship in other Buddhist traditions and among the Hindus does not feature in his writings and does not seem to have been studied by him. A very interesting set of taped talks, originally given to the monks at Gethsemani in the course of his Sunday afternoon lectures, shows his interest in the Sufi master and his mode of teaching.[62]

The final essay I want to consider here is a paper Merton distributed in mimeograph in February, 1966, entitled 'The Spiritual Father in the Desert Tradition'.[63] This was written shortly after he embarked upon the eremitical life and moved up to the hermitage on the hill. It is in part an *apologia* for the eremitical life. In it, though, we see the insights emerging in his introductory essay in *The Wisdom of the Desert* now being directly applied to spiritual direction: 'every practice, every decision, every change in one's mode of life is to be judged in terms of . . . purity of heart, perfect charity, and quies, or the tranquility of the selfless and detached spirit.'[64] In the final paragraph he goes further:

> This freedom and tranquility are the 'good ground' in which the seed of grace and wisdom can bring forth fruit a hundredfold. This state of purity and rest is not what one can call the 'summit of perfection' whatever that may mean. It is simply the last stage of development that can be observed and discussed in logical terms. It is what John the Solitary calls 'integrity', but his integrity is not the end, it is really only the *beginning* of the true spiritual (*pneumatikos*) life. 'Beyond integrity is mystery which cannot be defined.'[65]

There is a point beyond which the spiritual father cannot guide, he can only point into the Mystery.

In this essay we note two areas where Merton shows an evolution of thought. He moves from a strongly negative attitude towards the director making severe demands to a more open position: 'In fact the Spiritual Father must of necessity be uncompromisingly severe, and make extremely difficult demands upon the disciple in order to test his vocation . . . and help him make rapid progress.'[66] He does add cautions against excess on the next page. One wonders how much influence his contact with the harsh way of the Zen master had on his opening to the harshness in his own tradition which he earlier found more repugnant.

The second area is closely related to this. Earlier he carefully distinguishd between obedience due superiors and others with jurisdiction or ecclesial authority and the docility due the director.[67] Now he calls for obedience; there is to be

> uncompromising and complete obedience to the demands and advice of the Spiritual Father no matter how disconcerting any might appear. . . . If he [the disciple] can put up with rough treatment, realizing the Spiritual Father knows

what he is doing, he will rapidly come to a state of detachment from his own will and his own ego.[68]

He goes on to defend this from the charge of being blind obedience:

> This is not the blind, unreasoning and passive obedience of one who obeys merely in order to let himself be 'broken', but the clear sighted trusting obedience of one who firmly believes that his guide knows the true way to peace and purity of heart and is an interpreter of God's will for him. Such obedience is 'blind' only in the sense that it puts aside its own limited and biased judgement; but it does so precisely because it sees that to follow one's own judgment in things one does not properly understand is indeed to walk in darkness.[69]

This would seem to limit the scope of the obedience somewhat. I must confess I am more comfortable with Father Louis' earlier distinction but we are confronted with a monk who became more radical and traditional even as he became more prophetic and evolutionary. We need to let ourselves be challenged by him.

In the light of this added authority and role Merton does demand more of the spiritual father:

> The Master must be extraordinarily humble, discerning, kind, and in no sense a despotic character. The 'hard sayings' which he administers must spring from genuine kindness and concern for the interests of the disciples and not from a secret desire to dominate and exploit them for his own egotistic ends. The Master must, in other words, be himself one who is no longer in the least attracted by 'superiorship' or by the desire to rule and teach others.[70]

In his early work on spiritual direction Merton urged the directee to develop the virtue of prudence to 'guide himself when he cannot or need not seek guidance from another'.[71] Now he resorts to an earlier monastic term, a more descriptive one: '*diacrisis,* or the discernment of spirits'.[72] As we have seen, all along he has emphasized that ultimately the director is the Holy Spirit and the human director is to help the directee to learn how to hear the Spirit and follow his lead. For such, *diacrisis* is obviously essential. There is within us, besides the indwelling divine Spirit, our own very humam spirit, and if not within us certainly close by, the evil spirits. Discernment is necessary if we are to hear and follow the Spirit of God. Merton saw the way for the disciple to develop this to be by complete openness with the spiritual father, making known to him 'all that is going on in his heart'. Together with him, step by step, the disciple would learn to identify the inner movements and their origins.[73]

We could look at other texts. Spiritual direction in a more Cistercian context would be seen in his work on Adam of Perseigne and monastic formation.[74] Passages from *Conjectures of a Guilty Bystander*[75] and the *Asian Journal*[76] are of interest, too. But I think what we have seen here give sufficient sense of Merton's practice, his evolution, and his basic teaching on spiritual direction. Once he left the office of novice master in 1965 he did little in the way of giving regular direction. There are some letters—he responded generously to correspondence—which contain excellent direction.[77] But his energies now were directed to broader dialogue.[78] Merton's growth is fascinating to watch. In this very particular study we catch only glimpses of it. He grew from a late-traditional, by-the-book spiritual director to a truly traditional, generative spiritual father first of monks, then of ever widening circles and whole movements, to new currents of life in Church and society.

In his early years at Gethsemani, as a man very much part of the pre-Vatican II Church, Merton had no difficulty with the term 'spiritual direction' and 'spiritual director.' As we have seen he evolved through a fuller grasp of not only his own tradition but other spiritual traditions. In his later years this terminology became foreign to him. I must admit I feel very uncomfortable with it. No man is worthly to direct another human person nor does he know enough to do it fully. 'Eye has not seen, nor ear heard, nor has it entered into the heart of the human person what God has prepared for those who love him; but he makes it known to us through the Holy Spirit.'[79] Only God has the authority and the knowledge to direct a person. He may share that authority and knowledge in part, but the best thing a human person who is called to such a sharing can do is to help us to learn how to listen to the Divine Director. I rather stay with the more traditional terminology of spiritual father or mother for this better expresses the role of collaborating with God in bringing forth life, nurturing and educating it, and evolving into an adult relationship with it. As we have seen this terminology was more common to Father Louis in his later writings and talks, as he himself evolved to become, even in his life time, an almost legendary spiritual father.

Assumption Abbey
Ava, Missouri

NOTES — The Spiritual Father

1. Thomas Merton, *The Seven Storey Mountain* (New York: Harcourt, Brace and Company, 1948) p. 53.
2. *Ibid.*, pp. 229ff.
3. Thomas Merton, *The Sign of Jonas* (New York: Harcourt, Brace and Company, 1953) p. 329.
4. *Ibid.*, p. 335.
5. Thomas Merton, 'Spiritual Direction' in *Sponsa Regis*, (now *Sisters Today*) 30 (1959) 249–254.
6. Collegeville, MN: The Liturgical Press, 1960.
7. *RB. 1980. The Rule of St. Benedict,* ed. Timothy Fry, osb (Collegeville, MN: The Liturgical Press, 1981) chap. 2, pp. 170ff.
8. *RB,* chap. 21, pp. 216ff.
9. *RB,* chap. 58:6, pp. 266f.
10. *RB,* chap. 27:2, pp. 222f.
11. James Fox, 'The Spiritual Son' in *Thomas Merton, Monk. A Monastic Tribute,* ed. Patrick Hart (New York: Sheed and Ward, 1974) p. 144. Fox says of Merton he was 'a gifted director of others in the spiritual life'.
12. *Ibid.*, pp. 149ff. In the same volume Matthew Kelty, one of Merton's novices, says, 'I recall that in periods of spiritual direction when I was a novice he always seemed to know before I did when the matter was over. It never seemed to end without a kind of abruptness which I had later to admit was simply a quick and sure grasp of the situation; that we had reached a point of terminus' — 'The Man,' p. 20.
13. *Jonas,* p. 337.
14. *Ibid.*

15. *Ibid.*, p. 330. One of the monk-priests who was a scholastic at that time attests that he was certainly highly gifted for active listening and made one feel listened to.
16. *Ibid.*
17. *Ibid.*, p. 333.
18. *Ibid.*, p. 337.
19. *Ibid.*
20. *Ibid.*, p. 9.
21. *Ibid.*
22. *Ibid.*, p. 330.
23. *Ibid.*, p. 338.
24. *Ibid.*, p. 229.
25. *Ibid.*, p. 333.
26. *Ibid.*, p. 229.
27. *Ibid.*, p. 344.
28. *Ibid.*, p. 337.
29. *Ibid.*, p. 333.
30. *Ibid.*
31. *Direction*, Preface, n. p.
32. *Ibid.*, p. 13.
33. *Ibid.*, Preface.
34. *Ibid.*, p. 15.
35. Cf. Bernard of Clairvaux, 'Cistercians and Cluniacs: St. Bernard's *Apologia* to Abbot William' in *Bernard of Clairvaux: Treatises I*, Cistercian Fathers Series, 1 (Cistercian Publications, 1970).
36. *Direction*, p. 12.
37. *Ibid.*, p. 30.
38. *Ibid.*, p. 9.
39. *Ibid.*, p. 25.
40. *Ibid.*, p. 24.
41. *Ibid.*, p. 29.
42. *Ibid.*, p. 9.
43. *Ibid.*
44. *Ibid.*, p. 6.
45. *Ibid.*, pp. 40f.
46. *An Introduction to Christian Mysticism (From the Apostolic Fathers to the Council of Trent)*, Lectures given at the Abbey of Gethsemani. The author's name is not given. The date at the end of the Foreword is Vigil of Assumption, 1961.
47. *Ibid.*, p. 141.
48. Thomas Merton, *Mystics and Zen Masters* (New York: Farrar, Straus and Giroux, 1967).
49. Keith Egan, *Solitude and Community. The Paradox of Life and Prayer* (Kansas City, MO: NCR Casettes, 1981) tape 3, "The Desert: Place of Discovery."
50. Thomas Merton, *What Ought I To Do? Sayings of the Desert Fathers* (Lexington, KY: Stamperia del Santuccio, 1959).
51. Thomas Merton, *The Wisdom of the Desert* (London: Hollis and Carter, 1961).
52. *Ibid.*, p. 5.
53. *Ibid.*, p. 7.
54. *Ibid.*, p. 6.
55. *Ibid.*, p. 8.
56. *Ibid.*, p. 9.

57. Sergius Bolshakoff, *Russian Mystics,* Cistercian Studies Series, no. 26 (Kalamazoo, MI: Cistercian Publications, 1977) pp. ix–xvii.

58. *Masters,* p. 186.

59. *Ibid.,* p. 217.

60. '. . . interviews with the Roshi. These are deliberately humiliating and frustrating, for the spiritual master is determined to waste no time tolerating the illusions and spiritual self-gratifications that may be cherished by his disciples. If necessary, he will resort (as did famous Zen masters in the past) to slapping, kicking, and other forms of physical violence.' —*Ibid.,* p. 229.

61. *Ibid.,* p. 215.

62. *The Mystic Life.* 12 casettes (Chappaqua, NY: Electronic Paperbacks, 1974). Note especially tape three: 'Community Life and Spiritual Direction': 'They [the Sufis] have a man around who knows the score and can tell them: here is what is happening to you, here is how you fit this into the circumstances where you live. This is what spiritual direction is. That is what the spiritual life depends on — having somebody to tell you that in the beginning. After a while you can tell yourself. In Sufism, therefore, direction is very important.'

63. This was published after Merton's death in *Contemplation in a World of Action* (Garden City, NY: Doubleday, 1971) pp. 269–293, with some editorial changes.

64. Thomas Merton, *The Spiritual Fathers in the Desert Tradition,* manuscript, February, 1966, p. 14.

65. *Ibid.,* p. 29.

66. *Ibid.,* p. 23.

67. *Direction,* p. 40.

68. *Spiritual Father,* p. 23.

69. *Ibid.,* pp. 24f.

70. *Ibid.,* p. 25.

71. *Direction,* p. 17.

72. *Spiritual Father,* p. 22.

73. *Ibid.*

74. 'The Feast of Freedom. Monastic Formation According to Adam of Perseigne' in *The Letters of Adam of Perseigne, 1,* Cistercian Fathers Series, 21 (Cistercian Publications, 1976).

75. Garden City, NY: Doubleday, 1966; Image Paperback, 1968.

76. *The Asian Journal of Thomas Merton* (New York: New Directions, 1973).

77. Some examples of this may be found in 'Letters in a Time of Crisis' in *Seeds of Destruction* (New York: Farrar, Straus and Giroux, 1965) pp. 237–328 and William H. Shannon, ed., *The Hidden Ground of Love: The Letters of Thomas Merton on Religious Experience and Social Concerns* (New York: Farrar, Straus and Giroux, 1985).

78. This was primarily through his writings and through contact with influencial persons: 'I am more concerned with dialogue with selected groups of people — intellectuals, etc. and *not* with large numbers or with a movement. This may sound like an aristocratic approach but I think it is a traditional monastic one. I think the monk is concerned with *personal* contacts with people who exercise influence over groups, rather than directly with groups' —*Ibid.,* '34. To a Priest,' pp. 319f.

79. 1 Cor 2:9.

Robert E. Daggy

The Road To Joy
Thomas Merton's Letters to and About Young People

IN 1966 a high school sophomore from Niskayuna, New York, wrote to thank Thomas Merton for his help with a poetry unit in English class, for Merton's 'wonderful, gracious letter', expressing particular gratitude because Merton cared to help him 'in a world where so many adults treat us like young adults'.[1] And it is obvious as one reads through Merton's rather extensive correspondence with and about young people (a correspondence mostly from the 1960s amounting to over 100 surviving letters) that he cared. He did care despite the scepticism that shows through on occasion about the motives of some of the youths who wrote to him. He, in fact, prepared a 'form letter' in the early 1960s to send to some of the young people and students who asked for answers to an astounding variety of questions. He sent a copy of this letter to his friend (later a Trustee of the Merton Legacy Trust), Tommie O'Callaghan, with the notation: 'This may amuse you — I send it to High School kids who want me to write essays for them.' In 1964 he had written to another high school sophomore, this one in Waterloo, Iowa:

I don't know how most authors feel about this 'write to an author' deal, but my own feelings about it are a bit mixed. However, I must say this, you are very simple about it, you just ask for a note back. Most of the letters I get are usually asking me in some way to write them an essay they have been assigned to write about me. Thus the author writes your homework and saves you the trouble of reading his stuff, which is pretty neat. . . . Just for kicks I enclose the paper I send them when they do.[2]

Part of his scepticism may have stemmed from his feeling that many of these 'kids' wrote to him, not from any real interest in Thomas Merton and his writings, but because they had been prompted by adults. A Massachusetts eighth grader, for instance, said that 'Sister seemed to favor you more than the others, so I decided to do my report on you'. A sixth grader from Connecticut added: 'I was asked to write you. I guess you know why'. A fifth grader from Michigan was given an assignment to write to a famous person. She told Merton: 'Some people are writing to movie stars and some to famous authors. My dad has read some of your books. And he visted Gethsemine Monastery, in Kentucky. And he told me about you. So I think your famous.' A fifteen-year-old sophomore from Brooklyn was given an assignment to write on Merton and took it upon herself to write him a letter. When she wrote back to thank him for his reply, she said: 'After I wrote you my English nun told me I had a lot of nerve because of it. But she became so excited when she read your letter that I thought she was going to faint.'

He did care despite his ambivalence about writing letters, an ambivalence not, of course, just toward young people but one which extended to all his correspondents, including at times his oldest and closest friends. His saying he was too busy, his complaining that he received too much mail, his insisting that he did not have time to answer—all became a litany, a frequent and boring recitation, with which he began, and also sometimes ended, nearly all his letters. For example: 'I wish I had time to give you a detailed answer'; 'Sorry for the delay in answering your letter. I get so many requests, questions etc that half the time I never get around to answering'; 'I have far too much mail'. 'Though I don't have much time to answer your letter, I don't want to leave you in the lurch with your first term paper'. He could get snippy, though amusing, when pressed about answering a letter which had been around for a while. In 1967 a young 'poet' wrote to inquire why Merton had not answered his requests to read his poems and suggest a publisher for them. Merton fired back an answer:

> Most sorry. If you knew. I get buried under manuscripts every day of my life, they are lying all over the place, they are blocking the view, they are falling in my food. It happened that the other day yours fell out of a pile when I was looking for some drawings, so I knew just where it was when your letter came . . . Sorry again. I'm really not that much in touch with publishing etc. For some reason people imagine that I know everybody. Am better acquainted say with the possum who came up and sniffed at me during my meditation at 3.45 am today. He does not publish books as far as I know. Very gentle delicate dumb possum.[3]

Yet the irony of the situation, the inexplicable contradiction, is that often, after saying that he had no time, that he could not go into detail, that he had not much to say, Merton would proceed to write a page-long (sometimes more than a page) letter answering the person's question, writing frequently the very essay he had said they were trying to inveigle him to write. This, again, is not unique in his letters to young people since he would say to most of his correspondents that he could not write much in detail and would then pound out on his typewriter a letter the length and polish of which is staggering.

Merton cared despite the fact that, since he gained much of his information through correspondence, he would often use an exchange to get information he wanted — information from the letters themselves, from books and records he requested. A young Swede wrote to him from Lund in 1963 and Merton, after dutifully answering his letter, ended by asking: 'Sometimes we need a book or so published in Lund. Would you want to help us? We can send something in exchange.'[4] In what is perhaps his best-known exchange with a young person, that with Suzanne Butorovich, a sixteen-year-old high school student from Campbell, California, there is a mutual exchange of strokes and information and affection. In his first letter to her, after she had told Merton he needed to know more about the music of the 60s, he said:

> Go on then educate me in pop music. I don't know much about pop music. I am a confirmed jazzman but I need to know more about pop also. Like some of those outfits you have out there that I hear such a lot about Grateful Dead and all those: tell me about them.[5]

Evidence of Merton's attitudes toward and relationships with young people may be found partly in his writings (particularly in his poetry), partly in anecdotes but, since he actually met few young people other than novices during his monastic years, primarily in his letters. These letters range, as all his letters do, over an astonishing range of subjects: Kentucky, jazz, ecumensim, Bob Dylan, Ayn Rand, J. D. Salinger, David Jones, Stevie Smith, Norman Mailer, Milarepa, the Beatles, Lenny Bruce, Bud Powell, peace and war, conscientious objection, apartheid, Zionism, Arthurian legend, poetry, writing, the hermitage, sexuality. He was sometimes asked to comment or to provide information on subjects about which he knew little. A seventh grader form Ashland, Kentucky, asked Merton to send him 'all the information about Kentucky music'. Merton responded:

> You are the first person who ever picked me out as an authority on music. I cannot even play a mouth organ properly, though I can play bongo drums. I admit that. All I know is that I like Country Music when I hear it, which is rarely. I like Johnny Cash, but I guess he is not from Kentucky. Here in the monastery we have sung Gregorian chant which is an ancient form of Catholic Church music.[6]

Yet these letters to young people are written somewhat differently—with gentleness, understanding, reciprocity, simplicity, care,
and, frequently, allowance for less experience—but he never
patronizes, condescends, preaches. Kathleen Gillard, a high
school senior, had read *The Seven Story Mountain* and felt it 'had
a great effect on my way of thinking, especially as regards
Catholicism'. She wrote Merton for advice, particularly about her
father's accusing her of being 'too intense'. He replied:

> As you say, I don't have a lot of pre-cooked answers. Your
> letter makes plenty of sense, and you sound as though you
> are right. Or in the right way. My grandfather didn't use the
> word 'intense' but he told me that in equivalent terms. He
> wanted to know why I didn't read something like the news-
> papers—relaxing you know. I couldn't get across to him
> that even in 1935 the news made me vomit. Still don't be
> too intense in the sense of trying to find out the key to
> everything by sheer concentration. I don't think you'll try
> that.
>
> The important thing is not to play a role: not to fit in with
> the role imposed on you by this or that crowd. But obviously
> you have to find out the truth for yourself, not just buy
> somebody else's answers. I can't go into a lot of details. . . .[7]

Cindy McElhose, a gradeschooler, wrote to ask Merton his opinion on how a young person might 'become a better teenager'.
After saying 'If I wait much longer to answer your letter you may
cross the line and become a teenager and then you will be in the
midst of that crucial experience and my letter will be useless', he
continued:

> How to be a better teenager: well first of all too much fuss is
> made out of this business of being a teen ager. This is
> because there are a lot of people who want to make money
> out of teen agers. Therefore they promote a special teen age
> consciousness, and play up the idea that teen agers are very
> different from everyone else, which is not true. I am afraid
> we are all pretty much in the same boat: human beings who are

uncertain of ourselves, looking for the meaning of life, worried about the things we feel in ourselves, worried about what others think of us. Only in teen agers this is all more acute because they are vulnerable. You'll find out. All I can say is, don't take it too seriously or tragically. You'll make out ok. You are not alone. You will make some mistakes but they won't matter too much if you don't get carried away . . . Don't be in a big hurry to be completely grown up. Don't worry, you'll be grown up soon enough. Enjoy yourself being young while you are still young.[8]

Merton tried to confront young people, as he seems to have done all people, on their own ground granting them their own identity, dignity and integrity—in short, as one human writing to another human. In this sense he demonstrates in his letters to young people that quality which Sister Thérèse Lentfoehr dubbed 'delicate compassion'. To my mind he demonstrated that quality nowhere more strongly than in his letter to an unidentified homosexual, a letter written with understanding and restraint and without condemnation. Significantly he addressed the person as 'Dear Friend'.

First let me try to answer your question as it was put: the first name that occurs to me off hand of a 'proven homosexual' who probably saved his soul, is Oscar Wilde. The poor man suffered greatly and was certainly sincere. I don't know all the details of his later years but the impression I have is that he went through them with a martyr's nobility. I can think of others whom I think did the same though I am not sure if they were Christians so I won't go into that.

In other words, the pitch is this. Homosexuality is not a more 'unforgivable' sin than any other and the rules are the same. You do the best you can, you honestly try to fight it, be sorry, try to avoid occasions, all the usual things. You may not always succeed but in this as anything else, God sees your good will and takes it into account. Trust His mercy and keep trying. And have recourse to all the spiritual aids available. Maybe psychiatric help would be of use.

As I see it, there is a special sort of masochism that gets built into this pattern of inversion. A sort of despair that robs you of any urge to fight back. I'd say that was probably the problem and it is probably psychological in its root. That is what has to be handled, that need to fold up and give up resistance. But why? That is for you to find out. I am not a psychiatric counsellor. All I can say is that God will surely understand your good intentions as well as your weakness, and He is on your side. So have courage and don't give up. And don't waste energy hating yourself. You need that energy for better purposes.[9]

And why was Merton able to respond to young people in a way that impressed them — at a time when many perceived a 'generation gap', distrusted anyone over thirty, thought 'awareness' was available only to the young, and remained unimpressed by the attitudes and opinions of the middle-aged? He did it then, and my experience has shown me that he does it now in continually attracting young readers. I would like to suggest that several factors contributed to this capacity of Merton's: his unhappy childhood, his perceived lack of family, his duties as novice master, his writing itself, his ability to empathize with all different sorts of people, and his hope for a future world that would be better than the one in which he had grown up and in which he lived.

Much of Merton's subsequent experience, I feel, can be explained in light of his childhood, a childhood which, though unhappy, undoubtedly wildly unhappy at times, was probably no unhappier than that of many children in the twentieth century, another fact which causes Merton to mirror the period in which he lived. He tells us himself of some of the unhappiness as in his description of the lycee at Montauban.[10] Michael Mott has helped to fill in some of the details of his childhood in *The Seven Mountains of Thomas Merton* and Anthony Padovano points out in *The Human Journey:* 'His lost childhood was the object of his yearning, a childhood richly revealed in *The Seven Storey Mountain,* symbolically relived in *The Geography of Lograire*. His long pilgrimage for a home to settle him was also a journey back to the home he never had as a child.'[11] Part of the rootlessness of Merton's childhood may be found in loss, the loss of his mother at six, the loss of his father at sixteen, the loss of his Great Aunt Maud, the loss of his maternal grandparents in his early twenties. In his late poem *Cables to the Ace*, he says:

'Another sunny birthday. I am tormented by poetry and loss.'[12] But it was not simply loss that marred Merton's childhood for he grew up in a family strangely at odds with itself. Neither his New Zealander grandmother nor his American grandparents seem to have been delighted at the prospect of the marriage of Owen Merton and Ruth Jenkins. Ruth wrote to Owen's mother, Gertrude Merton: 'Please may I write to tell you how sorry I am to be, even innocently, the cause of your unhappiness about Owen? . . . My own Mother has worried some about it all.'[13]

Some of this antipathy remained in the family, reappearing nearly sixty years later when Merton's uncle, Harold Jenkins, wrote to John Howard Griffin in 1970: 'I note in Ka [Merton's] letter something about getting information from her sister. If that is Gwynne you should know that Ruth & Gwynne were not very good friends, & anything G. may say about Ruth may be suspect.'[14] Donald Grayston has pointed out that 'Merton's own family experience was not unmarked by violence of a number of kinds'.[15] Uncertainty, insecurity, hostility, as well as loss, marred Merton's childhood. His mother was demanding but peculiarly ungiving—echoes of this appear in the mid-60s when Merton asks, in *Cables to the Ace,* a series of questions more or less directed to a mother, his mother: 'What do you teach me', 'What do you want of me', 'What do you seek of me.'[16] Though Merton, rather feebly, says that his father gave him some erratic 'training', evidence indicates that Owen Merton's paternal skills were minimal. D. A. Callard has stated: 'Ruth Merton's death freed Owen in part from family responsibilities which he was tempermentally and financially unable to sustain'.[17] Letters written by Owen Merton and his mistress, Evelyn Scott, who might have

been Merton's stepmother, indicate that Tom had become, by
the mid-1920's, a fractious and rebellious boy, jealous of his
father, determined to prevent his father's marrying a woman
whom his mother's family considered a 'whore'. The pain, in fact,
brought on by the *menage* in which his father entangled them
with Scott was so great that Merton never mentioned her again by
name, never faced the fact that he had effectively prevented his
father's remarriage, never confronted his own role in keeping the
family at loose ends. Years later, when her son, Creighton Scott,
attempted to reestablish contact with Merton, Merton ignored
the overtures.[18] Psychically jarred and bruised Merton saw
himself surrounded by loss and hostility which took away the 'innocence' of his childhood, an innocence, indeed an Edenic
guilelessness, in which he was later to believe and in which he
came to see redemptive power for the individual and society.

Such themes run through much of Merton's writing, particularly through the recently and privately published poems he
wrote for Margie Smith or 'M' or 'S' or whatever initial the next
writer may choose to give the young student nurse with whom he
became involved in 1966. In one such he wrote:

> So all theology
> Is a kind of birthday
> A way home to where we are
>
> Epiphany and Eden
> Where two lost questions
> Make one orbit
> In the middle of nothing
> Is this the answer?
>
> No one ever got born
> All by himself: It takes more than one.
> Every birthday
> Has its own theology.[19]

Death took Merton's immediate family when he was young.
By 1943, with the death of his only brother, he was left with no
close relatives. He had managed to alienate his English guardian

and his American uncle and, though he may have been responsible for much, even most, of what led to the estrangements, he himself harbored wounds which prevented his corresponding with his guardian's widow or his uncle for twenty years and, even then, his letters are timorous and circumspect. While he was, by that time, willing to live with his old wounds, it is obvious that they were still there. He wrote a nice enough letter to Iris Weiss Bennett in 1966 in response to a strident one from her, but later confided to his aunt, Gwynned Merton Trier, she who had supposedly not liked his mother: 'For years I have been on such utterly bad terms with her that I cannot begin to deal with her.'[20] Aunt Gwyn's comment on Iris was simply that Iris had always been 'très difficile'. He did correspond with his remaining relatives in New Zealand (his grandmother did not die until 1956 at the age of 101), but they were not and had never been close to him. He harbored a sentimental attachment to New Zealand and wrote in 1964: 'New Zealand is where my father came from and I have lots of relatives there, it is a kind of homeland in a way.'[21] But that way had had little effect or influence on Merton. Rather it seems that he felt himself bereft of family and that he sought to find his 'family' in his friends and, because of his limited contact with those outside the monastery except by letters, through the 'friends' established by his correspondence. In 1949 he wrote to his mentor and teacher, Dan Walsh: 'I have no relatives and so close friends count as family.'[22]

In many ways he looked to his friends to substitute as family, usually careful to send greetings to their wives and children if they had them, delighting often in anecdotes and pictures of children, such as the picture which his friend Seymour Freedgood sent him of his daughter and her horse. And, through his friends, he came to experience vicariously something of family life. He became especially close to Tommie and Frank O'Callaghan and spent considerable time at their home just off Eastern Parkway in Louisville. Much of the time at the O'Callaghan's was spent with their seven children. Tommie has said:

> Thomas Merton was very comfortable at our home and was very much a part of the family. He helped the children with

their history lessons, played guitar with them or swung
them on his wrists. Our family often joined him for picnics
at Gethsemani. The children knew him as Father Louis
[elsewhere she says that they called him 'Uncle Tom'] and
always liked him . . . We often discussed the responsibilities of marriage and the Christian training of young
children.[23]

Michael Mott states that Merton's private journals suggest that he
'adopted' Diane O'Callaghan and Alice Willett, daughter of a
Bardstown family, as daughters in his imagination.[24] Nancy
O'Callaghan, however, was the only one of the O'Callaghan
children to whom he seems to have written a letter. All this
became very important to Merton. Anthony Padovano suggests:
'He holds fast to friendships because he had lost so soon and so
tragically all three members of his family.'[25]

The young people, of course, with whom Merton came into
the most direct contact were the novices at Gethsemani. He wrote
in his 1963 'Form Letter':

Doubtless I could go on to explain what I think about Jazz (I
like it) the movies (haven't seen one in years, don't miss
them) smoking (don't miss it) TV (never watched it, don't
want to), the newspapers (seldom see one), modern youth
(I like them, at least the kind we've got around here — they
are the only ones I know) cars (I never had one) wives (never
had one, can get along without.)[26]

He was for several years their novice master and spiritual director,
and there is no doubt that his feeling was often paternal. He
shared their concerns and enjoyed the contact with young people. He came, in time, to be called 'Uncle Louie', a name which
amused him. He was always concerned with the education of the
young and the Gethsemani novices became the youth he tried to
educate. He wrote letters to several former novices, one to former
monk Richard Loomis in 1958:

Real small children have become for me something remote
and mysterious which I tend to idealize. The smallest that

come my way are a couple of fifteen year olds from Detroit who take their vacations in the novitiate and are very lively. I like to have them around, one does feel more like a father going out to work with one trotting at each side of you and both talking their heads off, while the silent line of novices trails off behind. They scandalize all by an interest in wildlife and professional football and no obvious signs whatever of piety. Good solid prospects! They really are very good kids. My only moments of annoyance with them are when they insist on shooting tin cans with a twenty two within earshot of the novitiate. This I cannot brook. They have renounced the twenty two, (I fondly delude myself) after one shamefaced expedition for tin-can shooting at the lake. The rabbits are not hard put to it to avoid such talkative huntsmen.[27]

Merton's writing, particularly his poetry, was at times occasioned and informed by children. Sister Thérèse Lentfoehr, Anthony Padovano and others point out that a frequent theme in Merton's poetry is that of children. Sister Thérèse said: 'It has been said that in every poet there is a child, since in some fashion he invariably retains a child's vision. Merton is no exception, and with this vision comes an empathy with children that characterizes his most sensitive poems.'[28] She points to images of children in such early poems as 'The Winter's Night', 'Aubade: Lake Erie', 'Evening' and 'Aubade: Harlem'. Merton's letter to Jan Boggs, mentioned at the beginning of this paper, attempted to answer for a high-school sophomore what a poem is.

I would say that a poem was any piece of writing or spoken utterance which, in symbolic and rhythmic language seeks to communicate a deep and direct experience of life in some aspect or other. A poem however cannot be confined to mere teaching, nor is it necessarily 'inspirational' or serious. It must however in some way or other strive to be more memorable and more challenging than mere prose.[29]

Many of his poems were directly inspired by children. The murder of four black children in Birmingham, Alabama, in September

1963 moved him so deeply that he wrote the poem 'And the Children of Birmingham'. According to Sister Mary Luke Tobin, this incident led Merton to even greater involvement in the race crisis in the United States. 'I think he came to a special consciousness about blacks specifically at the time the Birmingham children were killed. It seemed such an outrage to him; you could see it in his eyes when he talked about racial injustice.'[30]

Black children, members of Sister Marialein Lorenz's high school class in Mobile, Alabama, had sent Merton an amice, a corporal, a purificator, and a finger towel at the time of his ordination in 1949. He used them in his first mass and later wrote a long letter to the class. In that letter he said: 'One of the main reasons why I am glad to hear from young fellows and girls is that you have all the same problems that I once had and I think that God has shown us all the same way out of it.'[31]

One member of that class, Gloria Sylvester Bennett, struck up a correspondence with Merton in the 1960s and he wrote to her in 1967:

What you say about the children is so maddening to me. That they have to be taught that there is nothing wrong with having a black skin, and that even the nuns don't know enough to help. I have had my own very small share of being beyond the pale in various societies — foreigner in French and English schools and so on — and I have some experiences of what it feels like. But I was always able to develop the right accent and the right protective feathers in a few months. Only in nightmares do I really experience it as it must be. You are certainly right that Negro children should grow up knowing enough to love themselves and be glad that they are themselves.[32]

When pictures of the Birmingham bombing appeared in the March 4, 1964, issue of *Look,* he cut out a picture of one of the children, Carole Denise McNair, and carefully kept the photograph in his journal. He captioned it: 'Carole Denise McNair, one of the four bomb-murdered Negro children, never learned to hate'. This was because she was holding a white doll in

the picture and it moved Merton to write his poem 'Picture of a
Black Child with a White Doll'. On October 12, 1964, he wrote
to Carole Denise's father, Chris McNair, who had taken the
photograph:

> This is not exactly an easy letter to write. There is so much to
> say, and there are no words in which to say it. I will say it as
> simply as I can, in the hope that you will understand this
> message from a total stranger.
>
> I saw the pictures you took of Carole Denise in 'Look' several
> months ago. One of them meant so much to me that I cut it
> out, and kept it. It seemed to say so much, principally about
> goodness, and about the way in which the goodness of the
> human heart is invincible, and overcomes the evil and
> wickedness that may sometimes be present in other men.
>
> Being a writer, and a writer of poems, I eventually was
> moved to write a poem, and now that it has been published
> I want to send at least this copy of it. It is a somewhat angry
> poem, because I think that a little anger is still called for. I
> hope that love and compassion also come through, for
> anger is not enough and never will be.
>
> At any rate, I wanted to say what you already know and
> believe, that the mercy and goodness of the Lord chose
> Carole Denise to be with Him forever in His love and His
> light. Nor is she forgotten on this earth. She remains as a
> witness to innocence and to love, and an inspiration to all of
> us who remain to face the labor, the difficulty and the
> heart-break of the struggle for human rights and dignity.[33]

Not all Merton's poems connected with children were serious and
inspired by tragic events. Merton's friend, Amiya Chakravarty,
held a 'Merton Session' in the Spring of 1967 and Merton wrote
and sent him his poem 'A Round and a Hope for Smith Girls'.
Merton said to Chakravarty on April 25:

> I am grateful to you for bringing me in contact with so many
> new friends at Smith. I am touched by their response and
> feel very close to them and grateful to them. Living alone in

the woods, I am more appreciative of friendship than ever before. . . . As to the poem, it was rather inadequate, as it had in mind people less mature, but still no matter how mature we are we need to know that we are not as helpless as we may sometimes feel.[34]

An interesting codicil to the Smith poem is that Merton was asked by a Vassar group that next summer to send a holograph poem which might be sold for a peace benefit. In a lapse from what would have been considered appropriate with Ivy League sister schools in the late 1960s, he sent them the Smith poem.

I am sending along a poem — in holograph, or kakography, or just plain a-graph: a piece of non-writing. . . . [A] possible misfortune is that is is a poem for Smith, and here it goes to Vassar. I mean, do not take this to be an expression of aggressive loyalty to Smith. I love Vassar too, but I happen to have more friends at Smith at the moment. Though maybe by now they are all flown away.[35]

Correspondence with Suzanne Butrovich seems to have prompted the prologue of the 'North' section of *The Geography of Lograire,* that poem with the unlikely title 'Why I have a Wet Footprint on Top of My Mind'. As stated earlier, themes and images of childhood and children run through the poems Merton wrote to the young nurse, possibly because she was herself only nineteen years old and a student. In one of these, called 'Louisvile Airport/May 5, 1966', he weaves the innocence of childhood with its redemptive power together with his newfound love for the nurse.

> Here on the foolish grass
> Where the rich in small jets
> Land with their own hopes
> And their own kind
>
> We with the gentle liturgy
> Of shy children have permitted God
> To make again His first world
> Here on the foolish grass

After the spring rain has dried
And all the loneliness

Is for a moment lost in this simple
Liturgy of children permitting God
To make again that love
Which is His alone

His alone and terribly obscure and rare
Love walks gently as a deer
To where we sit on this green grass
In the marvel of this day's going down
Celebrated only
By all the poets since the world began.

This is God's own love He makes in us
As all the foolish rich fly down
Onto this paradise of grass
Where the world first began
Where God began
To make His love in man and woman
For the first time
Here on the sky's shore
Where the eternal sun goes down
And all the millionaires in small jets
Land with their own hopes
And their own kind

We with the tender liturgy
And tears
Of the newborn
Celebrate the first creation
Of solemn love
Now for the first time forever
Made by God in these
Four wet eyes and cool lips
And worshipping hands
When one voiceless beginning
Of splendid fire

Rises out of the heart
And the evening becomes One Flame
Which all the prophets
Accurately foresaw
Would make things plain
And create the whole world
Over again

There is only this one love
Which is now our world
Our foolish grass
Celebrated by all the poets
Since the first beginning
Of any song.[36]

Finally, my personal favorite among his poems inspired by young people is the deceptively simple and haunting 'Grace's House'. Elbert Sisson, a friend and correspondent of Merton's, had enclosed some drawings done by his children, Grace and Clare, in a letter to Merton. Merton replied:

I was very happy with your letter and above all with the pictures, especially the drawings of the children. I was so moved by Grace (pun) and by her house and by her lovely little self that I wrote a poem which I enclose. And as for Clare, even more than Grace, she has just stolen my heart completely and I don't know what to do or say. What a blessing it is to be surrounded with so many images of God and to live in the midst of the loves and sorrows and complications and simplicities that God has given you in them. May He preserve our world a little longer for the likes of such beautiful beings, whom He so loves.[37]

The poem meticulously describes Grace's drawing of a house and its surroundings—animals, trees, grass, sun—and Merton ended it, commenting on her failure to provide access to the house, a bittersweet and poignant line: 'Alas, there is no road to Grace's house.'
     The empathy which Sister Thérèse says that Merton has with children, growing in part in her view from his own childlike simplicity,

was another factor in Merton's response to young people. Not that he did not claim empathy with all sorts of groups (and they with him), usually groups outside of what he perceived as the 'establishment'. He claimed empathy with Latin Americans, with Chinese, with blacks and others so it is not surprising that he also claimed empathy with another non-establishment group, young people. There is no evidence that Merton knew much of the underground student writing and he died about the time that Jerry Faber's 'The Student as Nigger' hit college campuses with force, but he knew something was in the air in the 1960s, knew that things were 'happening' at Berkeley and other campuses, knew about Hippies, LSD and other drugs. He was sympathetic with the organization known as SDS (Students for a Democratic Society) and wrote to one of its members at Seton Hall: 'What I know of SDS looks pretty good to me. I feel much closer to you people than to the big block of squares that stands between our generations.'[38] Or again: 'One thing I do like about the world these days is that your generation is protesting louder and better and more intelligently than most of the others have so far.'

Merton was able to remember what it was like to be young, to be a student, to feel excluded from the larger society. Edward Rice has recorded of their friends at Columbia that 'to a man [they were] fighting the Establishment and [were] young, rebellious, alienated misfits and (in their own eyes) downtrodden and poor'.[39] Merton always identified with and felt sympathetic toward those whom he perceived to be marginal to society and he found promising the attempts on the part of some young people to be marginal. And, as he did with other groups, he identified himself with that marginality. He said to Suzanne Butorovich:

I love Bobby D[ylan]. I have lots of his stuff here and what do you think I am: six hundred years old or something, that I don't know Paul McCartney is a Beatle? I have their record 'Revolver' — only one I have. I like them fine . . . You are right you probably don't have to take LSD you sound real alive without it . . . I live alone in the woods and borrowed a record player I am a real sneaky hermit and oh yes I love the hippies and am an underground hippy monk but I don't need LSD to turn on either the birds turn me on.[40]

In his 'Advent-Christmas 1967' circular letter to his friends, he made some of these views more widely known:

Other opinions: I don't think the Hippies are a menace to the nation. If Lyndon Baines Johnson suddenly went into nirvana and abandoned politics it would not be a disaster. However the 'hate Johnson' trend in some quarters is repugnant and infantile. I like the Beatles (what I have heard of them). The mere mention of LSD does *NOT* make me break out in a cold sweat. Several friends of mine were in the peace march on the Pentagon in October. . . . In other words a great deal of noise is being made about issues that are peripheral.[41]

Merton's sympathy toward and empathy with young people led him to hope that the young could eventuallly bring about a better world, or, to put it another way, that the world could become better by everyone's recovering childhood and thus recovering 'paradise'. He sent his old friend and teacher, Mark Van Doren, a copy of 'Grace's House' in 1962, saying in the letter that accompanied it:

Here is a poem. That is all. I have no other pretext for writing, but glad to have this one. It is a poem about a drawing of a house by a five year old child. What a drawing, what a house, what suns and birds. It is true that we do not know where we are.

That there are circles within circles, and that if we choose we can let loose in the circle of paradise the very wrath of God: this is said by Boehme in his confessions. We are trying to bear him out, but children can, if they still will, give us the lie and show us our folly. But we are now more and more persistent in refusing to see any such thing. All we will see is the image, the absurd image, the mask over our own emptiness.[42]

Merton was impressed by young people and realized, without fear and anxiety, that a new generation would rise and the old generation, his generation, would pass. He just hoped it would be a generation bent on making a better world and he was sanguine that what he saw in young people indicated that. He wrote in 1967 in the same circular letter: 'A new generation is sooner or later going to take over, and I think the youngest generation in religion and elsewhere (those born about 1940–1947) look very good indeed. The old guys like me have had it anyway.'[43]

Finally, Merton's sanguinity led him to conceive of a mystical union with children and with our own childhoods in which we might find again our innocence and come to know again the truths which he felt children instinctively know. In 1967, five years after she had drawn her first picture for Merton, Grace Sisson, who had obviously read or had pointed out to her Merton's last line to 'Grace's House', sent him another drawing, again with trees, grass and animals, but also, this time, with a road. She called it 'The Road to Joy'. Merton responded in a letter, picking up her phrase and avering his sense of oneness with Grace and by extension with all young persons:

> I want especially to thank you for your note and for your new drawing which is very significant. I like the way you see all the little creatures tending toward a tree which is sort of a tree of life. I am glad you still draw things with love, and I hope you will never lose that. But I hope you and I together will secretly travel our own road to joy, which is mysteriously revealed to us without our exactly realizing. When I say that, I don't want you to start thinking about it. You already know it without thinking about it.[44]

In the end, Thomas Merton called on us all to recover the innocence of childhood and to travel, without thinking about it, that road to joy, that road on which Jesus 'teaches us again the lesson of spiritual childhood'.[45]

Thomas Merton Studies Center
Bellarmine College
Louisville, Kentucky

NOTES — The Road to Joy

TMSC = Thomas Merton Studies Center, Bellarmine College
1. Jan Boggs to Thomas Merton, February 11, 1966 [TMSC].
2. Thomas Merton to Jim Frost, January 7, 1964 [TMSC].
3. Thomas Merton to John Allen Eastman, September 13, 1967 [TMSC].
4. Thomas Merton to Sven Heilo, October 20, 1963 [TMSC].
5. Thomas Merton to Suzanne Butorovich, June 22, 1967 [TMSC].
6. Thomas Merton to Tony Boyd, March 20, 1967 [TMSC].
7. Thomas Merton to Kathleen Gillard, September 19, 1967 [TMSC].
8. Thomas Merton To Cindy McElhose, April 10, 1967 [TMSC].
9. Letter to an Unidentified Homosexual, January 9, 1967 [TMSC].
10. Thomas Merton, *The Seven Storey Mountain* (New York: Harcourt Brace & Company, 1948) pp. 48–61.
11. Anthony T. Padovano, *The Human Journey: Thomas Merton, Symbol of a Century* (Garden City: Doubleday, 1982) p. 81.
12. Thomas Merton, *Cables to the Ace* (New York: New Directions, 1968) p. 7.
13. Ruth Calvert (Jenkins) Merton to Gertrude Hannah (Grierson) Merton, June 17, 1912 [Humanities Research Center, Austin, Texas].
14. Harold Brewster Jenkins to John Howard Griffin, December 9, 1970 [TMSC].
15. Donald Grayston, 'Thomas Merton and Family Violence.' *Merton Seasonal* 8 (Autum 1983) 3, p. 4.
16. Merton, *Cables to the Ace* pp. 6–7.
17. D. A. Callard, *Pretty Good for a Woman: the Enigmas of Evelyn Scott* (New York: Norton, 1985) p. 72.

18. Conversation with Brother Patrick Hart, OCSO
19. 'Untitled Poem' in *Eighteen Poems* (New York: New Directions, 1985).
20. Thomas Merton to Gwynned (Merton) Trier, December 20, 1966 [TMSC].
21. Thomas Merton to Father Placid, OCSO. [TMSC].
22. Thomas Merton to Daniel Clark Walsh, February 24, 1959 [TMSC].
23. Thomasine 'Tommie' O'Callaghan, 'From Lamb Chops to Peanut Butter,' *St. Anthony Messenger* 86 (December 1978): 77, p. 37.
24. Michael Mott, *The Seven Mountains of Thomas Merton* (Boston: Houghton Mifflin, 1984) p. 472.
25. Padovano, *The Human Journey* p. 98.
26. Thomas Merton, 'Form Letter' to Friends, 1963.
27. Thomas Merton to Richard Loomis, January 4, 1958 [TMSC].
28. Thérèse Lentfoehr, SDS, *Words and Silence: On the Poetry of Thomas Merton* (New York: New Directions, 1979) p. 85.
29. Thomas Merton to Jan Boggs, February 9, 1966 [TMSC].
30. Paul Wilkes, ed., *Merton, By Those Who Knew Him Best* (San Francisco: Harper & Row, 1984) p. 97.
31. Thomas Merton to 'My Dear Friends', Members of Sister Marialein Lorenz's High School Class, June 2, 1949 [TMSC].
32. Thomas Merton to Gloria Sylvester Bennett, January 19, 1967 [TMSC].
33. Thomas Merton to Chris McNair, October 12, 1964 [TMSC].
34. William H. Shannon, ed., *The Hidden Ground of Love: The Letters of Thomas Merton on Religious Experience and Social Concerns* (New York: Farrar, Straus and Giroux, 1985) p. 116.
35. Thomas Merton to Meg Shore, August 3, 1967 [TMSC].
36. 'Louisville Airport/May 5, 1966' in *Eighteen Poems*.
37. Thomas Merton to Elbert R. Sisson, June 1962 [TMSC].
38. Thomas Merton to Michael Hodder, January 26, 1967 [TMSC].
39. Edward Rice, *The Man in the Sycamore Tree: The Good Times & Hard Life of Thomas Merton* (Garden City: Doubleday, 1970) p. 30.
40. Thomas Merton to Suzanne Butorovich, June 22, 1967 [TMSC].
41. Thomas Merton, 'Advent-Christmas Letter 1967' [TMSC].
42. Thomas Merton to Mark Van Doren, August 9, 1962 [TMSC].
43. 'Advent-Christmas Letter 1967.'
44. Thomas Merton to Grace Sisson, May 13, 1967 [TMSC].
45. Thomas Merton to Sister Thérèse Lentfoehr, December 19, 1953 [Columbia].

John Albert

The Christ-Filled Decadence of Thomas Merton

C HRISTIAN LITERATURE FROM as early as the second
century *Epistle of Barnabas* has warned believers not to
give rein to their natural instincts lest they feel free to
mix with rogues and sinners and grow to resemble them. The
Didache — perhaps the earliest post-testamental text, in harmony
with *Psalm One* and the *First Letter of John* — speaks of two
Ways: the Way of Life and the Way of Death, emphasizing that
the difference between these two ways is great. Echoing Saint
Paul, the author of the *Epistle of Diognetus* describes Christ's
followers as 'aliens' in this world, citizens of heaven on their way
home. And spiritual masters throughout the centuries have
rightly pointed out dangers, realized and potential, in Christian
lives, informing the faithful in their awareness of evil, guiding
them in their behavior.

Yet the desire to be, to live, to grow, impels each human person
to seek a significant place in the time process. And 'belief in the soul's
immortality is intimately linked with the place of the human person
in an ongoing historical process which has two terminals — an

individual one in death and a universal one in the end of the world'.[1]

Thomas Merton's mature development as monk and artist will always be linked to the age during which he died in Bangkok, Thailand on December 10, 1968. The nineteenth-century aesthetic and religious revolt which took place in Europe came to full force in America in the 1960s. It was an era of rattling instability and angry reaction on every side, a time of the reassertion of personal values and a quest for human freedom, but also a time when all religious, moral, social and psychological restrictions were thrown off. A spirit of 'common sense', complacency and restraint eroded as people gorged themselves on an excess of sex, drugs, alcohol, and ego. The 1960s was an apocalyptic age of messiahs and enemies of the state. The Jefferson Airplane sang: 'We are all outlaws in the eyes of America. In order to survive we steal, cheat, lie, forge, . . . , hide and deal. We are obscene, lawless, hideous, dangerous, dirty, violent and young.'[2] But Alvin Toffler saw the youth rebellion in perspective: 'The successful "sale" of the hippie style model to young people all over the technological societies is one of the classic merchandising stories of our time.'[3]

Many voices were heard, many mantles worn. It was the time of gurus in saffron and gurus in black, of Zen postures and chemical mysticism. Many of every generation posed their way through the decade, not unlike those long ago denounced by Saint Cyprian of Carthage: pseudo-prophets and charlatan sooth-sayers, serpent-tongued deceivers of youth, skilled corruptors of the truth filling their hearers with visions unreal and undesirable.[4]

The 1960s is recognized as an era of unparalleled social upheaval and spiritual promise in the history of the United States of America. The Cuban missle crisis, the Civil Rights Movement, the U.N. visit of Paul VI, the Viet Nam War, the Second Vatican Council, the moon landing, the invasion of the Beatles, the Chicago Convention, the assasination of the Kennedys and Martin Luther King, Jr., all made life afterwards seem derivative, repetitious, void of value and conviction. Focusing solely on the

Black Panthers Trial, New Haven, Connecticut in April-May, 1970, Sydney E. Ahlstrom retrojected the dilemma of producing an historically accurate account of the 1960s:

> Too few introspective diaries were kept, too many levels of actions were proceeding at once, too many conflicting forces impinged on the university community. It meant too many different things to various groups of people; and from beginning to end the events had no physical or spiritual boundaries. Only with the passage of time, if ever, will it become clearer which elements of the situation had the most enduring effects and which ones, therefore, should have registered their impact on would-be historians. How much more impossible is it to account for a whole nation's turmoil during an entire decade![5]

And while many in the 1960s evinced irresponsibility and ir-resolution, there were authentic voices, persons making genuine religious and artistic attempts at capturing and reflecting the reality of their times. These attempts had validity and succeeded in their trial, establishing standards of influence for everything that had followed.[6]

In his *Poetry and Contemplation: A Reappraisal* (1958) Thomas Merton delineated a second-order reflection on his own experience as monk-poet and a method by which it can be inter-preted:

> A sincere and efficacious desire to enter more deeply into the beauty of the Christian mystery implies a willingness to sacrifice the things which are called 'beautiful' by the deca-dent standards of a materialistic world. Yet the Christian contemplative need not confine himself to religious, still less to the professionally 'pious' models. He will, of course, read Scripture and above all the contemplative saints: John of the Cross, Teresa of Avila, John Ruysbroek, Bonaven-ture, Bernard. But no one can be a poet without reading the good poets of his own time — T. S. Eliot, Auden, Spender,

Rilke, Pasternak, Dylan Thomas, Garcia Lorca. One might add that a fully integrated vision of our time and of its spirit presupposes some contact with the genious of Baudelaire and Rimbaud, who are Christians inside out.[7]

Thus Merton linked authentic religious experience with aesthetic experience and demonstrated his growing conviction that he who arrogates the total truth to his own understanding of it has lost it. In religious experience ontological, epistemological, moral and biblical truth become one as quest, knowing and unknowing equal components of the same experience. Merton's declaration dissolves the realms of truth through an inverson of value. Merton himself had helped to effect the renascence of the mystical writers he mentions as counter-balance to the professionally 'pious' authors whose works largely and limitingly formed the content of monastic *lectio*. The 'non-religious' authors he lists balanced the monastic world-view with the modern world. But for a 'fully integrated vision of our time and of its spirit' Merton himself looks to the 'contra-religious' and 'contra-secular' witness of the decadent poets, past and present, who sacrifice the 'beautiful' in spirit and matter in their confrontation with Mystery. The shift in value Merton delineated was not only the vertical shift in the poet's own apprehension of truth but also the horizontal shift that concerned the poet in his relationship with his society. The 'decadent standards of a materialistic world' must be redressed by the 'decadent standards' of the poet in confrontation with it.

Thomas Merton was no *flamen summus* of the absurd, no priest of paradox and perversity as ends in themselves. When he burned flax in the face of images, it was as reminder of his own. Idolatry — given and received — was to be shattered. Merton kept the aesthete and the ascetic in constant tension within himself, and reflected this in a logically consistent contemplative appreciation of decadence.

The following essay surveys 1.) Thomas Merton's principles for a criticism of decadent aesthetics; 2.) decadence as a mode of self-expression for Merton; 3.) some keys for an interpretation of decadence in the art and life of Thomas Merton.

1.   THOMAS MERTON'S PRINCIPLES FOR A CRITICISM
OF DECADENT AESTHETICS

In *Poetry, Symbolism, Typology,* used as a chapter in *Bread in the Wilderness* (1953), Merton described in terms of the 'paradisal' and the 'post-technological' the confrontation between the 'decadent standards' of modern society and the poets of decadence. For Merton, all the animals and elements of creations, the whole of natural economy, have so impressed themselves upon the spirit of man that they tend to mean to him much more than they mean in themselves. And that is why they enter so mysteriously into the substance of our poetry, visions, dreams:

That too is why in an age, like the one we live in, in which cosmic symbolism has been almost forgotten and submerged under a tidal wave of trademarks, political party buttons, advertising and propoganda slogans, and all the rest — is necessarily an age of mass psychosis. A world in which the poet can find practically no material in the common substance of everyday life, and in which he is driven crazy in his search for the vital symbols that have been buried alive under a mountain of cultural garbage, can only end up, like ours, in self-destruction. And that is why some of the best poets of our time are running wild among the tombs in the moonlit cemeteries of surrealism. Faithful to the instincts of the true poet, they are unable to seek their symbols anywhere save in the depths of the spirit where these symbols are found. These depths have become a ruin and a slum. But poetry must, and does, make good use of whatever it finds there: starvation, madness, frustration, and death.[8]

In *Theology of Creativity* (1960) Merton confronted the problem of self-expression and the myth of the genius as hero and as high priest in a cult of art that tends to substitute itself for religion. Merton judged this delusion serious and claimed that here 'creativity' sometimes takes on a 'demonic quality' which makes it one of the most tragic temptations of our era. Merton was quick to point out that one of the most tragic aspects of this problem is the fact that 'the weaknesses of conventional religiosity are in some sense to blame for this apostasy of the artist'. It is the inarticulateness of the preacher that moves the artist to assume a prophetic irresponsibility intended to justify not so much his art as his cult of himself. What comes to matter is no longer art or the work of art as such but art as the 'monument of genius', not as the symbol of transcendent spiritual reality but as the ikon of the artist himself. The artist thus renounces everything else, including morality and sanity, in order to devote himself exclusively to the magic of his artistic gifts, perceived as having superhuman quality. His life becomes then a deliberate cultivation of experience intended to open up new depths of his genius:

> Indeed it sometimes seems to him that a full, connatural acquaintance with evil and with despair has become a sacred obligation for him because only in this way can he fullly assert his protest against the conventions and hypocrisies of a society he despises. His vocation is to devote his magic gifts as fully as possible to negation and to defiance, and if in saying 'no' he can also explode with self-satisfaction, then all the better for him and for his art. He is a professional mystic-in-reverse.[9]

It does not matter how sombre or perverse his experiences may be. What matters is not their beauty, their significance, or even their reality, but the fact that they are *his* experiences. If they are sinful, degraded, subhuman, this makes no difference. Indeed it makes his experiences even more significant. The genius with his magic soul has descended into hell for a season of satanically detached lucidity which frightens ordinary men. This assures him of his own superiority and confirms him in his 'prophetic' vocation. The artist who descends into the hell of experience for experience sake proves himself no less complacent for being impure, concluded Merton, and:

> . . . offers no escape from bourgeois smugness, for it is the same smugness turned inside out. This accounts for the dullness, the

sameness, the conventionality, and the absurdity of all the second-rate followers of the few rare ones whose voices, speaking out of the shadows with Baudelaire and Rimbaud, impose upon the hearer the silence and the awe that are fitting in the presence of tragedy.[10]

Two aesthetic principles in *Answers on Art and Freedom* (1965) further developed Merton's attitude toward decadence. With regard to his society: the poet who rebels against conventional Western society (Rimbaud, Baudelaire, the Beats) establishes that society more firmly in its conviction 'that all artists are by necessity opium fiends and feeds its sense of magnaminity in tolerating such people'. The enemies of the artist's freedom are those who 'most profit from his *seeming* to be free,' whether or not he is:

And the artist himself, to the extent that he is dominated by introjected philistine condemnations of his art, pours out his energy and integrity in resisting these tyrannical pressures which come to him from within himself. His art then wastes itself in reaction against the anti-art of the society in which he lives (or he cultivates anti-art as a protest against the art cult of the society in which he lives).[11]

With regard to his art: the impiety of the Sartian who chooses the ugly, the absurd, and the obscene as an act of which he is the 'incontestable author' rejoins the piety of the monastic novice who chooses the most arbitrary and most pointless acts of self-mortification in order to see himself as pleasing to God. In either case there is a naive and narcissistic emphasis on the pure voluntaristic choice for its own sake. The supposed purity of this voluntarism is not purity at all — it is merely abstract willfulness:

True artistic freedom can never be a matter of sheer willfulness, or arbitrary posturing. It is the outcome of authentic possibilities, understood and accepted in their own terms, not the refusal of the concrete in favor of the purely 'interior'. In the last analysis, the only valid witness to the artist's creative freedom is his work itself. The artist

builds his own freedom and forms his own artistic conscience, by the work of his hands. Only when the work is
finished can he tell whether or not it was done 'freely'.[12]

Thomas Merton continuously stressed that the task of
Catholic theology is to preserve, as well as explain, Mystery. A
theology which seeks to render all the answers to Mystery other
than Mystery Itself has abdicated its position as orthodox, and
true liturgy — properly celebrated — is that locus for the 'religious'
person to express in public fashion that which is held in the
secrecy of the heart. And as early as 1959, in 'Easter: The New
Life', he made the declaration: 'The most important thing that
strikes us when we read the Pauline Epistles objectively, is that
most of the things that many sincerely pious Christians worry
about are things which do not matter.'[13]
Repeatedly Merton also warned against the catastrophic
results of misapplication of ascetical and mystical principles
learned from saints, Zen masters, hesychasts and desert fathers.
The *Dark Night of the Soul,* the koan collections, the Jesus
Prayer and the 'sayings' of the desert abbas have been sources of
personality disintegration. Thus, of itself, a religious work is
morally and psychologically neutral, a truth attested to over and
over again by the disparate responses of more than one perceiver,
by the discrepancies of response experienced by one perceiver at
various times. Merton was aware of his own — seemingly inconsistent if not contradictory — various appraisals of the same master
or school of spirituality.
The Parable of the Wheat and the Darnel (Mt 13:24–30) —
biblical basis for any discernment of religious experience — ad-
vises against any 'too quick' action, in the believer's own life or
against others. Merton's sensitivity to the perplexity of religious
experience and its discernment is demonstrated in 'The Ranters
and Their Pleads' and 'A Clever Strategem: Or, How to Handle
Mystics' (both published after his death as part of *The Geography
of Lograire*). Ranter Jacob Bauthemly, punished for his
'abominable' doctrines by being burned through the tongue,
says: 'O God what shall I say thou art when thou cans't not be

named/For if I say I see thee it is nothing but thy seeing of thy-self. . . .'[14] Basing his text on a passage in *The Soul of the Bantu* by W. C. Willoughby, Merton presents an open-ended nar-rative. Responsibility for gathering the deleterious darnel from the righteous wheat is forced upon the reader:

> When I was out in the Nyasaland Missions we held a meeting of five thousand converts at which religious fervor naturally mounted to the highest pitch. So much intensity of religious feeling required to be carefully channeled to prevent disturbances. Fervor must not be permitted to dissipate itself in wasteful, even riotous disorders. One mor-ning two of the leading teachers came to report some ex-periences they were having. They had been out in the bush all night praying and they had felt their bodies lifted up from the earth while bright angelic beings came to meet them as they ascended. What did this mean? I replied not in word but in deed. I went to the dispensary, took down the salts, gave them each a stiff dose and sent them off to bed. The visions and ascensions immediately ceased, and were replaced by a sweetly reasonable piety that disturbed no one. A missionary must combine spiritual passion with sound sense. He must keep an eye on his followers.[15]

Soto Zen Master Dogen (1200–1253) joins the giants of the West in *Cables to the Ace* (1967), Number Sixty-Two. Merton was fond of him. Compassion and the impermanence of all things, self-knowledge, self-discipline and self-abandonment are domi-nant themes of his doctrine. Dogen was accustomed to tell his monks: 'You should establish your practice in delusion'.[16] This is the antidote to man's refusal to confront his naked self, the *diver-sion* Merton borrowed from Pascal: the dread, the flight from ig-norance and wretchedness and death (*Pensees* 8:132). Thomas Merton knew that it is only by looking within ourselves that we find the possibility of genuine happiness, for it is within ourselves that we encounter God—a doctrine Merton found majestically ar-ticulated in Book Ten of Saint Augustine's *Confessions*.

2.　　　DECADENCE AS THOMAS MERTON'S
MODE OF SELF-EXPRESSION

The 'modern man', we know, is not any and every man,
woman and child who lives in the present epoch but only the person who lives on the leading edge of contemporary experience.
Every epoch will have its modern man since the leading edge of
experience will constantly change like a wave front. The *standpoint* of the modern man of one epoch will appear to have been
the *myth* of that period to the modern man of another epoch. It
is the most important element of a culture, the primary expression of its experience that we regard as the myth of the past and
the standpoint that makes the modern man modern. It is 'the
thing about which we are most serious, the point of view which
constitutes our enlightenment and our emancipation'.[17] The
epochal man, the man of the moment, is brought to life by the
moment itself: 'the readiness is all!' declares Shakespeare's
Hamlet (5:2). He is the *Zufallsprodukt,* the living result of his
circumstances, determined by them as much as determining
them.

That Thomas Merton stood at the leading edge of contemporary experience has been sufficiently established, specific studies
indicating his impact as 'Social Critic' (James Baker — 1971); 'Different Drummer' (Robert Voight — 1972); 'Prophet in the Belly of
a Paradox' (Gerald Twomey, editor — 1978); 'Symbol of a Century'
(Anthony Padovano — 1982). Merton, as 'Solitary Explorer' (Elena
Malits — 1980), became archetype of the spiritual search: to think
monk was to think Merton. Thomas Merton remains prominent
not so much because he influenced his epoch — and that he certainly did — as because his epoch — our times — has recognized in
his art and in his life the reflection of its spirit. Merton kept what
Sydney Ahlstrom described as 'introspective diaries' — found not
only in the still unpublished private journals (properly so-called)
but in highly personal and immensely appealing published works
such as *The Seven Storey Mountain* itself, *The Secular Journal,
The Sign of Jonas* and *Conjectures of a Guilty By-Stander.*

The prevailing myth of our times, at least as sharply focused in the 1960s, is FREEDOM. Where freedom has been reduced to bondage—psychological, in anxiety; political, in oppression; theological, in sin—the myth is articulated as LIBERATION. And decadence—psychological non-restraint; political revolution; theological dissent—becomes the means to new freedom. Disintegration precedes reintegration. Having examined his principles for a criticism of decadent aesthetics, we can now look to decadence as Thomas Merton's mode of self-expression.

Thomas Merton was no abecedarian in sin and human willfullness. His was no ideational awareness of evil. Sin and suffering were modes of identification for him. As early as 1941, before entering Gethsemani Abbey, he scrutinized himself in *My Argument with the Gestapo* (his earlier title was *Journal of My Escape from the Nazis*):

> But what most of all struck me dumb were the two questions that I even feared to ask myself: If I am here to have a good time without hurting other people, why is it, first, that you can't have the pleasures everybody believes in without hurting somebody? And why is it, second, that you never get the pleasure you expect anyway?[18]

In this work Merton established the two polarities, the two modes of life, that would hold him, pull him, energize him and thrust him into ever deeper awareness his entire remaining years: he was a 'waiter'—contemplative—and a 'seeker'—artist.[19] The *person* Merton was waiting for was himself, the other at his side, and in both, ultimately, Christ. The way to this meeting of the person was his inquiry expressed through writing:

> 'What do you see that you write?' '. . . I am still trying to find out: and that is why I write.' 'How will you find out by writing?' 'I will keep putting things down until they become clear.' 'And if they do not become clear?' 'I will have a hundred books, full of symbols, full of everything I ever knew or ever saw or ever thought.' 'If it never becomes clear, perhaps you will have more books than if it were clear

at once.' 'No doubt. But I say if it were all clear at once, I would not really understand it, either. Some things are too clear to be understood, and what you think is your understanding of them is only a kind of charm, a kind of incantation in your mind concerning that thing. This is not understanding: it is something you remember. So much for definitions! We always have to go back and start from the beginning and make over all the definitions for ourselves again.[20]

On July 23, 1961, Merton wrote to Dorothy Day about his increasing skepticism concerning his own writings as representative of the 'Catholic position': 'I find myself more and more drifting toward the derided and probably quite absurd and defeatist position of a sort of Christian anarchist. This of course would be foolish, if I followed it to the end. But it is no less foolish to hang in midair halfway to it.'[21]

In his 'First and Last Thoughts: An Author's Preface' to *A Thomas Merton Reader* (1962) Merton confessed what was already self-evident: the struggle between Father M. Louis Merton, OCSO, the monk, and Thomas Merton, the writer:

I have had to accept the fact that my life is almost totally paradoxical. I have also had to learn gradually to get along without apologizing for the fact, even to myself. And perhaps this preface is an indication that I have not yet completely learned. No matter. It is in the paradox itself, the paradox which was and still is a source of insecurity. I have become convinced that the very contradictions in my life are in some ways signs of God's mercy to me: if only because someone so complicated and so prone to confusion and self-defeat could hardly survive for long without special mercy. And since this in no way depends on the approval of others, the awareness of it is a kind of liberation.[22]

As a monk Thomas Merton knew the *chiarascuro* quality of Christian spirituality: the black surround of limited human existence and fallen nature, the negative affects that formed him and shaped him and set him in his struggle. Merton prayed the psalms because all their dark images and feelings reflected his own heart, if not his actions. Though 'Light' and 'Love' and 'Joy' characterized him — they are the marks of the true Cistercian — Merton knew that authentic Christianity is a movement into ever-widening absorption of the believer in obscurity and loneliness and sorrow as walker with Christ to Calvary. By the time he officially began full residence in his cinderblock hermitage in the woods of Gethsemani Abbey (Feast of Our Lady of Mount Carmel, July 16, 1965), Merton considered himself an ecclesiastical and social outlaw. In 'The Author's Advice to His Book' (Fall, 1965) used as Prologue to *Raids on the Unspeakable,* he indirectly addressed his readers from his new standpoint:

> You are not so much concerned with ethical principles and traditional answers to traditional questions, for many men have decided no longer to ask these questions. Your main interest is not in formal answers or accurate definitions, but in diffficult insights at a moment of human crisis. Such insights can hardly be either comforting or well defined: they are obscure and ironic. They cannot be translated into a program for solving all the problems of society, but they may perhaps enable a rare person here and there to come alive and be awake at a moment when wakefulness is desireable — a moment of ultimate choice, in which he finds himself challenged in the roots of his own existence. You have considered the critical challenge of the hour, that of dehumanization, and have dealt with it as you could, with poetry and irony rather than tragic declamation or confessional formulas.[23]

As Thomas Merton tasted the first fruits of his newly-won solitude, poet-guitarist Bob Dylan (1941–   ) stood a musical outlaw, playing the pounding rhythms of his new electric music at the Newport Folk Festival, July 25, 1965, and at Forest Hills Stadium, New York, August 27, 1965. With the release of *Highway 61 Revisited* — his first fully 'rock 'n roll' album — in

September, it became clear that all the forms and images present and active in the collective psyche, archetypes transmitted from tradition to his generation, had met in Dylan's lyrics and lifestyle. At this period, perhaps, Dylan knew his own realities, and he continued to break himself. Working deliberately like Rimbaud at the dissolution of his senses within a society whose very ethical foundations were crumbling, he made no public attempt to exonerate himself. Being at the vanguard of the moral demolition, Dylan needed no justification.

Though Thomas Merton never published his study of Dylan, begun in 1966 for Editor Ed Rice of *Jubilee Magazine,* there is evidence of the poet-musician's presence in the monk's life during his final years. In Merton's hermitage there was an image of Dylan and the song title "The Times They Are A-Changin'" carved in wood by a Sister friend from Loretto. In the photographs taken by John Howard Griffin of the 1966 visit of Jacques Maritain, it can be seen resting on the fireplace mantel, the Dylan image forming the peak of a triangle above the heads of the hermit and the philosopher.[24] Among Merton's effects at Gethsemani Abbey was found a large full-color Dylan magazine photograph from the *Blonde on Blonde* street camera sessions, taken shortly before Dylan's July 26, 1966 near-fatal motorcycle accident—with Medusa's hair and flowing scarf, Dylan looked quite obviously the decadent poet in the tradition of Rimbaud.[25] Found among his papers was a manila envelope with Merton's script in red ink: 'Dylan, Rilke, Muir'. Though the envelope was empty, there are traces of Dylan in Merton's study of Muir and other poets, in his letters and comments to friends.

Thomas Merton recognised Bob Dylan as an 'important new voice' in America, and although an unruly young man in angry reaction against his society, certainly gifted with an authentic poetic vocation and able to bring his audiences to a deeper awareness of their true selves. Bob Dylan provided Thomas Merton with the manner of *hardness* for his later experimental poetry, e.g. *Cables to the Ace* (1967) and *The Geography of Lograire* (1968); the matter of alienation and entrapment as expressed in Dylan's songs of the 1960s period; and the metaphor for himself as outlaw poet both as churchman and as American citizen in a nation at war.[26]

From John Howard Griffin — using the hermit monk's private journals as source for his information — we learned that in imitating Dylan's love songs for his own love poems, Merton was also aided by Dylan in the expression of his deep care for the one other human person who came to occupy the central focus of his life during his last years.[27] Using the same source, biographer Michael Mott comments: 'Merton's poems to S. were falling into Dylan's style at the time, while after one particularly tortured passage in his "Midsummer Diary" he broke in with 'Even Bob Dylan is not perfect!"' Mott continues that Merton had hoped that Dylan would set to music a poem which appears as Number Sixty-Eight in *Cables to the Ace*.[28]

In September of 1967, Merton wrote to Naomi Burton about his hope to have *My Argument with the Gestapo* published: 'I have gone over it making a few minor changes, and it is now being typed. I do think it reads well, just as well as it ever did (at least to me) and I think this is a reasonable time to try it out again.'[29] A macaronic work already obscure in itself, the unpaginated manuscript was accidentally dropped by a secretary in Louisville, and never restored to its original order. This bizarre autobiographical novel parallels parts of *Cables to the Ace* and *The Geography of Lograire*. Because of the period in which Merton worked at its revision, the structure and content suggest post-Dylan interpolations.[30] Most strikingly, *My Argument* has: 'The water wells are forgotten, and the suffering of the thirsty wounded echoes in the barrels of the gate like the anger of guitars.'[31] In Number Fifty-Four of *Cables* Merton has: 'Amid the cries of gang walls and surprises the echoes come forward. They are nude. A brazen charm expands. It invests the unguarded senses. Twin stars rise over the library. Another day lives. It questions the waterworks, it knows the fevers of Vegas.'[32]

In 'Solitary Life', a self-parody published only after his death, Merton wrote:

> White-collar man blue-collar
> Man I am a no-collar man
> (least of all a *Roman* collar!)

Shave twice a week
Maybe
Yes, I had beer in this place
A while back and once
Whiskey
And I worry about the Abbot
Coming up here to
Inspect
And finding
A copy of *Newsweek*
Under the bed.[33]

Toward the end of his life Thomas Merton confided to a friend: 'I'm in jail and sitting on the faggots while the head Inquisitor fumbles with the matchbox which is luckily in his other pair of trousers.'[34] Full poetic expression of his estrangement and psychological imprisonment is given by Merton in *Cables to the Ace*. In Number Nine he has:

'I am doubted, therefore I am. Does this mean that if I insist on making everybody doubt me more, I will become more real? It is enough to doubt them back. By this mutual service we make one another complete. A metaphysic of universal suspicion!' (These words were once heard, uttered by a lonely, disembodied voice, seemingly in a cloud. No one was impressed by them and they were immediately forgotten.)[35]

And in Number Seventy-Nine Merton wrote: 'O it is not lazy to be a messenger or to live out of the shadow of some town. Other masks would be less trouble. This one is never allowed to be familiar: it is often the most naked. It is not without risk in a season of frost. Nothing that is chosen is unbearable.'[36] But for all the gloom, don't miss that twist of triumph, the turn of a smile in the final line!

3. SOME KEYS FOR AN INTERPRETATION OF DECADENCE
IN THE LIFE AND ART OF THOMAS MERTON

Throughout history, whenever a nation has been forced with a cataclysm, prophets, eschatologists, and apocalypticists have called their peoople to a religious re-awakening and political change through a literature uniquely their own — cryptic and symbolic of their people's aspirations. Unrestrained by normal literary conventions, they have permitted their minds to revel in figurative and imaginative situations. All reserves set by a sense of reality are abandoned in favor of a content and form which sometimes appears to be most bizarre. As Shailer Mathews once pointed out, to a mind dominated by syllogistic consistency, such a complex of war, politics, religion, cosmology, Persian dualism and psychological symbolism seems so logically inconsistent as to be incredible. And it is not difficult to find in this literature 'nonpolitical expectations of the future which may well give rise to doubts as to the writer's sanity'.[37]

Never merely religious or simply political, the call to repent, to revolt, to renew, is addressed to individuals, but as members of a nation which has lost its way. The prophet issues no program of religious or political reform, any more than he lays down precise regulations for individual behavior. He makes no attempt to reshape a religious institution or political system to his own design.[38] The revolutionary mind shunts aside programs of administration and seeks freedom from institutionalization in whatever form. Its basic dogmatic foundation is of absolutes, abstract ideas expressed in a language code that is lean, concrete and carries a tremendous emotional appeal.[39] In this context, then, his intelligence and his feeling make the poet the philosopher and the theologian by confronting his hearers with belief or unbelief through words wherein are expressed 'love and hate and all the shades between', to use a phrase from William Butler Yeats.[40] Rooting his language in his own experience of sadness and pain, the poet of the apocalypse seeks to comfort by setting forth the final triumph of his nation. His first function is to explain the 'sacred history' of his people. His second: to propose positive action, 'religious experience' that is shared.

Having now considered Thomas Merton's principles for a criticism of decadent aesthetics and decadence as Merton's mode of self-expression, in light of the preceding comments concerning the prophetic function of the poet, to what understanding can we arrive concerning Thomas Merton's intentions as a cloistered contemplative monk and 'decadent poet'?

Just five lines into the opening chapter of *The Seven Storey Mountain* Merton says of his parents: 'My father and mother were captives in that world, knowing they did not belong with it or in it, and yet unable to get away from it. They were in the world and not of it — not because they were saints, but in a different way: because they were artists. The integrity of an artist lifts a man above the world without delivering him from it.'[41]

And in writing of his father in the chapter entitled 'The Harrowing of Hell' Merton says: 'He was a man of exceptional intellectual honesty and sincerity and purity of understanding. And this affliction, this terrible and frightening illness which was relentlessly pressing him down into the jaws of the tomb, was not destroying him.'[42]

Two further passages from *The Seven Storey Mountain* bear significance in this context. Again, in 'The Harrowing of Hell', this time speaking of his adolescent willfulness, Merton comments:

But in Scotland I had begun to bare my teeth and fight back against the humiliation of giving in to other people, and now I was rapidly building up a hard core of resistance against everything that displeased me: whether it was the opinions or desires of others, or their commands, or their very persons. I would think what I wanted and do what I wanted, and go my way. If those who tried to prevent me had authority to prevent me, I would have to be at least externally polite in my resistance: but my resistance would be no less determined, and I would do my own will, have my own way.[43]

The final selection — from Chapter One, 'Prisoner's Base', — shows us Merton reflecting from the perspective of a monk at Gethsemani Abbey:

The bias which my will was to acquire from the circumstances of all its acts would eventually be the direction of my whole being towards happiness or misery, life or death, heaven and hell.

More than that: since no man ever can, or could live by himself and for himself alone, the destinies of thousands of other people were bound to be affected, some remotely, but some very directly and near-at-hand, by my own choices and decisions and desires, as my own life would also be formed and modified by theirs. I was entering into a moral universe in which I would be related to every other rational being, and in which whole masses of us, as thick as swarming bees, would drag one another along towards some common end of good or evil, peace or war.[44]

Taking his comments about his parents and applying them to Merton himself, joining these with his two statements of self-critique, we find the cluster of impulses and identifications that shaped the entire life of Thomas Merton. He was artist, intellectual, sufferer, rebel, and man of universal compassion. How he juggled these powerful forces is his unique story. And as has already been demonstrated, Thomas Merton's story is also the story of our times: it is the story of continuous change and conversion, the groping of the human person for ever-greater freedom in the love of God.[45]

In *The Seven Storey Mountain* Merton recalled his discovery of France as a child: 'I discovered that land which is really, as far as I can tell, the one to which I do belong, if I belong to any at all, by no documentary title but by geographical birth'. And Merton drew significance from the fact that he and his father sailed for France from America during his early childhood, on the twenty-fifth of August, the Feast of St Louis of France — patron of his native place and name he would be given in Trappist life.[46]

But properly to understand 'decadence' in the life and art of the mature hermit monk of the 1960s, we cannot divorce Thomas Merton from his English past. For it was in England as a schoolboy at Ripley Court and Oakham that Merton came to his intellectual and moral awakening, and, as a student at Cambridge, his spiritual dissolution. Merton himself is clear about his identification. Recalling personal sadness and the endurance of brutish behavior at the French *lycée*, Merton wrote of himself: 'After this everybody accepted me and became quite friendly and pleasant, once they were used to my pale, blue-eyed and seemingly stupid English face'.[47]

Thomas Merton was linked historically with post-World War I England, and the nation that prepared itself for the new war. If he could look back with appreciation to Crashaw and Blake, Newman and Hopkins—literary lights along his way—he scorned the dark and terrible realities of modern life on that ancient island:

> And so I became the complete twentieth-century man. I now belonged to the world in which I lived. I became a true citizen of my own disgusting century: the century of poison gas and atomic bombs. A man living on the doorsill of the Apocalypse, a man with veins full of poison, living in death. Baudelarie could truly address me, then, reader: *Hypocrite lecteur, mon semblance, mon frère.*[48]

Elsewhere in his autobiography, Merton describes his shedding of illusions about English life: 'Its fragile web of charmed associations had been broken and blown away and I had fallen through the surface of old England into the hell, the vacuum and the horror that London was nursing in her avaricious heart.'[49] Like Brian Howard and Rupert Brooke, the Prince of Wales and Guy Burgess, Evelyn Waugh and T. S. Eliot, the Lords Acton and Randolph Churchill, W. H. Auden and Christopher Isherwood, Thomas Merton was one of England's *Sonnenkinder*—her 'Children of the Sun', all born in the years of 'the great war'; all bright and beautiful in their brilliant rebellion against all the values their culture held dear; ever restless, ever in reaction against their upbringing, yet always tethered to it.[50] These were the inheritors of Oscar Wilde's legacy.[51]

Paul Wilkes, in his *Merton: A Film Biography*, powerfully portrayed the conflict within Merton between a growing consciousness of Christ—imaged in the sun rising behind the dome of Saint Peter's Basilica in Rome—and Merton's moral degeneration—conveyed through the background sounds of 'swing music' and bubbling wine, and images of a winsome blond-haired youth and a pensive co-ed in the midst of chattering couples at a Cambridge garden party.[52] Another aesthetic vehicle of similar kind is *Another Country,* a 1984 film based on the play by Julian Mitchell. Set in an English boys' school in the 1930s, starring Rupert Everett as 'Guy Bennet', it is a *roman à clef* portrayal of the early life of Guy Burgess, infamous as a spy for Russia. The site is different, but the cultural environment could well be Merton's Oakham or Cambridge — as Merton described them in *The Seven Storey Mountain* — and is little removed from the Oxford of Oscar Wilde's England. The story is that of youthful idealism (homosexual affection, nascent communism) pitted against the bitter realities of actual life. Here, the aging Bennet opens the story with a quotation from *Henry V* — 'a most patriotic play' he calls it — and asks: '. . . treason to what, loyalty to whom? That's what matters. . . .' A simple pastiche of lines forcefully conveys the parameters of young Merton's school-boy England:

> Our parents send us here to get an education, and we spend our days playing games . . . sportsmanship . . . it's all hy-pocrisy . . . militarism from twelve to half-past four . . . I'm a school boy, not a soldier . . . Not empire builders, but empire rulers. It takes imagination to be an empire builder . . . contemptible synchophant of the bourgeoisie . . . grovelling about the kings and queens, walking backwards, kissing hands . . . utterly imbued with the spirit of servility . . . self-perpetuating oligarchy . . . Life is ladders, that is all![53]

In the original play, Julian Mitchell has: 'This whole place is *based* on contradictions. It's a complex network of irreconcilable values. The only surprising thing is how few suicides there are.'[54]

The Prince of Wales, in this group of *Sonnenkinder* to which Merton belonged by age and acumen and attitude, became King Edward VIII, and abdicated for the love of a woman. In her autobiography *The Heart Has Its Reasons,* written in 1956 (just eight years after Merton's), Bessie Wallis Warfield, Duchess of Windsor, summed up the political and social climate of the 1930s: 'There is something steely and unhuman in the monarchial principle. No form of discipline can be more repressive of the simpler instincts of the heart than that of a monarchy in defence of its institutional self.'[55]

Like John Donne's *A Hymne to Christ, at the Authors last going into Germany,* Thomas Merton sealed the bill of his divorce with England as he crossed the sea for America, recounted as a salutation to Blessed Mary in *The Seven Storey Mountian:* 'Lady, when on that night I left the Island that was once your England, your love went with me, although I could not know it, and could not make myself aware of it. And it was your love, your intercession for me, before God, that was preparing the seas before my ship, laying open the way for me to another country.'[56]

If from the perspective of time Thomas Merton appears in *The Seven Storey Mountain* as callow and a cad — which he certainly does — his critique of Church and State in the England of his youth had objective validity. And here Merton, as dissenter, was in direct line with John Henry Cardinal Newman. For Newman held that there was no religious principle involved in the Oath of Recognition of God taken by members of Parliament. In Newman's view, the Personal God of the Jewish religion and Christianity was regarded with as little concern by politicians as any 'Impersonal or Material, or Abstract Ideal Something or other' to which men swore their allegiance. In old age, when accused of contemplating a return to Anglicanism, Newman responded:

> Return to the Church of England! no; 'the net is broken, and we are delivered.' I should be a consummate fool (to use a mild term) if in my old age I left 'the land flowing with milk and honey' for the city of confusion and the house of bondage.[57]

In 'Learning to Live', an essay written near the end of his life, Merton revealed a still prevailing negativity toward the educational years about which he had written in 1948: 'I always felt at Columbia that people around me, half amused and perhaps at times half incredulous, were happy to let me be myself. (I add that I seldom felt this way at Cambridge.)'[58]

In introducing his edited version entitled *Elected Silence*, Evelyn Waugh described Thomas Merton's autobiography as 'essentially American', typical of what is newest and best in his country. For Waugh, Columbia and not Cambridge formed Merton's literary style. And for Waugh, Merton's spirituality — though French (Trappist) in discipline — is a 'flower of the New World'. Americans, contended Waugh, no longer become expatriates in their quest for full cultural development. Rather, he said: 'They are learning to draw away from what is distracting in their own civilization while remaining in their own borders.' Waugh described Merton's words as: 'fresh, simple, colloquial', and expressive of a 'disgust with the modern world'. For Waugh, it was a prodigy of the new spirit of the New World that Merton's book should have been read by hundreds of thousands of interested people. There is an ascetic tradition deep in the American heart, wrote Waugh, which has sometimes taken odd and unlovable forms. Here in the historic Rules of the Church lies its proper fulfillment. In the natural order, according to Waugh, the modern world is rapidly being made unthinkable by the scientists and politicians. As in the Dark Ages, the cloister was once again offering 'the sanest and most civilized way of life'. And Waugh concluded: in the supernatural order the times require more than tepid and dutiful piety. Prayer must become heroic.[59]

In the United States of America Thomas Merton discovered intellectual freedom, the Roman Catholic Chuch, and monastic life. For the young Frater Louis, OCSO, the monastery was a bastion of orthodoxy and orthopraxy, and monks guardians of tradition ever entrenching themselves against the onslaught of the dangerous ideas and evil mores of 'the world', preserving primary religious values in their base of reaction against change. This was, in his view, all to the benefit of humankind. History reminded Merton that it was the monks who preserved Western Civilization by adapting the best of the past to present needs. And the young Merton projected an image of the Cistercian, in white cowl with hood up, illuminating a manuscript at his Gothic desk, frankincense and beeswax candles nearby, a choir of muffled voices humming Gregorian chant in the distance.

But history and his own experience also taught the maturing monk of the decadence and decline of monasteries once religious experience has become solidified. Material prosperity and political power result, as Merton well knew. Not bad in themselves, they could be deadly when misused. Then, the monk is no longer spiritually a sign of contradiction to the world, no longer threatening: his religious experience has become institutionalized, regularized, and recognized by society as acceptable. The monk is then found at the center of established religious and established secular society, his very existence a vicarious participation of all in some vague union with God that requires no personal accountability.

Merton's on-going study of the monastic tradition throughout his twenty-seven years at Gethsemani Abbey taught him of responses to this decadence and decline in each period of history. In each age, a call has come forth from new voices for a counter-reaction and new growth through a return to simplicity, decentralization of power, and a recognition of the primary religious experience of each person with God—both in the monastery and in 'the world'. Restoration to the 'primitive monastic ideal' takes place in history though the discovery and development of new charisms within institutional monasticism and within organized society, a discovery and development which is of itself a counter-decadent movement. For those who resist it, this 'new movement' is interpreted as heterodoxy and heteropraxy, leading to a new kind of decadence, decline and disorder. Within religious culture, then, this 'new monk' becomes a heretic. For secular culture, he becomes a social critic and a threat once again. In the end, by free-choice and by condemnation, he has become an ecclesiastical and social outlaw and outcast.

If the monk Thomas Merton was a Frenchman 'by geographical birth' and an Englishman by aspect and pre-adulthood formation, he was indeed an American citizen by 'documentary title'. And as he progressed in the exploration of the American intellectual tradition, he aligned himself with dissenters so much a part of our heritage as, for example, Henry David Thoreau.[60]

If many of the early American settlers are recognized as religious dissenters from England, subsequent generations in the first and second hundred years of our history can be seen as dissenters from the established culture brought over from 'the Old Country'. As they moved further west, scouring the vast open spaces, dashing to sequestrate land and secure gold, the American people — linked as they were to an identification with the land itself — personified its 'Spirit' in folk heroes — historical and mythic — who had in some way wedded and tamed this immense continent. Robert Rogers and his Northwest Rangers, Meriwether Lewis and Roger Clark, Daniel Boone and Davy Crockett, 'Buffalo Bill' and 'Mark Twain', Thoreau himself, and Walt Whitman all somehow epitomize the energy and the awesomeness of the land itself.

But already by the mid-nineteenth centry, America witnessed the birth of an entirely new and decidedly different generation of heroes and 'anti-heroes' with the laying of the iron nails of the locomotive. All of the righteousness and all of the rebelliousness of the 'American Spirit' has been confected around the railroad ethos. Thoreau lamented the incursion of the Fitchburg Railroad into his Walden solitude, but was not the less fascinated by the train's mellow night-time call. In his later years he travelled by the iron tracks in his excursions to Canada and the midwestern states. Walt Whitman conveyed his poetic sensibilities toward the 'steam beast' with its 'swelling pant and roar, now tapering in the distance. . . .'[61] For a people naturally restless, locked in a vast prison of land, the railroad was much more than a convenient means of transportation: it stood for freedom, opportunity, wealth, romance, adventure and progress. In the words of Alan Lomax: '. . . country boys regarded Casey Jones and his kind as so many Lancelots mounted on magnificent iron horses'.[62]

But this great American adventure with its own poetry had its dark side too. Through collapse of companies half a million railroad workers lost their jobs. Unemployment hit the foundaries. Hundreds of thousands of American men — homeless and hungry — roamed the nation. With the industrial age and the railroads came the 'tramp', the almshouse, and prisons. Hamlin Garland called the hoboes and tramps: '. . . a flight of alien, unclean birds. . . .'[63] The locomotive promised not only new opportunities and even *escape*, but also maiming, gang violence, and police-enforced murder. Jack London — who lived to tell it in a breathless tale — wrote of 'train jumping', slipping away into the night as 'disappointed pursuers . . . howl curses up at me and say unsocial things about my ancestors'.[64]

The locomotive also brought the merger of audacity and depradation, producing such American 'anti-heroes' as the Reno Brothers, Jesse James, 'Butch Cassidy' and 'The Sundance Kid' — men immortalized in song and film as American Robin Hoods. In truth, they were men of brutal stripe, far more akin to England's Dick Turpin.

For the poor and imprisoned Blacks particularly — another kind of outcast and outlaw — the poetry of the railroad offered a spiritual liberation from the pain of life, and added to the wealth of the Gospel Music tradition. And it was Woody Guthrie who gave the railroad myth its strongest voice during the Depression and 'Dust Bowl' years of this century. And it was Bob Dylan who — with his 'spit-without-polish, and ambisexual appearance, and social protest in the Woody Guthrie tradition'[65] — linked the hermit monk Thomas Merton in the 1960s with the anti-materialistic poetic heritage of America's past and its contemporary expression in the folk-rock idiom.

The concomitant publications in the fall of 1984 of Michael Mott's *The Seven Mountains of Thomas Merton* — the long-awaited 'official biography' written in cooperation with The Merton Legacy Trust — and Jonathan Cott's *Dylan* — the most lavish photo-essay yet produced — is fitting. Each, in his respective realm was (and Dylan still is) an artist and social critic caught in a tension with his times and expected identities, each involved in great personal transitions. Merton's increased solitude — yet by no means isolation — in the Kentucky woods — and Bob Dylan's metamorphosis from American 'folk hero' to counter-cultural rock star signalled significant life-changes that affected the lives of many other persons who looked to Merton or Dylan for direction in troubled times. Both Merton and Dylan identified with the down-trodden, the abused, the scorned, on whatever side of the predicament. Both sacrificed their reputations for new identities, consistency for openness to truth. Both have been denounced as impostors wanting the people's applause without their problems. Both have borne the agony of apotheosis, and both have repudiated the prophet's role — Merton in such self-chronicles as 'Day of a Stranger' and 'Rain and the Rhinoceros', Dylan in 'It Ain't Me, Babe' and 'My Back Pages', [more recently with 'Sweetheart Like You' (1983) and 'Trust Yourself' (1985)]. Bob Dylan — for Thomas Merton — was one of the 'few rare ones whose voices, speaking out of the shadows with Baudelaire and Rimbaud, impose upon the hearer the silence and the awe that are fitting in the presence of tragedy'.

The apparent incongruity of the hermit Trappist Merton linking himself with rock musician Bob Dylan (and of another Trappist expending so much time and energy explicating the connection) may strike many observers as bizarre. Is this thing to be taken so seriously? By approaching this connection as a new means of hearing the Word of God speaking to him, as metaphoric experience and as 'mask' for him, we can attribute to Merton the seriousness of consideration he deserves.

In 1966 — the year that Merton became acquainted with the work of Dylan — Robert W. Funk published *Language, Hermeneutic, and Word of God: The Problem of Language in the New Testament and Contemporary Theology,* calling for a fresh apprehension of the gospel. 'In short', he wrote, 'the only course ever open to those who are concerned with the proclamation of the gospel, whether or not they believe this is a time of the failure of the word of faith, is to learn as never before, with ears sharply tuned for the tones that are suspected of having fallen on deaf ears; to seek to hear the silent tolling of grace as it echoes faintly from the traditional language of the church.'[66] Funk invited his reader not to 'founder on the words and sentences of his essays:

The 'logic' does not aspire to a rigid dialectic. What is to be listened for is what is struggling to come to expression. If it is borne in mind that something is being talked about which requires a deformation of our common speech, and thus our way of looking at reality, it may be possible to accord imprecise language a certain latitude. In any case, it is a curious not-knowing and not-having that is seeking its way into the clarity of expression.[67]

Thomas Merton listened to 'the silent tolling of grace' as it echoed faintly from the traditional language of the Church he criticized out of love as a faithful member. And Merton listened to Bob Dylan's 'Chimes of Freedom': tolling for the rebel, the rake, the luckless, the abandoned, the forsaken; tolling for 'the outcast, burnin' constantly at stake'; tolling for the deaf and blind, for the mute, the mistreated, mateless mother, the 'mistitled prostitute'; tolling for 'the searching ones, on their speechless, seeking trail'; and most poignantly, perhaps, 'tolling for the aching ones whose wounds cannot be nursed. . . .'[68]

At the time of their metaphorical meeting, Merton would find that in the art of Bob Dylan chemical visions, mythology, religious tradition and music transcend the level of ordinary intelligibility: 'Inside the museum, Infinity goes up on trial/ Voices echo this is what Salvation must be like after a while/But Mona Lisa musta had the highway blues/you can tell by the way she smiles.'[69] Of itself often unintelligible and untranslatable, Dylan's art flows in realms inaccessible and outside modes of ordinary communication. Sense dissolves into being, the hearer drawn into a new temporal dimension, both in self-awareness and apprehension of external reality. The external continuum is a theoretically unlimited series of historical events, or events believed to be historical, from which society takes a relevant number of happenings.[70] Thus, we have Dylan's anti-anthem: 'Because something is happening here/But you don't know what it is/Do you, Mister Jones?'[71]

While Altizer and associated 'Honest to God' theologians wrote volumes on God's demise and power-politicians prevailed over peace-makers, Dylan made clear the message being received:

Disillusioned words like bullets bark as human gods aim for
their mark/Made everything from toy guns that spark to
flesh-colored Christs that glow in the dark/It's easy to see
without looking too far that not much is really sacred. . . ./
While preachers preach of evil fates teachers teach that
knowledge waits/Can lead to hundred-dollar plates/Good-
ness hides behind its gates but even the President of the
United States sometimes must have to stand naked.[72]

The inner continuum is based on the listener's psychological
development sequence. The length of the tale, the recurrent
themes, surprises, parallelisms, associations and differentiations
provoke psychic reactions, mental and bodily responses: the duality
of movement and stasis.[73] Dylan sings: 'Ain't it just like the night to
play tricks when you're trying to be so quiet/We sit here
stranded/though we're all doin' our best to deny it.[74]

The interconnectedness of these *continua* manifests itself
repeatedly in his art as Dylan's hearers listen to his vision flow.
There is an inversion of the relationship between sender (Dylan)
and the receiver (Merton), the latter discovering himself signified
by the message of the former, with the song/poem 'living' in the
hearer who hears himself through it. From Dylan, then, is heard
these words:

When you're lost in the rain in Juarez and it's Easter time
too/your gravity fails you and your negativity don't pull you
through. . . ./Everybody said they'd stand behind me
when the game got rough but the joke was on me there was
nobody there to call my bluff.[75]

As gradually becomes clear, Dylan's poetic myth and
musical work are like an orchestra whose audience are the silent
performers, and the poet and his reader/hearer are two moments
of the same operation. Once the poem is written, the song sung,
Dylan is alone and his reader/hearer recreates himself when he
reads and listens. The experience of creation—as we see—is
reproduced in opposite fashion. The aesthetic creation opens

itself up before the perceiver who enters into it, takes leave of himself and penetrates another self unknown until that moment. Thus, in the case of Merton listening to Dylan, the music and lyrics opened up doors of strangeness and recognition at the same time.[76] Merton, as we know from his own writings, was highly sensitive to upbeat music. As aesthetic experience, we can imagine Dylan's work addressed itself both to his mind and his body, with such lines as: 'Pointed threats/they bluff with scorn/ Suicide remarks are torn from the fool's gold mouthpiece/The hollow horn plays wasted words/Proves to warn that he not busy being born is busy dying.'[77] Such art calls forth not only thought and judgment as to meaning, but 'those forces of the self which are ulterior to the conscious'.[78]

Now Ophelia, she's 'neath the window/for her I feel so afraid/on her twenty-second birthday she already is an old maid/To her, death is quite romantic/she wears an iron vest/her profession's her religion/her sin is her lifelessness/ And though her eyes are fixed upon Noah's rainbow/she spends time peeking into Desolation Row.[79]

As metaphor, Dylan's art rapts attention, involves the entire person, is autonomous of preceding circumstances and even of the author itself, whose intention is neither available or desirable as a standard for judging the success of his work. Nowhere is the proper literal signification of a word, the proper literal sense of a text so inaccessible as in Dylan's poetics and the symbolist tradition he embodied for Merton. The intentionality of Dylan is rarely, if ever, explicitated, and as a living art-form his own intended meaning may shift from performance to performance. Dylan as the artist sees the reverse side of the verbal tapestry, his hearers the ordered threads according to who they are and how they perceive any aspect of reality, the degree of conformity between their mental grasp and the truth of the thing itself.

Realizing the immensity of Merton's creative imagination and his deep grasp of poetic values as we do, we can get a glimpse of how he drew meanings from Dylan and set them into motion in his own mythic compositions, such as *Cables to the Ace* and *The Geography of Lograire,* for example. Through the strange, non-linear patterns of Dylan's works, Merton communicated with himself, rediscovered and re-invented himself.[80] Tensive, hyperbolic, compressing past-present-future time into a moment of decision NOW — *kronos* into *kairos* — Dylan created a 'word event' for Merton. Listening to Dylan injected a new possibility into Merton's situation, calling for judgment that shook the security of past existence with risk and promise in a new existence. Ultimately, then, it was not Dylan or his text — written or sung — that was interpreted but Merton himself.[81] And this makes clear the importance for Merton of the wood carving that rested on his hermitage mantel: 'Your old road is rapidly agin'. / Please get out of the new one if you can't lend your hand for the times they are a-changin'.'[82]

Thomas Merton in his Vulgate Bible surely often read: *praeterit enim figura huis mundi,* from 1 Corinthians 3:7. But Saint Paul's doctrine of the world as we know it passing away was recharged with vitality and urgency as the monk aged. Merton linked himself with Saint Paul and Philoxenos and Christ as Outlaw in 'Rain and the Rhinoceros'. As an artist himself, the 'mask of Dylan' was a new synthetic self, created by Merton's vision of his own reality. Though not actualized — he was a Roman Catholic, a contemplative monk, priest and hermit — it was superior to ordinary life as a means of revealing inner feelings, of bringing into consciousness and mastery his inner conflicts. Wearing the 'mask of Dylan' harmonized his faculties, energized him to complement not only his moral but also his psychological opposite, his deficiencies and his idealized self. The mask of itself is cold and impersonal, an artifice which signifies the life of instinct, though in a personal way. But on it depends all happiness and fulfillment for the artist. Art reveals what the artist in real life cannot. Artistic creation is a rebirth as something not oneself, 'something which has no memory and is created in a moment and perpetually renewed'.[83]

Fabricating the mask, cultivating the antithetical self, is the path to greatness or to destruction. It can be a hiding from judgment, a forgetting of reality, a flight from the 'infinite pain of self-realization'.[84] The ordinary self and the antithetical self are encompassed by the buried self, the principle which drives a man to his opposite, its existence proof that the artist is already the self he is striving to become.[85] As Thomas Merton's life becomes more known to us — revealed in ever greater detail by his biographers and commentators — we better understand that in the end he had at last embraced his own humanity. Finally he had won a full capacity to love and to be loved. He had — in conformity with Christ's suffering through years of conversion — liberated himself from the false young monk who in *The Seven Storey Mountain* had written:

> As a child, and since then too, I have always tended to resist any kind of possessive affection on the part of any other human being — there has always been this profound instinct to keep clear, to keep free. And only with truly supernatural people have I ever felt really at ease, really at peace.[86]

THOMAS MERTON'S CHRIST-FILLED DECADENCE: SOME FINAL REFLECTIONS

Just seven months after Thomas Merton's death, Astronaut Neil Armstrong walked on the moon. 'It's one small step for a man, one giant leap for mankind', are the first words he beamed back to us. Not many years later came the Computer Revolution. It is exciting to wonder how Thomas Merton would have reacted to these monumental social 'happenings'. The redoubtable anti-poet would have rebelled with loud vituperations, no doubt. But the 'Solitary Explorer' would have wanted to be the first hermit monk in outer space. And despite — like so many people of poetic temperament — being intimidated by machines, the boy in Merton would have wanted the latest super word-processor.

Thomas Merton was a humanist in the classical sense. Like Terence's comedian in *The Self-Tormentor,* nothing human was alien to him (I:1,23). The lust and self-indulgence through drugs and alcohol and sex he found as themes and factors in the life of

Bob Dylan were recognized as cries of the human person for permanence in love relationships, pleas for liberation from physical, emotional and spiritual suffering. Bob Dylan — one among many poets and prophets to whom the monk looked — became other eyes through which Thomas Merton was able to view his own fragmented existence. Not otherwise able to act on his convictions and feelings — he lived in the freely chosen solitude of his Trappist abbey and hermitage — Merton entered into the human condition metaphorically with Dylan in the realm of poetic truth, not unlike non-violent Henry David Thoreau's identification with insurrectionist Captain John Brown one hundred years before him. He could not articulate the full implications of his conjuction logically, nor even rationally. Rather, he recreated his existence, giving unique expression to his own troubled truth while remaining faithful to it in such works as *Cables to the Ace, The Geography of Lograire,* the posthumously published 'found', 'concrete' and 'anti-poems', in his writings for the woman he loved.

Has Thomas Merton become an embarrassment to the Trappists? Some, by their responses to the information now generally known about him since the publication of *Follow the Ecstasy* and *The Seven Mountains of Thomas Merton,* have said: 'Yes!' The 'stealthy egress' — to use a term from the old Trappist *Spiritual Directory* — and the drinking, the enormous letter-writing and publishing involvements, the love affair, have aroused anger, hurt, and feelings of betrayal in some monks. Certainly, judged against the model he first projected in his early published works, Merton in his final years was not a good monk. But for Merton, the Order of Cistercians of the Strict Observance and monasticism itself, like all things in the human order, were means and not absolute ends in themselves.

As a Christian believer — there is no reason to doubt he was — Merton found God manifest in all creation (Rm 1:20) and did not stifle the proddings of the Holy Spirit in his life. He chose, following Saint Paul's admonition, to test everything and he retained what was good and to his purposes, while avoiding evil as intended deed (1 Th 5:19-22). As a monk, Merton steeped himself in the teachings of the spiritual and mystical masters of Christianity, Judaism, Hinduism, Buddhism, and Sufism, in the *mores* of primitive traditions and third world cultures. Following the guidance of the giants of his own Cistercian tradition, Merton labored seriously at the profession of self-knowledge as Christ's follower, examining his conscience to the very depths—and despite the pain—sparing himself nothing of the truth that he hoped would set him free from self-assumed and other-imposed identities (Jn 8:32; Aelred of Rievaulx, *The Mirror of Charity* II.1). And, as sensitive as he was—his ruthless side not to be denied—Merton came to knowledge of himself by learning the truth of other persons through sympathy for their suffering. And he, being a man of prayer, contemplated with never-ending efforts truth itself through purity of heart (Bernard of Clairvaux, *The Steps of Humility* III.6).

Wherever there are human persons desiring their own truth, wherever there are Christians who pummel their minds and hearts in the hope that—along with Saint Paul—they who preach to others not find themselves rejected (1 Co 9:27), the art and the influence of Thomas Merton will be welcomed.[87] And, in his own words:

> After that we'll meet in some Kingdom they forgot and there the found will play the songs of the sent. Surely a big bird with all the shades of light will beat against our windows. We will then gladly consent to the kindness of rays and recover the warm knowledge of each other we once had under those young trees in another May. (It is a big bird flies right out of the center of the sun.)[88]

Holy Spirit Abbey
Conyers, Georgia

NOTES — The Christ-Filled Decadence

1. Marjorie Reeves, Preface to *Apocalyptic Spirituality*, translation and introduction by Bernard McGinn. The Classics of Western Spirituality Series (New York: Paulist Press, 1979) p. xiii. The texts of the *Epistle of Barnabas*, the *Didache*, and the *Epistle to Diognetus* are conveniently available in English in *Early Christian Writings: The Apostolic Fathers*, translated by Maxell Staniforth. New York: Penguin Books, 1968.

2. 'Volunteers of America' copyright 1969 by Icebag Corporation.

3. *Future Shock* (New York: Bantam Books, 1971) p. 310.

4. *Treatise on the Unity of the Church* 10–11. *PL* 4:523–524. English translation in *Christian Readings* 4:1 Edited by John E. Rotelle, OSA (New York: Catholic Book Publishing Company, 1973) p. 147.

5. *A Religious History of the American People* (New Haven: Yale University Press, 1972) p. 1095, note 14.

6. Some of these principles of aesthetic criticism are expressed by Jacques Barzun in *Classic, Romantic and Modern* (Garden City, NY: Doubleday/Anchor Books, 1961) p. 112. Cf. Jacques Barzun, *The Energies of Art: Studies of Authors Classic and Modern* New York: Random House/Vintage Books, 1962.

7. *The Literary Essays of Thomas Merton* Edited by Brother Patrick Hart. (New York: New Directions, 1981) p. 346. In subsequent notes this source will be abgreviated as *LE*.

8. *LE*, p. 333.

9. *LE*, p. 360.

10. *LE*, p. 361.

11. *LE*, p. 376.

12. *LE*, p. 380.

13. *Seasons of Celebration* (New York: Farrar, Straus, Giroux, 1965) p. 154.

14. *The Geography of Lograire* (New York: New Directions, 1969) p. 66.

15. *Lograire*, p. 21.

16. *Cables to the Ace or Familiar Liturgies of Misunderstanding* (New York: New Directions, 1968), p. 62. Merton quotes a different comment from Dogen. My citation is from Shunryu Suzuki's *Zen Mind, Beginner's Mind* Edited by Trudy Dixon with an introduction by Richard Baker. (New York: Weatherhill Books, 1970) p. 125. Cf. *Zen Master Dogen: An Introduction with Selected Writings by* Yuho Yokoi with the assistance of Daizen Victoria. New York: Weatherhill, 1976; and: *Shobogenzo (The Eye and Treasury of the True Law)* Translated by Kosen Nishiyama and John Stevens. Tokyo: Nakayama Shobo. Volume 1, 1975. Volume 2, 1977.

17. John S. Dunne, csc, *The City of the Gods: A Study in Myth and Mortality* (Notre Dame: University of Notre Dame Press, 1965) p. v.

18. (New York: New Directions Paperback Edition, 1975) p. 149.

19. *My Argument*, pp. 51, 58.

20. *My Argument*, pp. 52–53.

21. *The Hidden Ground of Love: The Letters of Thomas Merton on Religious Experience and Social Concerns* Selected and Edited by William H. Shannon. (New York: Farrar, Straus, Giroux, 1985) p. 139.

22. Edited by Thomas P. McDonnell. (New York: Image Books, Revised Edition 1975) p. 16.

23. (New York: New Directions, 1966) pp. 2–3.

24. *A Hidden Wholeness: The Visual World of Thomas Merton* Photographs by Thomas Merton and John Howard Griffin. (Boston: Houghton Mifflin Company, 1970) pp. 107, 109.

25. The Merton-Dylan-Rimbaud connection has been analyzed in my essay: 'Mind Guards Against the White Knight: Thomas Merton and Bob Dylan', *The Merton Seasonal* (Thomas Merton Studies Center, Bellarmine College, Louisville, Kentucky). 9:3 (Autumn, 1984) 4–10. For further sources on Jean-Nicholas-Arthur Rimbaud (1854–1891) see also: *Oeuvres Complètes D'Arthur Rimbaud* Texte établi et annoté par Rolland De Renéville et Jules Mouquet. Paris: Bibliothèque de la Pléiade, Editions Gallimard, 1963; and: *Arthur Rimbaud: Une Saison en Enfer, Les Illuminations/A Season in Hell, The Illuminations* A new translation by Enid Rhodes Peschel. New York: Oxford University Press, 1973.

26. 'The American Villon' was the epithet Thomas Merton used to describe Bob Dylan to Jacques Maritain. Villon (1431–vanished 1463), along with supporting detail and cultural resonances from the French poetic tradition, was used as key to an understanding of Merton's study of Dylan in my essay: 'Ace of Songs — Ace of Freedoms: Thomas Merton and Bob Dylan', *The American Benedictine Review* (Part One) 37:1 (March 1986) 67–95; (Part Two) 37:2 (June 1986) 143–159. Some further sources on Villon are: *Villon (OEUVRES)* Illustrations De Dubout. Paris: Gilbert Jeune — Libraire d'Amateurs, Limited Edition No. 824, 1959: *The Poems of Master Francis Villon of Paris* Done into English Verse, in the original forms by John Payne. London: Reeves & Turner, 1881; Carco, Francis, *The Romance of Villon* Translated by Hemish Miles. New York: Alfred A. Knopf, 1927; and : Chaney, Edward F. *Francois Villon in His Environment* London: B. H. Blackwell, Ltd., 1946.

27. *Follow the Ecstasy: Thomas Merton, The Heritage Years — 1965–1968* (Fort Worth, TX: JHG Editions/Latitudes Press, 1983) pp. 115, 120.

28. *The Seven Mountains of Thomas Merton* (Boston: Houghton Mifflin Company, 1984) p. 451; *Cables*, pp. 43–46.

29. *My Argument,* Introduction, pp. 14–15.

30. *My Argument,* e.g., pp. 27, 30, 31, 89.

31. *My Argument,* p. 235.

32. *Cables,* p. 54.

33. *The Collected Poems of Thomas Merton* (New York: New Directions, 1977) pp. 808–809.

34. Quoted by Edward Rice in his *The Man in the Sycamore Tree, The Good Times and Hard Life of Thomas Merton.* (Garden City, NY: Doubleday, 1970) p. 92.

35. *Cables,* p. 6.

36. *Cables,* p. 54.

37. *Jesus on Social Institutions* Edited with an introduction by Kenneth Cauthen, in *Lives of Jesus Series* Leader E. Keck, General Editor. (Philadelphia: Fortress Press, 1971) pp. 26–27.

38. C. H. Dodd, *The Founder of Christianity* (New York: Macmillan Publishing Company, 1970) p. 86.

39. *Mathews,* pp. 23–24–25.

40. *The Ten Principal Upanishads* Put into English by Shree Purshit Swami and W. B. Yeats. (London: Faber and Faber Limited, 1937) p. 8.

41. (New York: Harcourt Brace Jovanovich, Publishers, A Harvest/HBJ book, 1976) p. 3.

42. *Ibid.,* p. 83.

43. *Ibid.,* p. 76.

44. *Ibid.,* p. 12.

45. Of course this is the story of the human person, ancient as well as modern. As patristic source and modern novel set in early twentieth-century England, the following provide background to this Merton study: *The Confessions of Saint Augustine* Translated by Edward B. Pusey, D. D. Macmillan/Collier Books, 1961; Ethel Mannin, *Late Have I Loved Thee* Garden City, NY: Image Books, 1962. This novel—inspired also by Augustine as well as by Merton's autobiography—was originally published by G. P. Putnam's Sons in the year that *The Seven Storey Mountain* was released.

46. *The Seven Storey Mountain,* pp. 31, 29.

47. *Ibid.,* p. 49; One of the Trappist Founders of Holy Spirit Abbey—before coming to Georgia in 1944—assisted at the Mass of First Holy Communion of John Paul Merton. The following recollections are pertinent here and cast light on Merton's self-image in contrast to the appearance of his brother: 'The day after his baptism (at a local church) John Paul received his First Holy Communion at the private (low) Mass of Dom Frederic Dunne, Abbot of Gethsemani. There were two servers, one of whom was Frater Louis Merton. (I think he was still a novice at that time, which must have been about 1942.) Abbot Dunne offered his Mass at the Altar of Our Lady of Victory in the transept of the Abbey Church. Only a few monks were present. John Paul was tall (about 6 ft), slender, and well-built. He had bright yellow (blond) hair. Was rather a good-looking, handsome young man. He wore his best, new military uniform. It was the light gray uniform of the Royal Canadian Air Force. He was a bomber pilot, and was scheduled to go to the war in Europe very soon. One interesting feature: John Paul was wearing his combat sword in a scabbard suspended from the left side of his belt. Evidently this was an important occasion, both for Thomas Merton (Fr. Louis) and his younger brother, John Paul. Tom's deep affection for his brother could be read between the lines during the liturgical ceremony. Although First Communion is always a joyous occasion, yet there was an unmistakable note of sadness underlying this particular First Communion.

John Paul would very soon be going to Europe to fight in the terrible war. I believe he died that same year when his plane crashed over the North Sea.' Merton's Father Master of Novices who was so kind and instrumental in John Paul's conversion later became the second Abbot of the Georgia community. *The Father Himself Loves You,* Notes on the Life of Dom Robert McGann [unpublished manuscript] by William Reams, Monk of Holy Spirit Abbey, has provided useful background source material for this study.

48. *The Seven Storey Mountain,* p. 85.

49. *Ibid.,* p. 121.

50. Martin Green, *Children of the Sun: A Narrative of 'Decadence' in England after 1918* (New York: Wideview Books, 1980). Merton is discussed in conjunction with Evelyn Waugh on p. 354. Green states that some, like C. S. Lewis, avoided dandyism and allied themselves with Christianity and with creative mythopoeia: 'They set themselves to create cultural images for Christ, and for a Christian temperament, that would be meaningful for the age. . .' (p. 430). The linking of Merton with the *Sonnenkinder* is mine, not Green's. Cf. related ideas in my book review of *Blaze of Recognition – Through the Year with Thomas Merton: Daily Meditations* Selected and Edited by Thomas P. McDonnell. (Doubleday & Company, 1984) in *Cistercian Studies* 20 (1985) Bulletin of Spirituality 311: 691–692.

51. Though at first seemingly quite unlikely, there are interesting literary and prophetic parallels between Merton and Wilde, which I have explored in: 'Two Studies in Chuang Tzu: Thomas Merton and Oscar Wilde' *The Merton Seasonal of Bellarmine College* [Louisville, Kentucky] 12:1 (Winter, 1987) 5–14.

52. PBS Premiere: June 5th, 1984; Cf. especially the reminiscences of John Barber in the film text: *Merton By Those Who Knew Him Best* Edited by Paul Wilkes. (San Francisco: Harper & Row, 1984) pp. 81–84. For biographical material on Merton in England see: Monica Furlong, *Merton: A Biography* (San Francisco: Harper & Row, 1980) Part 1, Chapters 3 and 4, and Oakham photograph; *The Seven Mountains of Thomas Merton,* Part 3 – 'Brooke Hill'.

53. Goldcrest Films. Screenplay by Julian Mitchell. Music by Michael Storey. Also starring Colin Firk and Cary Elwes. In 1968, Lindsay Anderson's film 'IF', starring Malcolm McDowell, David Wood, and Christine Noonan, gave a more violent portrayal of the English school system.

54. (Oxford: Amber Land Press, 1982) p. 33.

55. Quoted by John Ezard in: 'The other woman in the royal house', *Manchester Guardian Weekly* 134:18 (Week ending May 4, 1986) 5.

56. *Seven Storey Mountain,* p. 129.

57. Letter of 1862 published in the *Globe,* quoted by Brian Martin, *John Henry Newman: His Life and Work* (New York: Oxford University Press, 1982) p. 113.

58. *Love and Living* Edited by Naomi Burton Stone and Brother Patrick Hart. (New York: A Harvest/HBJ Book, 1979) p. 13. Like Newman—who retained a respect for persons within the Anglican tradition, and experienced an amelioration of relationships in his later years—Merton could distinguish between ideas and values on the one hand, and human persons on the other, of whatever religious persuasion. Cf. Canon A. M. Allchin, 'Whale of a Book: Review of *The Seven Mountains of Thomas Merton* by Michael Mott', *The Merton Seasonal* 10:1 (Winter 1985) 4–5.

59. *Elected Silence* The Autobiography of Thomas Merton. With a Foreword by Evelyn Waugh. (London: Burns & Oates, 1949) pp. 5–6.

60. Though Merton never wrote an extended essay on Thoreau, he felt they were kindred spirits. I have explored their relationship in: 'Inauguration of

Prayer House', *Theology Activities Organization Newsletter*, Saint Meinrad School of Theology, Indiana (Fall 1971) 2; 'The Contemplative Witness of Henry David Thoreau', *Monastic Exchange* 8:3 (Fall 1976) 7–14; 'Thomas Merton's Journey Home', *The Georgia Bulletin* (Catholic Archdiocese of Atlanta Weekly Newspaper) 22:43 (Tuesday, December 6, 1984) 5; 'Lights Across the Ridge: Thomas Merton and Henry David Thoreau' [Publication forthcoming, *The Merton Annual*, 1988 (New York: AMS)].

61. Roger A. Bruns, *Knights of the Road: A Hobo History* (New York: Methuen, 1980) p. 35.

62. *The Penguin Book of American Folk Songs* Compiled and edited by Alan Lomax. (Baltimore: Penguin Books, 1966) p. 117.

63. *Bruns*, p. 28.

64. *Bruns*, p. 38.

65. Charles Winick, *The New People: Desexualization in American Life* (New York: Pegasus Books, 1969) p. 69.

66. (New York: Harper & Row, 1966), p. 9.

67. *Funk*, p. 7.

68. Bob Dylan, *Lyrics, 1962–1985* (New York: Alfred A. Knopf, 1985) pp. 132–133. Hereafter, the citation will be: *Lyrics.*

69. 'Visions of Johanna', *Lyrics*, p. 223. For an historical perspective on Bob Dylan's role in the 1960s see: Jonathan Cott, *Dylan*, Garden City, NY: Doubleday/Rolling Stone Press, 1984; Anthony Scaduto, *Bob Dylan: An Intimate Biography*, New York: New American Library/Signet Books, 1973. And: Randall H. Alfred, 'The Church of Satan,' in *The New Religious Consciousness* Edited by Charles Y. Glock and Robert N. Bellah. Berkeley: University of California Press, 1976; John Gruen, *The New Bohemia: The Combine Generation*, New York: Grosset & Dunlap, 1967; William Manchester, *The Glory and the Dream: A Narrative History of America, 1932–1972*, New York: Bantam Books, 1974; Theodore Roszak, *The Making of A Counter Culture: A Reflection on the Technocratic Society and Its Youthful Opposition*, New York: Doubleday/Anchor Books, 1969; Milton Viorst, *Fire in the Streets: America in the 1960s*, New York: Simon and Schuster, 1979. For a General background see Ronald B. Flowers, *Religion in Strange Times: The 1960s and 1970s*, Macon, Georgia: Mercer University Press, 1984. Merton's place in the radical movement is discussed by Charles A. Meconis in *With Clumsy Grace: The American Catholic Left, 1961–1975*, New York: Seabury Press, 1979. I have written about Merton as inheritor of the ancient spirituality of 'voluntary imprisonment' in 'In the Heart of Christ: The Monk, the Outcast, The Prisoner', *Hospitality* (Publication of the Atlanta OPEN DOOR Community). (Part 1): 5:2 (February 1986) 4–7; (Part 2) 5:3 (March/April 1986) 8, 12. See also my review of *Portraits of Those I Love* by Daniel Berrigan, SJ in *Cistercian Studies* 21 (1986) Bulletin of Spirituality 26: 27–28.

70. Octavio Paz, *Claude Lévi-Strauss: An Introduction* Translated from the Spanish by J. S. Bernstein and Maxine Bernstien. (Ithaca, NY: Cornell University Press, 1970) pp. 63–64.

71. 'Ballad of a Thin Man', *Lyrics*, p. 198.

72. 'It's Alright, Ma (I'm Only Bleeding)', *Lyrics*, pp. 176–177.

73. *Paz*, pp. 65, 67–68.

74. 'Visions of Johanna', *Lyrics*, p. 223.

75. 'Just Like Tom Thumb's Blues', *Lyrics*, pp. 207–208.

76. *Paz*, pp. 67–68.

77. 'It's Alright, Ma (I'm Only Bleeding)', p. 176.

78. Elizabeth Sewell, quoted by Dan Otto Via, Jr. in *The Parables: Their Literary and Existential Dimension* (Philadelphia: Fortess Press, 1980) pp. 74–75.

79. 'Desolation Row', *Lyrics*, pp. 204–205.
80. William K. Wimsatt and Monroe C. Beardsley, authors of *The Verbal Icon*, cited in *Via*, p. 77.
81. *Via*, pp. 53–55; For related sources on metaphor see: Wesley A. Kort, *Narrative Elements and Religious Meaning*, Philadelphia: Fortress Press, 1975; Philip Wheelwright, *Metaphor and Reality*, Bloomington: Indiana University Press, 1962.
82. 'The Times They Are A-Changin'', *Lyrics*, p. 91. In the Fall of 1985 CBS, Inc. released *Bob Dylan: Biograph*. In the twenty-five year commemorative collection of his songs, Dylan gives a thirty-six page photo-essay and liner notes for the fifty-three songs included which serves as an excellent introduction to his work. In this study I have limited selections to material known to Merton. Since 1968 Dylan has released more than twenty albums, has excited interest in his conversion to Christianity, and has been the object of study in more than two dozen books. In 1985 he participated in the 'We Are The World' recording and performed before an audience of 100,000 spectators and a billion and more viewing via satellite at the Live Aid concert to raise money for people starving in Africa. He inspired Farm Aid and was interviewed in a special 20/20 television program dedicated to him. In 1986 he received the ASCAP award for his contribution to music, participated in the celebration of the first Martin Luther King, Jr. National Holiday, and travelled to New Zealand and Australia where his concerts were filmed by HBO for a television special. And Dylan toured the United States and began work in England on 'Hearts of Fire', a film also starring Rupert Everett of *Another Country*.
83. W. B. Yeats, quoted by Morton Irving Seiden in *William Butler Yeats: The Poet as Mythmaker, 1865–1939*, New York: Cooper Square, 1975, p. 61.
84. *Ibid.*
85. The doctrine of Yeats presented by John S. Dunne, C.S.C. in *A Search for God in Time and Memory*, Notre Dame: University of Notre Dame Press, 1969, p. 150.
86. *The Seven Storey Mountain*, p. 57.
87. The scripture texts used in this study are:
Biblia Sacra Iuxta Vulgatam Versionem, Editio Minor. Stuttgart: Deutsche Bibelgesellschaft, 1984.
The Holy Bible Authorized King James Vesion edited by Rev. C. I. Scofield, D. D.; Scofield Facsimile Series No. 2. New York: Oxford University Press. Scofield's Preface is dated: 'Greyshingles', Douglaston, L. I., January 1, 1917.
The New American Bible New York: Catholic Book Publishing Co., 1970.
The New English Bible With the Apocrypha. Cambridge, England: At the Univeristy Press, 1970.
88. *Cables to the Ace*, Number Seventy-Six, p. 52.

George Kilcourse

Spirituality and Imagination Thomas Merton's 'Sapiential Thinking'

W ITH THE CHARACTERISTIC bluntness that col-
ored his mature writings, Thomas Merton addressed
the prospect of lay contemplatives near the conclusion of 'The Inner Experience'. He mapped for us an adventurous
route: 'If you are waiting for someone to come along and feed you
the contemplative life with a spoon, you are going to wait a long
time, especially in America. You had better renounce your inertia, pray for a little imagination, ask the Lord to awaken your
creative freedom. . . .'[1]

Spirituality and imagination grew more intimately connected in Merton's career and his vision for contemplative life.
How far he had travelled from the lament of the tortuous *The
Sign of Jonas* where he declared, 'it is no fun to live the spiritual
life with the equipment of an artist'.[2] In his posthumously
published reflections on monastic renewal, *Contemplation in a*

World of Action, he had reclaimed the constructive role of imagination in responding to the question, 'Is the Contemplative Life Finished?' Merton called imagination a 'discovering faculty, a faculty for seeing relationships, for seeing meanings that are special and even quite new'.[3]

His script for the education of contemplatives (specifically monastic postulants) reversed the culture's neglect of imagination. Merton observed that we cannot any longer presuppose access to a liberal education: 'Imagination needs to be reformed and educated along normal, natural lines'. He insisted such cultural formation was 'absolutely necessary as a basis for higher spiritual development'.[4] Merton quipped that the destruction of a child's imaginative response to reality was followed by twenty years of 'overstimulated vegetation'.[5]

To complicate the task, Merton found much to distress him in monastic prayer life. The preponderance of those he dubbed 'juridical contemplatives'—'they live in a "contemplative monastery" and follow its exercise. . . . The great thing is to sing loud, observe the rubrics, and beg God seven times in the day to punish Communists'[6]—discouraged imagination and mired contemplative life in banality, triviality, and pettiness. Merton identified the 'one great defect—a failure of imagination. Our prayer life itself', he confessed, 'is poor in imagination'.

In a very telling entry near the end of his earlier journal, *Conjectures of a Guilty Bystander,* Merton had applied familiar terms from his spiritual lexicon to our topic. He wrote, 'to assume that my superficial ego—this cramp of my imagination—is my real self is to begin by dishonoring myself and reality'.[7] From one who habitually exercised the imagination, this metaphor of the 'cramp of the imagination' proves intriguing. Indeed, the muscular life of imagination mobilized Merton's spirituality. And it would be the limber, lithe life of imagination (his own and that of other literary artists) which Merton ventured to appreciate as a most authentic (if unconventional) source of spiritual communion and dialogue.

The inspiration for this study originates with Merton's use of the term 'sapiential thinking' as he employed it in an essay the year before his death, ' "Baptism in the Forest": Wisdom and Initiation in William Faulkner' in George Panichas' *Mansions of the Spirit*.[8] That essay stands as a unique piece in the Merton canon. Highly exploratory, it articulates Merton's mature thought on the relationship between spirituality and imagination. Its limits as an essay are obvious: it is tentative, probing, in dialogue with other points of view and theories rehearsed in the collection of articles that follow in the volume. Nevertheless, it plots coordinates on the frontiers of Merton's most mature reflections.

My purpose is two-fold: (1) to come to an understanding of Merton's evolving sense of the intimate connection between spirituality and imagination; essential to that relationship is the new context of a 'post-christian' diaspora in which he pursued the discussion; and (2) an evaluation of Merton's method of 'sapiential thinking', borrowing insights from David Tracy's important theological study, *The Analogical Imagination*.

Let me begin with the notion of the Church in 'diaspora'. The Second Vatican Council's pastoral constitution *Gaudium et Spes* (1965) radically re-oriented Catholic Christianity. An entirely new situation existed. When the official Church declared it was no longer threatened by or condemning of the secular world, Thomas Merton felt vindicated. His own instincts reverencing nature and creation had already lead him to this openness and dialogue with the world. Merton now embraced with enthusiasm what he found in Karl Rahner's seminal contributions to Vatican II's deliberations on this very issue. It remains curious that Merton's important essay, 'The Church and the "Godless World"', published in the 1966 British edition, *Redeeming the Time*, had not found its way into later editions of the American version of this material and other essays entitled *Seeds of Destruction* (1964).[9] It is this growing consciousness of a post-christian world that Merton will repeat in his later writing.[10] He quotes from Rahner, '*theologically* we are obliged to accept this fact of a diaspora as the starting-point for all conclusions about our behaviour as Christians in the modern world'.[11] With the demise of triumphal optimism and clericalism, Christians in the modern world face a new task: without the formal church structures the human person becomes all-important. In Rahner's language, theology becomes Christian anthropology.[12] 'The Second Vatican Council', concluded Merton, 'manifested a wholly new concern—man himself.' He delights in the irony: 'It is rather awe inspiring to see that a basic and permanent problem that once presented itself as a theoretical denial of the humanity of Christ now presents itself as a practical, concrete and existential denial of man.'[13] Then Merton develops his theology of the human person, a self-transcending orientation:

> The human ego, or the individual centre of man's natural being, is not (in Christian thought) the centre of personal freedom. Christian anthropology is not yet fully clear about the person, since what belongs to the whole Christian person has traditionally been ascribed to the soul (part of the person only) and to grace. The Christian theology of grace needs to be reviewed in the light of a new and deeper metaphysic of the person and of love.[14]

It was a declaration of independence for Merton's own developing existential theology. His reflections from the late 1950s forward would evidence that he had reclaimed more and more consciously this native style of theologizing. Recalling the youthful autobiography nearly twenty years later, Merton in a 1967 interview testified to his development. 'I was still dealing in a crude theology', he apologized, 'a clean-cut division between the natural and the supernatural, God and the world, sacred and secular, with boundary lines that were supposed to be quite evident.' 'Life is not as simple', he confessed, 'as it once looked in *The Seven Storey Mountain.*'[15]

I find this overlooked manifesto of Merton's theological agenda a key to his own creative and critical work in the last decade of his life. The narrative of grace in the person's life is precisely what Christian spiritual autobiography attempts to make intelligible. And, the engagement with another artist's imaginative world summons the theological critic at the crossroads of grace, a most intimate personal dialogue. Not only are we offered the artist's experience; but by recreating the experience in us the artist summons us to what Nathan A. Scott, Jr. has named 'the drama of interrogation'.[16] This new hermeneutic inverts the classical critical stance because now the work interprets the reader. Merton turned with renewed enthusiasm to artists, especially literary artists. Never again would he indulge in the scholastic vocabulary of his analytic, systematic and woefully detached study of St John of the Cross, *The Ascent to Truth* (1951). Merton was reclaiming his true idiom. He confessed it best in the introductions to his subsequent reflection. In the 1960 volume, *Disputed Questions,* he admitted coming back into contact 'through certain discrete readings and conversations' with the America he had once known.[17] Perhaps more revealing was his confession in the preface to *New Seeds of Contemplation* (1961). There he acknowledged the 'new perspective': 'the author's solitude has been modified by contact with other solitudes.'[18]

One recalls immediately the exchange of letters between Merton and Boris Pasternak at the end of the 1950s. His critical essays appraising Pasternak's post-christian environs in Soviet Russia freed Merton to recognize his 'problematical Christianity'. 'The protest of *Doctor Zhivago*', Merton wrote, 'is spiritual . . . religious, aesthetic and mystical.'[19] And yet, Pasternak's spirituality, Merton judged, used the Christian symbols more effectively than our 'ritualistic routine': 'It . . . is not perfectly at home with dogmatic formulas, but gropes after truth in its own clumsy way.'[20]

Writing later on Christian Existentialism Merton declared this insight more clearly: 'Existentialism has expressed itself most unambiguously in literature, where it is free from technicalities and quasi-formulas'. Claiming it 'an experience and an attitude, rather than a system of thought', he pointed to the devastating existential intuition and irony of Flannery O'Connor.[21] Along these same lines in his essay, 'The Church and the "Godless World"', Merton pointed to Rilke representing 'a certain type of modern religious consciousness'. 'It seeks to "create" a new symbolic language for the things of God', Merton claimed.[22]

In the published notes on Christian Existentialism which he entitled 'The Other Side of Despair', Merton returned to the theme of diaspora Christianity: 'One can certainly subscribe', he wrote, 'to correct dogmatic formulas without the intimate spiritual ground of one's own existence being called into question'.[23] But such gestures of religion, Merton worried, did not 'disturb man in the depths of his conscience'.[24] Existential theology such as we encounter in literary art, he insisted, 'unmasks' the flight from the true self which society promoted. (He wrote lucidly of this theme in his study of Ionesco's *The Rhinoceros* in an essay, 'Rain and the Rhinoceros', in *Raids on the Unspeakable*.[25]) In a very autobiographical voice Merton volunteered Existentialism's great contribution: 'The authentic person is not born in stoic isolation but in the openness and dialogue of love.' He concluded this essay diagnosing our spiritual inertia, again in terms of grace. Our openness to grace as an *event* 'is proportionate to our sense of our *need* for it', said Merton. 'This in turn depends on our awareness of the reality of the crisis we are in.'[26] Or, to use his earlier phrase, one must be aware of the 'cramp of the imagination'.

Merton's 1967 essay exploring Faulkner's 'The Bear' section in *Go Down, Moses* employed the method of existential theological criticism. We discover here an application of his 'sapiential thinking'. A systematic study of this methodology eluded Merton — as sustained systems would ever remain foreign to his writing. But here he focussed the issue. An inchoate theory tentatively auditioned.

First, Merton insisted that in the wake of 'troublesome questions' for this interdisciplinary field, 'literary' and 'religious' values must not be confused.[27] He broadened the term 'religious' beyond confessional or even ecumenical labels and particular dogmatic faith. He distanced himself from a sense of literature as moralizing or preaching and propaganda.[28] 'Basic problems of human destiny', he said, 'are embedded in human nature itself.'[29] These 'truths about man' constituted the religious dimension. He pointed to the dramatic power of 'enchantment' which religious (literary) artists have:

It brings you into living participation with an experience of basic and universal human values on a level which words can *point to* but cannot fully attain . . . . What the author means to convey is not a system of truths which explain life but a certain depth of awareness in which life itself is lived more intensely and with a more meaningful direction.

Without confusing this 'power of imaginative communion' with theological faith, Merton found the artist 'activiating the deepest centers of decision which faith calls into play'.[30]

Merton found the terms 'religious' and 'metaphysical' incapable of communicating the imaginative awareness of basic meaning. So, he volunteered the term 'sapiential', 'the highest level of cognition'. 'Wisdom', he stated with monastic conviction, 'is not only speculative but also practical: that is to say, it is "lived". And unless one lives it one cannot have it. . . . It proceeds, then, not merely from knowledge about ultimate values, but from an actual possession and awareness of those values as incorporated in one's own existence.'[31] In his imaginary conversation with Karl Barth (published in *Conjectures of a Guilty Bystander,* Part I, as 'Barth's Dream') Merton reminded this stern dogmatist that a child, the lover of Mozart, a hidden Sophianic wisdom in each of them would be their salvation—and not the celebrity of their many books!

Merton concluded his sapiential reading of Faulkner with a reminder. In our post-christian world 'most modern literature', he said, 'speaks a language that is neither Christian nor unchristian'. The challenge for the theological critic becomes a 'creative effort to penetrate the meaning of man's suffering and aspirations in symbols that are imaginatively authentic'. The God who appears in modern literature—if at all—is a God Merton found expressed 'negatively and obscurely'. (Hence, the ironic imagination he himself practiced in his own late poetry.) This age of doubt, as Merton dubbed it, offers 'authentic assurances of hope and understanding provided we are willing to tolerate theological discomfort.'[32]

William H. Shannon's masterful *Thomas Merton's Dark Path* has critically analyzed the monk's contemplative reflections in an era of such theological ferment. In studying his anthropology,

Shannon reviews 'The Inner Experience' and Merton's exegesis of Genesis 3, where the fall from paradise results in alienation. Redemption becomes for Merton a return to the paradisal state, a recovery of lost unity. The soul is awakened and begins on the illuminative way. In this context, Merton interpreted sin not as a moral lapse, but an ontological lapse. His complaint in 'The Inner Experience' that 'guilt' has replaced 'sin' in our age set in sharp relief his identification of the contemplative mission today — 'to keep alive a sense of sin' (as ontological lapse). Sin in this sense violates my very being, Merton insisted.[33]

What is particularly forceful here is the kinship between the contemplative and the existentialist. Merton quoted Paul Tillich:

> What unites contemplatives and existentialists is precisely the depth and sincerity of their 'concern.' Both reject any easy or convenient substitute for ultimate reality. Both face insecurity and the darkness of spiritual risk.[34]

Merton's warning against 'my superficial ego — this cramp of the imagination' echoed this contemplative insight. His multiple terms (false self, mask, illusion, empirical ego, Cartesian subject) conveyed a singular antithesis to the real or authentic self, the 'self in Christ' for Merton. 'Without bothering to question the deep mystery of our own identity', Merton observed, 'we fabricate a trifling and impertinent identity for ourselves with the bare scraps of experience that we find lying within immediate reach.' Merton was convinced that the artist and contemplative shared the antipathy to 'adjusting to a whole galaxy of illusions'.[35] He had earlier in *Conjectures of a Guilty Bystander* diagnosed our spiritual trouble:

> . . . We have to *die* to our image of ourselves, our autonomy, our fixation upon our self-willed identity. We have to be able to relax the psychic and spiritual cramp which knots us in the painful, vulnerable, helpless "I" that is all we know as ourselves.
>
> The chronic inability to relax this cramp begets despair. In the end, as we realize more and more that we are knotted

upon *nothing,* that the cramp is a meaningless, senseless, pointless affirmation of nonentity, and that we must nevertheless continue to affirm our nothingness *over against* everything else — our frustration becomes absolute. We become incapable of existing except as a 'no,' which we fling in the face of everything. This 'no' to everything serves as our pitiful 'yes' to ourselves — a makeshift identity which is nothing.[36]

Merton saw tragedy when,

the man-in-a-cramp of freedom knotted up in frustration, may obscurely *mean* his cramp to be a noble refusal. In a sense he may seem to be right in his protest. He may seem to be protesting against the iniquity of a situation that impoverishes and destroys him. With this as his justification he hardens himself in total refusal.[37]

One could so easily fail to recognize 'the nature of this cramp', Merton concluded, for

the 'refusal' is fundamentally a refusal of faith. Not necessarily of theological and Christian faith in the full sense of the word, but at least a refusal . . . to *believe in life.* . . . There is only one remedy — the surrender that seeks faith in God as a gift that is not our due, and that is willing to suffer great indigence and peril while waiting to receive it.[38]

Merton named this 'simply the ordinary way of human existence', threatened with despair but fruitful with the possibility of choosing new life.[39] He concluded a 1968 essay on symbolism with just such an insight.

The final answer does not remain entirely and exclusively in the hands of those who are still equipped to interpret ancient religious traditions. . . . The artist and the poet seem to be the ones most aware of the situation, but they are for that very reason the closest to despair.[40]

The finest evidence of Merton's sustained application of this method of 'sapiential thinking' can be found in his studies of Albert Camus.[41] In seven cogent and challenging essays Merton examines his 'typical "post-Christian" thinker',[42] Camus. And the concern of his critical engagement with Camus' imaginative world centers around a review of the Christian theology of grace in the light of a new and deeper metaphysic of the person and love.

Camus had exposed the soft underbelly of Christianity—masquerading-as-religion. Merton found him relentless but nonetheless he agreed—up to a point. There is a kindred spirit exchanged between Camus who condemns both Christianity and Marxism as absolutist, alienating *systems* evacuating human values; and Merton who was responding to the need to re-formulate Christian truth after the dry dogmatism which had robbed Christianity of its life and sources.

Here I must capture tersely Merton's interpretation of Camus as practical sapiential criticism. First, Merton refused to surrender his critical literary faculties in evaluating Camus with the methodology. He could speak of the artist's occasional artistic failure.[43] Nonetheless, Camus' talent overcame the limitations, Merton being generous in praise of the 'austere and ironic genius of Camus'.[44] At the religious level, Merton cautioned again: 'This is not to say that Camus was a secret Christian, but only that a Christian is free, if he likes, to understand Camus in a Christian sense which Camus himself did not realize.'[45] One might again borrow Merton's phrase and applaud Camus as one profoundly aware of the 'cramp of the imagination' and con-templative possibilities for the real self's relaxation. At issue is the ironic caricature of faith and grace which Merton (again, recognizing the post-christian milieu) blames not on Camus but on Christians themselves. We have embalmed, not renewed, Christianity, Merton exclaimed.[46] He remarked the development in Camus' ethic from the early nihilism of Meursault to the solidarity and communal commitment of *The Plague* and *The Rebel*.[47]

The essay, 'Three Saviors in Camus', signalled Merton's ability to fathom Camus' protest. It is a matter of awakening 'lucidity' or the lucid consiousness. And with piercing clairity he percieved Camus' drama: 'It depends most of all on the encounter and communion of persons.'[48]

The parable of *The Plague* unfolds as an exploration of the mystery of Evil and the Christian God of grace. Of course the metaphor of the 'plague' points to the *moral* crisis, not merely a physical contagion. Merton interpreted the response in quarantined Oran as the discovery of solidarity. A 'new order arises of freedom and love in which all who participate do so by deliberate choice. . . .' Their two possible motives are: (1) revolt against the absurd; and (2) self-sacrifice in service to others, affirming humanity's life and love.[49] Without such a response one became either victim or accomplice to the plague.

It is the Jesuit, Father Paneloux, who mimics the caricature of Christianity. No coincidence that Camus styles him as the personification of defective Christian faith. Without compassion, he lives alone with an abstract God. Alone he dies. The irony compounds with his declaration at the child's death bed, 'Now I understand what grace is.' Merton interpreted the priest as perverting faith and being 'fanatically loyal to a God that is stone dead'.[50] It is because nominal Christians (in a post-christian world) elect to revere *that* God who can be 'explained' as arbitrarily destroying the innocent that Camus revolts. Merton accepted the sting of his satire. But then he corrected. A Christian is not inevitably reduced to Father Paneloux's state of atrophied love. Ironically, Merton observed, Paneloux is without grace despite his claims of insight. Merton accepted the artist's awakening of recognition; and in the post-christian world fashion he saw the opportunity to re-articulate and reclaim the priority of grace as the *experience* of God's love and not abstract knowledge *about* God.[51] But Merton suggested that Camus' 'refusal' itself approached the peril of despair in refusing the possibility of faith. The contemplative Merton avoided the superficial ego of existing simply as a negation, a 'no' to the seduction of illusions.

By way of conclusion I will briefly measure Merton's achievement in light of salient points from David Tracy's theological study, *The Analogical Imagination*. Tracy assesses characteristics of the 'relgious classic' which offer a benchmark for weighing Merton's 'staying power', his permanent status and excess of meaning. But beyond such considerations as: What ultimate questions came alive again for the reader? How is the work a dialogue? How is the reader transformed? What does the classic cause you to 'recognize' in an entirely new way?; Tracy remarks the true achievement of the religious classic is its 'publicness'. The very public discourse entered through a religious classic invites readers to its paradigm of interpreted meaning. The religious classic captures the event of truth and understanding in a normative way, transforming, Tracy says, our perceptions of the real. Whether disclosing our present mode of being-in-the-world as 'inauthentic, spent, finished', or 'confirmed beyond any hope for confirmation', the religious classic makes possible an event of truth.[52]

Let me illustrate Merton's success at risking this very interpretation for his diaspora 'public' (which includes Tracy's three publics, Society, Academy, and Church). John Eudes Bamberger has assessed that Merton's spiritual autobiography (reflected throughout his diverse writings) achieves (to use Tracy's language) 'the always-already, not-yet reality of grace as manifestation, proclamation, and prophetic task'. In Bamberger's words:

> As he had a passion for spiritual beauty later on, he had a passionate nature for all kinds of things, and he'd indulged it too much. But he never totally identified with that: he always believed in innocence. And somehow he was able, because of the experience of God, to believe that God had recreated his innocence.[53]

Merton's reading public in the diaspora continues to be galvinized by the 'shock of recognition'[54] encountered in reading his narratives and intepreted categories through which he convinces us that God recreates our innocence as well. The existential truth of the horizon of grace, our conversion from alienation, overcoming our ontological lapse, these Merton concluded were to rid ourselves of the 'cramp of the imagination'.

My being is not an affirmation of a limited self, but the 'yes' of Being itself, irrespective of my own choices. Where do 'I' come in? Simply in uniting the 'yes' of my own freedom with the 'yes' of Being that already *is* before I have a chance to choose. . . . The Christian choice . . . is simply a complete, trusting, and abandoned consent to the 'yes' of God in Christ.[55]

Tracy's effort at 'Christian theology and the culture of pluralism' names the project Merton had accepted in the diaspora context. He surveyed the landscape of pluralism and resisted both temptations Tracy has identified: (1) indifferentism, or the 'lazy pluralism' of 'repressive tolerance'; and (2) brittle univocity, the path of dogmatism and ideology which had become synonymous with Tridentine Catholicism.[56] Without the label, Merton practiced Tracy's option of the 'analogical imagination'. Against the horizon of the contemporary, each different Tradition seeks to understand the other 'through analogy or not at all'.[57] It enters conversation with the other without abandoning its particular genius.[58] In Tracy's language, it becomes a 'journey of exposure to all the fundamental questions in the uncanniness of our contemporary situation.'[59]

Merton's expanding Catholicity[60] perhaps endures as the most visible result of this engagement with the culture of pluralism. His essays 'Apologies to an Unbeliever' and 'The Unbelief of Believers',[61] provoked and challenged the institutional Church. Without himself being systematic, Merton stood in the mainstream of Christian systematic theology; he dared to reinterpret the particular tradition of Catholicism and its self-understanding for the current horizon of the believing community and the wider public. But the 'shock of recognition' of a religious classic perhaps belongs more to works such as his 'A Letter on the Contemplative Life'.[62] There Merton writes 'only as a sinner to another sinner', disclaiming an official voice. Solidarity breathes from this 1967 epistle, proclaiming that 'we exist solely for this, to be the place He has chosen for His presence, his manifestation in the world, His epiphany'—echoes of Tracy's 'the always-already, not-yet reality of grace as manifestation, proclamation, and prophetic task'!

The existential theology of Merton radiated from his habit of questioning, exploration. Two examples. In introducing *The New Man* (1961) Merton revealed his preference for the interrogative voice.

> Religions do not, in fact, simply supply answers to questions. Or at least they do not confine themselves to this until they become degenerate. Salvation is more than the answer to a question. To emerge alive from a disaster is not just the answer to the question, 'Shall I escape?'[63]

And in the preface to *Conjectures of a Guilty Bystander* he wrote unashamedly:

> I do not have clear answers to current questions. I do have questions, and, as a matter of fact, I think a man is better known by his questions than by his answers. To make known one's questions is, no doubt, to come out in the open oneself.[64]

The strategy of Merton's 'sapiential thinking' and Tracy's 'analogical imagination' cultivates the habit of openness and dialogue, the risk of transformation.[65] In Merton's mind, the future of authentic Christian contemplative life and Christian humanism depended upon our ability to integrate spirituality and imagination in the environs of an irreversible (and welcome!) diaspora. Here one meets more than a quaint museum filled with neat fossils of imagination.

As we look *through* metaphor to the too often hidden ground of love, we discover a spiritual ground beyond explanations. This Merton celebrated as the energy and life of our imaginative symbols.

He phrased it well in one of his last articles:

> What is 'new' in the symbol is the ever new discovery of a new depth and new actuality in what *is* and always has been. . . . The function of the symbol is to manifest the union that *already exists but is not fully realized.* The symbol awakens awareness, or restores it. Therefore it does not

aim at communication, but at communion. Communion is the awareness of participation in the ontological or religious reality: in the mystery of being, of human love, of redemptive mystery, of contemplative truth.[66]

Or, as Merton put it more imaginatively in another context, his own poem inviting us to the contemplative's discovery:

Have you seen it? Then though my myrth has
    quickly ended you will live forever in its echo:
You will never be the same again.

('Night-Flowering Cactus,' 26–28)

Bellarmine College
Louisville, Kentucky

NOTES — Spirituality and Imagination

1. 'The Inner Experience: Problems of the Contemplative Life (VII)', *Cistercian Studies* 19 (1984) 279.

2. *The Sign of Jonas* (New York: Harcourt, Brace, 1953) p. 241.

3. *Contemplation in a World of Action* (New York: Doubleday, 1965) p. 357. He continues: 'The imagination is something which enables us to discover unique present meaning in a given moment of our life. Without imagination the contemplative life can be extremely dull and fruitless.'

4. 'The Inner Experience', pp. 269–270.

5. *Ibid.*, p. 271.

6. *Ibid.*, pp. 274–275.

7. *Conjectures of a Guilty Bystander* (New York: Doubleday, 1966) p. 265.

8. George A. Panichas (ed.), *Mansions of the Spirit* (New York: Hawthorn, 1967) pp. 19–44.

9. New York: Farrar, Straus and Giroux, 1964.

10. *Redeeming the Time* (London: Burns and Oates, 1966) pp. 7–92. Cf. *Faith and Violence* (Notre Dame: University of Notre Dame Press, 1968) pp. 142, 244, 263; *Conjectures,* pp. 329, 334, 335; *The Literary Essays of Thomas Merton,* ed. Brother Patrick Hart (New York: New Directions, 1981) pp. 218, 229, 230.

11. *Redeeming the Time,* p. 99.

12. For a recent interpretation of the Rahnerian Christian anthropology see R. Viladesau, *The Reason for our Hope* (New York: Paulist Press, 1984).

13. *Redeeming the Time,* p. 7. Cf. Merton's epigraph quoting Gabriel Marcel in *Raids on the Unspeakable* (New York: New Directions, 1964): 'Today

129

the first and perhaps the only duty of the philosopher is to defend man against himself: to defend man against that extraordinary temptation toward inhumanity to which — almost without being aware of it — so many human beings today have yielded.'

14. *Redeeming the Time*, p. 56.

15. Thomas P. McDonnell, 'An Interview with Thomas Merton', *Motive* 27 (1967) 32–33.

16. 'Criticism and the Religious Horizon', *Humanities, Religion and the Arts in the Future* (New York: Holt, Rinehart and Winston, 1972) pp. 39–60.

17. *Disputed Questions* (New York: Farrar, Straus and Cudahy, 1960) p. 12.

18. *New Seeds of Contemplation* (New York: New Directions, 1961) pp. ix–x.

19. *Ibid.*, p. 46.

20. *Ibid.*, p. 15.

21. *Mystics and Zen Masters* (New York: Farrar, Straus and Giroux, 1967) pp. 258–62.

22. *Redeeming the Time*, p. 41. Cf. 'Symbolism: Communication or Communion?' in *New Directions in Prose and Poetry* 20 (New York: New Directions, 1968) pp. 1–15.

23. *Mystics and Zen Masters*, p. 271.

24. *Ibid.*, p. 273.

25. New York: New Directions, 1966.

26. *Mystics and Zen Masters*, p. 280.

27. ' "Baptism in the Forest," ' pp. 19, 21.

28. See 'Message to Poets' and 'Answers on Art and Freedom', *Raids on the Unspeakable*, pp. 155–64, 165–78.

29. ' "Baptism in the Forest" ' p. 22.

30. *Ibid.*, p. 25. Cf. 'Symbolism: Communication or Communion?'

31. ' "Baptism in the Forest," ' p. 26, Cf. *Mystics and Zen Masters*, pp. 209–10; *Conjectures*, p. 83.

32. ' "Baptism in the Forest," ' p. 41.

33. 'The Inner Experience: Some Dangers in Contemplation (VI),' *Cistercian Studies* 19 (1984) 147–50. Cf. Merton's discussion of the paradise consciousness in 'Paradise Bugged', *Critic* 25 (1967) pp. 69–71.

34. William H. Shannon, *Thomas Merton's Dark Path* (New York: Farrar, Straus and Giroux, 1981) pp. 39–42, 97.

35. *Conjectures*, pp. 264–65.

36. *Ibid.*, p. 224.

37. *Ibid.*, pp. 224–25.

38. *Ibid.*, p. 225.

39. *Ibid.*, pp. 225–26.

40. 'Symbolism: Communication or Communion?' p. 15.

41. *The Literary Essays*, pp. 181–301.

42. *Ibid.*, p. 211.

43. *Ibid.*, p. 290, 297ff.

44. *Mystics and Zen Masters*, p. 257.

45. *The Literary Essays*, p. 202.

46. *Ibid.*

47. *Ibid.*, pp. 298–99.

48. *Ibid.*, pp. 275–76.

49. *Ibid.*, p. 195.

50. *Ibid.*, pp. 212–13.

51. *Ibid.*

52. *The Analogical Imagination: Christian Theology and the Culture of Pluralism* (New York: Crossroad, 1981) p. 115.

53. 'Wrestling With God', *Commonweal* 111 (October 19, 1984) p. 556.
54. *The Analogical Imagination*, p. 170.
55. *Conjectures*, p. 266.
56. *The Analogical Imagination*, p. 449.
57. *Ibid.*, p. 447.
58. *Ibid.*, p. 448.
59. *Ibid.*, p. 454.
60. See 'Thomas Merton's Expanding Catholicism' by E. Glenn Hinson in Patrick Hart (ed.), *The Message of Thomas Merton* (Cistercian Publications, 1981) pp. 55–71.
61. *Faith and Violence* (Notre Dame: University of Notre Dame Press, 1968) pp. 199–214.
62. *The Monastic Journey*, ed. Patrick Hart (Kansas City: Sheed Andrews and McMeel, 1977) pp. 169–73.
63. *The New Man*, p. 4.
64. *Conjectures*, p. 5.
65. *The Analogical Imagination*, p. 455.
66. 'Symbolism: Communication or Communion?' pp. 9–10.

M. Basil Pennington

Thomas Merton And Byzantine Spirituality

T HOMAS MERTON has been without doubt the most influential Catholic writer on the American scene in the twentieth century. His heart was indeed ecumenical. In fact it stretched beyond the bounds of ecumenism properly so-called to embrace all that is good in the human spirit even if that be found among so-called pagans or Marxists. I do not think it would be possible to exaggerate the importance of the influence of Byzantine spirituality and especially that of the Fathers of Eastern Christendom on the development of Merton's well-integrated spirituality. We might say that Merton's Christian life, writings, and spirit are marked from their first serious awakening to their end by the influence of the Christian East. When he went to Rome in 1933, still very much a hedonist, it was the great Byzantine mosaics that called him forth and changed the tourist into a pilgrim. In *Seven Storey Mountain* he tells us:

> I was fascinated by these Byzantine mosaics. I began to haunt the churches where they were to be found. . . . And

now for the first time in my life I began to find out
something of Who this Person was that men called Christ.
It was obscure, but it was a true knowledge of Him, in some
sense, truer than I knew and truer than I would admit. . . .
And now I think for the first time in my whole life I really
began to pray — praying not with my lips and with my intel-
lect and my imagination, but praying out of the very roots
of my life and of my being, and praying to the God I had
never known. . . .[1]

At the end of his journey in the last book which Merton
prepared for publication, *The Climate of Monastic Prayer*[2], Merton moves from the Fathers of the Desert to share the kernel of
the teaching of the *Philokalia*. As we progress through the text,
which offers a clear and relatively concise history of contemplative spirituality and the teachings of the masters, we come
upon such names as Isaac of Nineveh, Saint Ammonas, Evagrius
Ponticus, Saint Basil, Saint Gregory of Nyssa, the Pseudo-Dionysius, Saint Nilus, and others in the Byzantine tradition.

The influence of the great Fathers of the Eastern Church
first came to Merton mediated through the Cistercian Fathers
whom he read extensively in his early years in the monastery.[3] As
his studies moved forward he came, in part with the help of
Gilson,[4] to recognize and identify these Fathers' sources. But I
think it can also be said that it was the Fathers of the Desert,
whose delightful, pithy, and profound sayings so attracted him
who opened Merton to pursue the evolution of this strong, rich
current of spirituality. Keith Egan in his very interesting and informative series of taped talks, *Solitude and Community. The
Paradox of Life and Prayer,* has said of Merton: 'He began to read
the literature that came out of the desert, the Christian desert of
the fourth century. And one of the most important books he
wrote is his shortest and that is *The Wisdom of the Desert*. . . .
The study that lies behind the writing of this little book was
transforming and changed Merton's life forever.'[5]

In 1960, when he published this short collection of the *Sayings*, Merton wrote a very rich introduction of twenty-two pages.
He traced the spiritual path laid out by the Fathers in their sayings.

It begins with a 'clean break', compunction, a lament over the madness of our attachments to unreal values. Through solitude and labor, poverty and fasting, charity and prayer, the old superficial self is purged away and the true secret self is permitted to emerge. The monk moves toward purity of heart:

> a clean unobstructed vision of the true state of affairs, an intuitive grasp of one's own inner reality as anchored or rather lost in God through Christ. This leads to *quies,* the sanity and praise of a being that no longer has to look at itself because it is carried away by the perfection of being that is in it. And carried where? Wherever Love itself of the Divine Spirit sees fit to go. Rest, then, was a kind of simple nowhereness and no-mindedness that had lost all preoccupation with a false or limited 'self.'[6]

The terminology Merton uses here is not that of the Desert Fathers. By this time the Fathers had opened Merton to other even broader influences.[7] But first they opened him to their own immediate heirs. Merton went on to expand and deepen his vision through the developing theology of the Christian East, with the Cappodocians, especially Saint Gregory of Nyssa, and with Evagrius Ponticus, who really belongs to the desert tradition, and above all in Maximus the Confessor.

In his first full-length work on spirituality, a study of the teaching of Saint John of the Cross entitled *The Ascent to Truth,* Merton devotes many pages in the first and third chapters to those 'great theologians of darkness: Saint Gregory of Nyssa, and Pseudo-Dionysius'.[8] The former he hails as 'the most important and the most neglected of the early Christian mystical theologians, the Father of Christian apophatic mysticism'.[9] He also says of him: 'There are pages in the works of Saint Greogory of Nyssa which might easily fit into a context of Zen Buddhism of Patanjali's Yoga.'[10] He depends here largely on Gregory's scriptural commentaries, those on Ecclesiastes, Psalms, and the Song of Songs. He traces out Gregory's journey from light to darkness with the Mosaic imagery of the burning bush, the pillar of cloud, and finally the darkness of Sinai and suggests a parallel with the three dark nights of Saint John of the Cross. On page twenty-seven he speaks of *theoria physike*, distinguishing the positive and negative aspects of it. But I do not think at this time this important element of Eastern Christian spiritual teaching had had the impact on him that later was to be, in my opinion, very significant. In the introduction to the *Sign of Jonas*, Merton himself clearly indicated the shortcomings of the very dry intellectual approach to this teaching which he presented in the *Ascent*.[11]

Some years later Merton had the opportunity to study these Fathers more fully and reflect more profoundly on them as he prepared and gave a course to his fellow monk-priests on Christian Mysticism. We have only the notes of these lectures,[12] but they are quite full and, while they lack his usual rich literary style they do have his candid clarity and forceful impact. It is here that he highlights the central place of Saint Gregory more in detail, indicating his influence on the Cistercian Fathers — on Saint Bernard through Origen, on William of St Thierry through the Pseudo-Dionysius and John Scotus Erigena, and on all of them through Cassian through Evagrius — on the Syrians through Saint Macarius, and on the Greeks in general through Maximus the Confessor.[13] Here he studies extensively and deeply the meaning of the 'spiritual senses', disagreeing with the interpretations or understanding of previous Western writers such as Poulain and Olphe Gaillard. Merton adopts a more integrated view, seeing them closely allied with the bodily senses that have been freed and purified by mortification, virginity, and passive purification, and elevated and spiritualized by grace and the operation of the Holy Spirit till they approach a full restoration of that state of paradise where God was enjoyed by the senses 'deifying the body' (Saint Gregory Palamas).[14]

More important is the insight he attains into *theoria physike* under the tutelage of Evagrius Ponticus, whom he strongly defends,[15] and Maximus the Confessor. The spiritual life is seen to involve three stages: *bios praktikos — praxis —* the purification of the body, of the senses, of the passions — *apatheia —* the *puritas cordis* of John Cassian, something more than detachment, a positive openness to reality, to the Divine: *theoria physike* — a spiritualized knowledge of the created, a sort of natural contemplation, which does reach on to the divine *oikonomia,* God's plan for things, and the *logoi* of things, the Divine plan within things. At its higher levels it reaches to the contemplation of the spiritual: *theologia* — the contemplation of the Trinity without form or image.

I believe it was the understanding of *theoria physike* that enabled the zealous, ascetic, world-despising young monk who constantly fought with his own human gifts for poetry and literature to reintegrate his natural appreciation and love for the wonders of creation and all that the good God made and to go on to become the very full and integrated person he became. He himself said: 'We can in fact say that the lack of *theoria physike* is one of the things that accounts for the stunting of spiritual growth among our monks today.'[16]

He goes on to say:

> It is by *theoria* that man helps Christ to redeem the *logoi* of things and restore them to Himself. . . . This *theoria* is inseparable from love and from a truly spiritual conduct of life. Man must not only see the inner meaning of things but he must regulate his entire life and his use of time and of created beings according to the mysterious norms hidden in things by the Creator, or rather by the Creator himself in the bosom of His creation.[17]

I would like to quote more extensively from Merton in this place because I thing this matter is absolutely central to the understanding of his spiritual development and outlook.

> Man by *theoria* is able to unite the hidden wisdom of God in things with the hidden light of wisdom in himself. The meeting and marriage of these two brings about a *resplendent clarity* within man himself, and this clarity is the presence of Divine Wisdom fully recognized and active in him. Thus man becomes a mirror of the divine glory and is resplendent with divine truth not only in his *mind* but in

his *life*. He is filled with the light of wisdom which shines
forth in him, and thus God is glorified in him. At the same
time he exercises a spiritualizing influence in the world by
the work of his hands which is in accord with the *creative
wisdom of God* in things and in him.

No longer are we reduced to a purely negative attitude
toward the world around us, toward history, toward the
judgments of God. The world is no longer seen as purely
material, hence as an obstacle to be grudgingly put up with.
It is spirit there and then. But grace has to work with and
through us to enable us to carry out this real transformation. Things are not fully spiritual in themselves, they
have to be spiritualized by our knowledge and love in the
use of them. Hence it is impossible for one who is not
purified to 'transfigure' material things. On the contrary,
the *logoi* will remain hidden and he himself will be captivated by the sensible attraction of these things.[18]

In this last sentence we see the difference between these
Greek Fathers, and Merton with them, and the currently popular
'creation theology'. The Fathers and Merton emphasize that it is
impossible to enter into a true *theoria physike,* a true appreciation of the creation and the presence of God in creation, without
first embracing the *bios praktikos,* that purification that produces *apatheia,* a true purity of heart that enables us to appreciate the overwhelming beauty transfiguring the creation
without being ensnared by it. Otherwise we are in danger of
resting in the creation and becoming attached to it and ourselves
rather than finding all in God and God in all, being attached to
him alone.

Also, the Fathers and Merton never stop at the *theoria
physike,* the wonders of the creation, even transfigured by God,
but are ever conscious of this as a stage on the way to true
theologia, to finding our true place within the very life of the
Trinity, we who have been made truly and most mysteriously one
with the Son in baptism, we who have been 'deified'. In this context, and in this context alone does *theoria physike* or 'creation

theology' attain its full meaning. And human life comes to have its full meaning. May I quote Merton again:

> The 'will of God' is no longer a blind force plunging through our lives like a cosmic steamroller and demanding to be accepted willy nilly. On the contrary we are able to *understand* the hidden purpose of the creative wisdom and the divine mercy of God, and can cooperate with Him as sons with a loving Father. Not only that, but God himself hands over to man, when he is thus purified and enlightened, and united with the divine will, a certain creative initiative of his own, in political life, in art, in spiritual life, in worship: man is then endowed with a *causality* of his own.[19]

As I have said, I believe that Merton's 'discovery' and full perception of *theoria physike* had a profound formative and liberating influence on him. Later in this paper I will return to further indications of this. Let us now continue to look at the influences of the Eastern Christian spiritual heritage on Merton and his writings.

At the same time as Merton was preparing and teaching this course he was preparing one of his more significant and weighty theological volumes, *The New Man*.[20] In this study he does depend heavily on Western Fathers and theologians: Saint Augustine and Saint Bernard, Aquinas and Ruysbroeck. But the names of Eastern Fathers keep cropping up: Clement of Alexandria and Gregory of Nyssa, Cyril of Jerusalem and others. But the influence is perhaps more profoundly marked by the extraordinary frequency with which he employs Greek works in this text. We find *pneuma, pneumatikos, metanoia, antitypos,* and *parousia* all used more than once. More signficant is the very extensive study of *parrhesia*, which Merton well defines as 'free spiritual communication of being with Being'.[21]

Also at this period Merton wrote a rather poor piece on Mount Athos,[22] 'the last important Christian survival of the typical ancient monastic colonies'.[23] I do not think Merton can be blamed for the poverty and inaccuracies of this piece. He never had the opportunity to visit the Holy Mountain (something I am sure he would have loved to have done) and had to depend on the accounts of others of which he noted: 'In such books one rarely receives any insight into the profound religious mystery of Athos'.[24] He was enthusiastic about the idea of Athos and proposed a similar western monastic republic with a similar freedom of monastic expression. He was a bit pessimistic about the future of the Holy Mountain. I am sure he would be elated at its present vigorous revival, even to the inclusion of more monks from Holy Russia.[25]

In the same volume in which he published the Athos piece he added a study on 'The Spirituality of Sinai', largely a commentary on Saint John Climacus' *Ladder*.[26] The piece is rather rough, filled with slang (fanatical windbag, busting him in the teeth, Climacus was nuts, etc.) and homely details (such as the brethren's reaction to reading the *Ladder* in the community refectory at Gethsemani).[27] The piece was occasioned by the publication of Archimandrite Lazarus Moore's translation, which Merton praises. He appreciates more the stream of spirituality that Climacus represents then this 'tough, hard-hitting, merciless book,'[28] for 'all Russian literature and spirituality is tinged with the ferocity and paradox of Sinai.'[29] From Sinai, too, the practice of the Jesus Prayer came to Athos and to Russia: 'Let the remembrance of Jesus be present with each breath, and then you will know the value of solitude', says Climacus.[30]

Russia had a special place in Merton's heart. The only Athonite monk to whom he seemed to get close as a living reality was the humble and saintly procurator of the Russian monastery of Saint Panteleimon, Father Siloan. Through the writings of Father Siloan's disciple, Father Sophrony, Merton was able to appreciate this simple and profoundly prayerful man who never lost his love for solitude even in the midst of serving a monastery of hundreds of monks.[31] In his preface to Sergius Bolshakoff's *Russian Mystics*,[32] Merton gives evidence of an extensive knowledge of Russian monastic history. Saint Nilus, in his controversy with the institutional monasticism represented by Saint Joseph Volokolamsk, was of special interest, especially since much of Evagrius' teaching has come down to us under Saint Nilus' patronage. But for Merton

Saint Seraphim of Sarov was 'without doubt the greatest mystic of the Russian Church.'[33] In him there was a balance between the ascetic tradition and austerity (*podvig*), repentance and tears and a humanism filled with joy, open to life, gentle, and profoundly compassionate. He had 'evangelical and patristic purity, pure and traditional theology, ingenuous amazement of the divine light shining through the darkness.'[34] Saint Seraphim's was a mysticism of light (albeit based on the apophaticism of Pseudo-Dionysius and Maximus) which approached the Invisible as visible in a creation *transfigured* in Divine Light.

Merton's interest in the Russian writers ranged far beyond the monastic and even the so called religious. In the late fifties he even made an abortive attempt at learning Russian so that he could read them in their original language. *Conjectures* is sprinkled with names like Belinsky, Lenin, and Berdyaev, along with the pages devoted to Evdokimov.[35] His next published journal includes a quote from Yelchaninov in the Prelude.[36]

This broadening is indicated in a curious way in an interesting piece that reflects Merton's first days in his hermitage. He had never moved very far from the Desert Fathers. In those days he wrote a very fine piece on the Spiritual Father in the desert tradition.[37] Dom John Eudes rightly notes that the ideal of the spiritual father had become part of his own identity.[38] Merton also wrote a piece on the cell drawing from the same sources.[39] But the biographical piece that opens *Raids on the Unspeakable*[40] is the piece to which I am referring. In 'Rain and the Rhinoceros'[41] Merton tells us of sitting in his hermitage on the hill above the Abbey, reading by his Coleman lantern (he did not yet have electricity there). On this particular rainy night he was reading Philoxenos (a sixth-century Syrian Father), seeking to understand better the solitude he was so drawn to and finding more and more. On this night he read Philoxenos' ninth *memra* to dwellers in solitude. Merton heard again that 'there is no explanation and no justification for the solitary life, since it is without a law',[42]'. . . leave the rule of the world where he [Christ] has left the law, and go out with him to fight the power of error.'[43] Merton concludes his passage on Philoxenos saying:

'Today the insights of a Philoxenos are to be sought less in the tracts of theologians than in the meditations of the existentialists and in the Theater of the Absurd.'[44]

Without a shadow of doubt Merton's favorite among the modern Russian writers is Boris Pasternak. He wrote three articles[45] on this poet and novelist whom he saw as 'immensely more important that Sholokov.'[46] He found Pasternak's witness 'essentially Christian.'[47] The Christianity Pasternak presented was 'reduced to the barest and most elemental essentials: intense awareness of all cosmic and human reality as "life in Christ", and the consequent plunge into love as the only dynamic and creative force which really honors this "Life" by creating itself anew in Life's — Christ's — image.'[48] Merton sensed a very deep oneness with Pasternak and expresses it powerfully and beautifully in the first letter he addressed to the Russian, some months prior to the explosion over the Nobel Prize awarded to Pasternak:

> I feel much more kinship with you, in your writing, than I do with most of the great modern writers in the West. That is to say that I feel that I can share your experience more deeply and with greater intimacy and sureness. . . . With other writers I can share ideas, but you seem to communicate something deeper. It is as if we meet on a deeper level of life on which individuals are not separate beings. In a language familiar to me as Catholic monk, it is as if we were known to one another in God.[49]

I believe this is so because by this time Merton had fully integrated the outlook and experience of *theoria physike* and Pasternak comes out of the same living tradition; they experience the creation in the same basic way and express this in their poetry and writing. Merton actually points to this in his first article on Pasternak:

> Pasternak, whether he knows it or not, is plunged fully into midstream of the lost tradition of 'natural contemplation' [Merton's English expression for *theoria physike*, as we have seen above] which flowed among the Greek Fathers after it

had been set in motion by Origen. Of course the tradition
has not been altogether lost and Pasternak has come upon it
in the Orthodox Church. The fact is clear in any case: he
reads the Scriptures with the avidity and the spiritual imagination of Origen and he looks on the world with the illuminated eyes of the Cappadocian Fathers. . . .[50]

Merton appreciated this 'sophianic' view of the cosmos — a
creation impregnated by Santa Sophia, Holy Wisdom, the Word
and Love of God — in other Russian writers such as Soloviev and
Berdyaev (Merton's articles on Pasternak bring out his extensive
familiarity with the Russian authors) but he identified most
strongly with Pasternak's spirit so akin to his own. It is a question
of *sobornost.* This is perhaps why he shared with him in his second letter a secret he had shared with only three others. Because
of its important bearing on a significant turning point in
Merton's life and because it is relatively little known I would like
to quote the passage from the letter in full:

It is a simple enough story but obviously I do not tell it to
people — you are the fourth who knows it, and there seems
to be no point in a false discreteness that might restrain me
from telling you since it is clear that we have so very much in
common.

One night I dreamt that I was sitting with a very young
Jewish girl of fourteen or fifteen, and that she suddenly
manifested a very deep and pure affection for me and embraced me so that I was moved to the depths of my soul. I
learned that her name was 'Proverb,' which I thought very
simple and beautiful. And also I thought: 'She is of the race
of Saint Anne'. I spoke to her of her name, and she did not
seem to be proud of it, because it seemed that the other
young girls mocked her for it. But I told her that it was a
very beautiful name, and there the dream ended. A few
days later when I happened to be in a nearby city, which is
very rare for us, I was walking alone in the crowded street
and suddenly saw that everybody was Proverb and that in
all of them shone her extraordinary beauty and purity and

shyness, even though they did not know who they were and were perhaps ashamed of their names—because they were mocked on account of them. And they did not know their real identity as the Child so dear to God who, from before the beginning, was playing in His sight all days, playing in the world.[51]

Thus we have here a very intimate and, I think, a very important insight into that well-known experience on the streets in Louisville which Merton has reported elsewhere.[52] Not only was it impacted with the rich imagery of a dream but with the ever-deepening insight into *theoria psyike* that Merton was integrating into his perception of reality. Merton was in many ways a very private person, even in his many published journals. We owe to the extraordinary openness of a very unusual frienship this beautiful and touching revelation that throws so much light on the integration of its writer.

In the last journal that Merton himself prepared for publication, the one flowing from his two-week trip to the west coast and New Mexico in May of 1968, Merton is still with his Russian friends. He returns to Theophane the Recluse with his salutary advice for prayer of the heart:

Not to run from one thought to the next . . . but to give each one time to settle in the heart.
Attention. Concentration of the spirit in the heart.
Vigilance. Concentration of the will in the heart.
Sobriety. Concentration of the feeling in the heart.[53]

Here, too, in his constant quest for true freedom Merton writes: 'I wonder about the definition of Orthodoxy as hostility to rules. . . .'[54] His reference is to a quote from Yelchaninov: 'Orthodoxy is the principle of absolute freedom.'[55]

But the most important thing about this journal, especially as it has been published with inclusion of some of the photographs that Merton took on the journey, is that it is a magnificent witness to the full flowering of *theoria physike* in its author. It conveys his cosmic and earthy contemplation in the way it can best be conveyed: through poetics and artistry. This severe critic of technology (and in his criticisms I think he was not wholly off) does not hesitate with the true freedom of the son of God to use a bit of technology — the camera — to produce some real art that powerfully highlights and shares his contemplative insight.

The *Asian Journal,*[56] his last, posthumustly published book, is totally free from any mention of Russians or Eastern Christian Fathers. This may be due to the editors. In his notes for the talk he gave at the Spiritual Summit Conference of the Temple of Understanding in Calcutta he indicated his intention to speak on the Hesychast tradition, Mount Athos, and Orthodox monasteries.[57] And though in actual fact Merton did not employ these notes and rather spoke extemporaneously, the spirit of this tradition was not missing from his presentation that day.

In those same notes Merton speaks about the qualities needed for true dialogue between the different traditions: '. . . it must be reserved for those who have entered with full seriousness into their own monastic tradition and are in authentic contact with the past of their own religious community — besides being open to the tradition and to the heritage of experience belonging to other communities.'[58] Speaking of such a person in another article published after his death he adds:

> Such a man is fully 'Catholic' in the best sense of the word. He has a unified vision and experience of the one truth shining out in all its various manifestations, some clearer than others, some more definite and certain than others. He does not set these partial views up in opposition to each other but unifies them in a dialectic or insight of complementarity. With this view of life he is able to bring perspective, liberty and spontaneity into the lives of others. The finally integrated man is a peace-maker.'[59]

This certainly Merton was. He entered very deeply and lived deeply his own tradition. He also entered deeply into the traditions of others. In his introductroy essay to *The Wisdom of the Desert* Merton says: 'Love demands a complete inner transformation — for without this we cannot possibly come to identify ourselves with our brother. We have to become, in some sense, the person we love.'[60] Merton did this. He loved and he identified. Finally, in *Conjectures* he says: 'I am more convinced that my job is to clarify something of the tradition that lives in me and in which I live: the tradition of wisdom and spirituality that is found not only in Western Christendom but in Orthodoxy. . . .'[61] As Rowan Williams said in a comparative study of Evdokimov and Merton: 'Merton's spirituality . . . would not be what it is without his devoted and careful study of Greek patristic thought and the Desert Fathers'.[62] And, I would add, all that flowed out of them. And not only study but an assimilation and integration that produced a profound and profoundly beautiful lived synthesis.

Assumption Abbey
Ava, Missouri

NOTES — Merton and Byzantine Spirituality

1. Thomas Merton, *The Seven Storey Mountain* (New York: Harcourt, Brace, 1948) pp. 108–111.

2. *The Climate of Monastic Prayer,* Cistercian Studies Series (hereafter CS) no. 1 (Cistercian Publications, 1969).

3. John Eudes Bamberger, OCSO, 'Thomas Merton and the Christian East' in *One Yet Two. Monastic Tradition East and West,* M. Basil Pennington, OCSO, ed., CS 29 (Cistercian Publications, 1976) p. 443.

4. Etienne Gilson, *The Mystical Theology of St. Bernard* (London: Sheed and Ward, 1955).

5. Keith Egan, *Solitude and Community. The Paradox of Life and Prayer* (Kansas City, MO: NCR Casettes, 1981) tape 3, 'The Desert Place of Discovery.'

6. Thomas Merton, *The Wisdom of the Desert* (London: Sheldon Press, 1960) p. 8.

7. Merton goes on to say: 'In many respects, therefore, these Desert Fathers had much in common with Indian Yogis and with Zen Buddhist monks of China and Japan.' *ibid.,* p. 9.

8. Thomas Merton, *The Ascent to Truth* (New York: Harcourt, Brace, 1951) p. 25.

9. *Ibid.,* p. 319.

10. *Ibid.,* p. 26. I do not know if this is a slip of the pen, a typo (I have not yet been able to see the original manuscript for this piece) or an indication of how little Merton knew at this time of the Eastern masters, but to speak of the 'Zen Buddhism of Patanjali's Yoga' does not make much sense. In later English editions and in some of the translations the 'of' is changed to 'or', which makes perfect sense.

Thomas Merton and Byzantine Spirituality   147

11. Thomas Merton, *The Sign of Jonas* (New York: Harcourt, Brace, 1953) p. 9.

12. *An Introduction to Christian Mysticism (From the Apostolic Fathers to the Council of Trent)*. Lectures given at the Abbey of Gethsemani. Mss. At the end of the 'Foreward' we find the date: Vigil of the Assumption, 1961.

13. *Ibid.*, p. 31.

14. *Ibid.*, pp. 35–42.

15. 'Evagrius of Pontus is one of the most important, the least known (till recently), most neglected and the most controversial of Christian mystics. He merits, with Gregory of Nyssa, the title of ' "Father of Christian Mystical Theology" ' *ibid.*, pp. 42f. Merton does later (p. 56) say: 'There remains a considerable danger of misunderstanding him. He is an interesting and important source, but in forming young monks and in preaching the contemplative life it would of course be wiser to find the same things said much better in great saints like Gregory of Nyssa, Maximus, etc.'

16. *Ibid.*, p. 56.

17. *Ibid.*, p. 59.

18. *Ibid.*

19. *Ibid.* It is worthy of note that Merton includes here and in a primary place, 'political life'.

20. Thomas Merton, *The New Man* (New York: Farrar, Straus & Cuhady, 1961).

21. *Ibid.*, p. 76.

22. 'Mount Athos' in *Disputed Questions* (New York: Farrar, Straus and Giroux, 1960) pp. 68–82.

23. *Ibid.*, p. 70.

24. *Ibid.*, p. 69.

25. For a detailed description of this renewal of Athos, see my *O Holy Mountain* (Washington, D.C.: Michael Glazier, 1978).

26. *Disputed Questions*, pp. 83–93.

27. According to Merton's secretary, Brother Patrick Hart, Merton used this style for this piece because it was written for *Jubilee*.

28. *Ibid.*, p. 84.

29. *Ibid.*, p. 88.

30. *Ibid.*, p. 93.

31. Thomas Merton, *Conjectures of a Guilty Bystander* (Garden City, NY: Doubleday, 1966) p. 147. Merton refers to Father Siloan as 'Staretz Sylvan'; this is undoubtedly a slip of memory.

32. Sergius Bolshakoff, *Russian Mystics* CS 26 (Cistercian Publications, 1977) pp. ix–xviii. This preface was also published in *Mystics and Zen Masters* (New York: Farrar, Straus and Giroux, 1967) pp. 178–187.

33. *Russian Mystics*, p. xii.

34. *Ibid.*, p. xiii.

35. *Conjectures*, pp. 308–310. Merton gives the title 'Father' to Evdokimov, perhaps mistakingly thinking that this lay theologian was a priest.

36. Thomas Merton, *Woods, Shore, Desert. A Notebook, May 1968* (Santa Fe: Museum of New Mexico Press, 1982) p. 3.

37. 'The Spiritual Father in the Desert Tradition' in *Contemplation in a World of Action* (Garden City, NY: Doubleday, 1971) pp. 269–293.

38. Bamberger, p. 449.

39. 'The Cell' in *Contemplation in a World of Action*, pp. 252–259.

40. Thomas Merton, *Raids on the Unspeakable* (New York: New Directions, 1966).

148   *Toward An Integrated Humanity*

41. *Ibid.*, pp. 9–26.
42. *Ibid.*, p. 14.
43. *Ibid.*, p. 19.
44. *Ibid.*
45. 'The Pasternak Affair' in *Disputed Questions*, pp. 3–67.
46. *Ibid.*, p. 13.
47. *Ibid.*, p. 12.
48. *Ibid.*
49. Boris Pasternak/Thomas Merton, *Six Letters* (Lexington, KY: The King Library Press, 1973) pp. 3–4.
50. *Disputed Questions*, p. 17.
51. *Six Letters*, pp. 11f. Merton then adds with delightful humor: 'Thus you are initiated into the scandalous secret of a monk who is in love with a girl, and a Jew at that! One cannot expect much from monks these days. The heroic asceticism of the past is no more.'
52. 'In Louisville, at the corner of Fourth and Walnut, in the center of the shopping district, I was suddenly overwhelmed with the realization that I loved all those people, that they were mine and I theirs, that we could not be alien to one another even though we were total strangers. It was like waking from a dream of separateness, of spurious self-isolation in a special world, the world of renunciation and supposed holiness. The whole illusion of a separate holy existence is a dream. . . . I suppose my happiness could have taken form in the words: "Thank God, thank God that I *am* like other men, that I am only a man among others." To think that for sixteen or seventeen years I have been taking seriously this pure illusion that is implicit in so much of our monastic thinking.' — *Conjectures*, pp. 156f.
53. *Woods, Shore, Desert*, p. 16.
54. *Ibid.*, p. 20.
55. *Ibid.*, p. 3.
56. *The Asian Jouranl of Thomas Merton* (London: Sheldon, 1974).
57. *Ibid.*, p. 311.
58. *Ibid.*, p. 316.
59. *Contemplation in a World of Action*, p. 212.
60. *Wisdom of the Desert*, p. 18.
61. *Conjectures*, p. 176.
62. Rowan Williams, 'Bread in the Wilderness. The Monastic Ideal in Thomas Merton and Paul Evdokimov' in *One Yet Two*, pp. 452f.

David D. Cooper

Thomas Merton and the New Theology*

I N DISCUSSING Thomas Merton's reactions to the New Theology movement of the 60's, I must note from the outset that
the movement itself amounted to little more than a blip on
the radar screen of twentieth-century theological thought. I
believe it is a fascinating blip, something we might classify as a
near-collision of radical dissent and mainstream theological
thought during an era when traffic in dissent was considerably
more congested than it is today. Nonetheless, few tenets of the
radical theology have been historically assimilated during the
past twenty years, except perhaps for some trace elements showing up in such things as Liberation Theology, the sanctuary
movement, or even the facile new wave video evangelicalism.
Also, Merton himself was not terribly preoccupied with the work
of the New Theologians. He did engage them with care and
thoughtfulness and with his characteristic energy and thorough-
ness, but his writings on the radical theology hardly dominate the
Merton bibliography. I believe, however, that it is important to

149

examine such responses as there are because Merton, especially during the early 60's, was wrestling privately with many of the same issues that the radical theologians subjected to intense and lively public debate. Like the New Theologians, Merton struggled to reconcile himself to modernity in its fullest sense; he sought, as they, to accommodate his faith, rooted in centuries of Christian tradition, to what both he and the New Theologians recognized and accepted as a post-Christian era.

Merton became eventually, then, not willing to accept, in the words of Amiya Chakravarty, 'a fixed medieval line between the sacred and profane', precisely that separation challenged by a ferment of new ideas stirring in the theological arena of the time. In fact, Merton's entire three decades of monastic experience were cut against a contemporary backdrop of vigorous debate in theological circles, a debate sparked by a new generation of Protestant theologians, by and large, who sought to revise and revitalize Christian teaching and practice in the context of a modern secularized world. The movement, generally speaking, centered on efforts to accommodate centuries of tradition in Christian culture to the radically new demands and climate of modern life and to find a new language to describe the experience of faith as well as a more relevant vocabulary for the enterprise of formal religious scholarship. Most interestingly, the entire movement spanned Merton's monastic years, from the depths of World War II and the writings, initially, of Dietrich Bonhoeffer to the final years of the 1960's when the so-called New Theology movement was eclipsed by a growing fundamentalist retrenchment. The essential questions of most concern to the movement can be summarized by drawing from the contributions of two central figures whose writings bracket the period. Writing from a Nazi prison in 1944, Dietrich Bonhoeffer, returning to fundamental questions characteristic of the movement, asked 'What *is* Christianity, and indeed what *is* Christ, for us today?

The time when men could be told everything by means of words, whether theological or simply pious, is over, and so is the time of inwardness and conscience, which is to say the time of religion as such. We are proceeding towards a time of no religion at all: men as they are now simply cannot be religious any more. . . . Our whole nineteen-hundred-year-old Christian preaching and theology rests upon the "religious premise" of man. What we call Christianity has always been a pattern — perhaps a true pattern — of religion. But if one day it becomes apparent that this *a priori* 'premise' simply does not exist, but was an historical and temporary form of human self-expression . . . what does that mean for Christianity?[1]

Two decades later, John A.T. Robinson — in an immensely popular synthesis of the ideas of Bonhoeffer and other leaders of the movement, notably Rudolf Bultmann and Paul Tillich — also wrestled with the collision of tradition and modernity in Christian thought and wondered whether the old concept of God as 'a super-Being "out there" is really only a sophisticated version of the Old Man in the Sky?'

Suppose belief in God does not, indeed cannot, mean being persuaded of the 'existence' of some entity, even a supreme entity, which might or might not be there, like life on Mars? Suppose the atheists are right . . . ? [But] suppose that all such atheism does is to destroy an idol, and that we can and must get on without a God 'out there' at all? Have we seriously faced the possibility that to abandon such an idol may in the future be the only way of making Christianty meaningful?[2]

Variously labeled the New Theology, Death of God Theology, and Religionless Religion, other issues must be taken briefly into consideration if we are to appreciate the impact of this movement and prepare to assess its effect on Merton. First, the very word 'secular' in historical context and usage, had always been locked into a dialectical relationship with its opposite, the 'sacred'. The separation between the secular and sacred was so rigid and clear cut that in the medieval era, for example, the rhetorical interrelationship between the two remained essentially spacial. The sacred became the world of religious—of monks cloistered in monasteries, a space bounded neatly by the walls of the monastic enclosure; the secular encompassed the world outside the monastery. The cleavage between the two was further underscored by institutional sanctions and the church's establishment of a hierarchy of values: the secular realm, in effect, was subordinate to the sacred space of the monastery. Reacting against this historical context of the secular, the new generation of modern theologians sought to bridge the rigid separation between the sacred and the secular, to ease the tension of the old dialectics, and to liberate, in essence, the usage of the secular from its traditional rhetorical stigma rooted in the old spacial hierarchy. Dietrich Bonhoeffer could then argue, for example, that historical developments converging on the modern person's 'coming of age' must not be viewed as anti-Christian, but only that the reactionary polemics of Christian apologists, refusing to surrender the old dialectics, had made it seem so. And Robinson could insist that secularization must not be combated, but must be accepted dispassionately as a neutral historical fact.

Consider too, secondly, the ontological and psychological ramifications for men and women of faith living a Christian life in a fully secularized world. Secularization implies a fundamental, radical change in the modern person's sense of being and existence in the world. Historically, earthly life was viewed as subordinate and inferior to a higher metaphysical reality. For Christians coming of age in the context of a modern reality, this other, higher, truer, supraterrestrial reality is no longer present, it no longer imposes itself on the modern person's capacities to judge and decide and solve problems and, most important, to self-reflect. And, psychologically, secularization implies a profound liberation. Men and women are free to live their lives independently and assume full responsibility for their actions and shape their own destinies. With secularization comes a heightened sense of autonomous responsibility for moral and ethical, intellectual, familial, social, educational and aesthetic spheres of human existence, as well as a new freedom from authority where the burden of human responsibility is cut free from the approval or disapproval of a 'god' or any sacral reality.

Such ontological and psychological implications threatened, thirdly, to undermine the institutional footings of the church itself. Secularization tacitly assumed a new relationship between the church and its role in the lives of the laity, a relationship requiring the church to surrender its influence and control in all spheres of human life. Most obviously, science and politics, for example, become fully autonomous, independent entities no longer subject to the church's institutional approval or disapproval. Largely in response to a perceived threat to its tradition of authority and control, the church naturally reacted against the secularization movement. Christians were called upon to reject and fight secularization, and the resistance was frequently characterized in institutional pronouncements as tantamount to a struggle against the Devil himself. The battle lines stiffened during three decades of virulent debate. The reactionary wing of leadership in the churches, sensing the old framework of Christian society breaking up, waged a campaign to discredit the radical theologians. The new theologians, in turn, persisted in their efforts to accept the fact of secularization as historically inevitable, surrender the old dialectics, and search for new ways to accommodate Christian faith to the institutional, ontological and psychological realities arising from secularization. By trying to renegotiate Christian teaching and Christian practice in light of the modern secular world's experience of reality, this cadre of theologians continued to press their work beyond the religious premise of man. Like Bonhoeffer, they held that 'God as a working hypothesis in morals, politics or science, has been surmounted and abolished; and the same thing has happened in philosophy and religion. . . . For the sake of intellectual honesty, that working hypothesis should be dropped, or as far as possible eliminated'.[3]

The young Thomas Merton—the Merton of *The Seven Storey Mountain*, a contemporary of Bonhoeffer's—must surely have viewed the notion of eliminating God as a working hypothesis as heretical and greeted it with contempt. During the forties, committed as he was to a life within the sacred space of the monastery, Merton might have been a perfect caricature of what John A. T. Robinson later called a 'flat-earther', clingling, philosophically and theologically, to a distinctly pre-Copernican hierarchy of separation between both secular and monastic life and the relationship between God and the human person mediated by the institutional authority of the church. But given Merton's steady intellectual development and personal growth over three decades, it would be unfair and unwise to judge his response to this ferment of new ideas from the perspective of *The Seven Storey Mountain* and its bellicose apologetics. Merton came to share, especially during the 60's, in the spirit of the new theologians. Although he could never entirely accept the full range of conclusions argued by the new generation, he, too, nonetheless searched for new ways to adapt questions of faith and Christian practice to the realities of a modern, post-Christian era. Later in his life Merton remarked, on more than one occasion, how put off he was by the 'religiousness' of religion—a religion of tactics, external observances, formalistic rituals—a 'religiousness' that he, like the new radicals, dismissed as negative, ambiguous, moralizing, and, frankly, dysfunctional. Even as he looked back, in his journal of the 60's, to reconsider his own conversion, he was compelled to borrow the language of Bonhoeffer and Robinson, recalling then that 'God was not for me a working hypothesis. . . . Nor was He a God enthroned somewhere in outer space.'

How, then, did Merton respond to the new climate of religious thought? What was the precise course in the evolution of those responses? To what extent did he accommodate himself to the historical process of secularization coming to fruition in the context of a modern world that he had once vowed to reject? What shape did those accommodations take? What difficulties did he encounter and how did he resolve those difficulties? More important still, what principal influences worked upon Merton to temper his reconciliations to modernity?

Those are important questions, especially the latter one. It seems to me that Merton's reaction to the New Theology is best understood by examining first a range of mediating influences. Unfortunately, I do not have the time for that here, except to say that I have isolated what seem to me to be the most significant: namely, the German ethicist Dietrich Bonhoeffer, the Swiss theologian Karl

Barth, the French Algerian novelist Albert Camus, the humanist psychotherapist Erich Fromm, and the neo-Marxist philosopher Herbert Marcuse. With that said, I must move on to the claim that Thomas Merton's response to the Radical New Theology, judging at least from his pivotal public journal of the 60's, was, although not without substantial reservations, largely sympathetic and understanding. His preferential treatment of Bonhoeffer's 'holy worldliness', over and against the relative conservative orthodoxy of Karl Barth, situates Merton rather more neatly in the fold of the moderns. And the ardor of his Camus essays further aligns Merton with the new radicals, many of whom utilized Camus' writings to fashion a Christian existenialism compatible with the New Theology. Other journals show Merton equally hospitable to a movement which, at first glance, may seem entirely anathema to his monastic agenda.

But Merton's overall reactions to the movement are complicated considerably by the context of his responses. As he shifted perspectives and personae — from self-reflective, introspective journal writing or literary criticism, for example, to a more formal and authoritative public discourse — Merton's sympathetic understanding gave way to a sustained, near-polemical critique, especially as he discussed the Death-of-God theologians (the most radical wing of the new radicals) in a collection of late essays to which we will presently turn. In examining the full range of Merton's reactions, we encounter, in a word, his return to a familiar posture of ambivalences. Merton could accommodate the radical theologians in the context of private self-reflection where his aim was to reconcile himself to modernity, and where he could more freely reckon with the personal experience of religious crisis central to the Radical Theology. And he could be less obliging in the context of direct discourse, when adopting the persona of an influential Catholic writer who had amassed a considerable following and who recognized his responsibility to such a wide readership. Many of those readers had repeatedly turned to Merton to shore up a flagging belief. How could he, in good conscience, endorse a movement that preached the efficacy of unbelief?

Such a pattern of ambivalences can be seen in other contexts as well. In his letters Merton routinely tailored his comments concerning the Death-of-God movement to his correspondents' sympathies. For example, Merton could share with Marco Pallis, who as deeply devoted to Tibetan monasticism, how utterly struck he was 'by the limitless depth of despair . . . implicit in the pitiful "hopes" of so many moderns, Christians, who are trying to come out with justifications for a completely secularized and optimistic eschatology of psuedo-science, in which the eventual triumph of religion is to discover that God is "dead" and that there is no religion anyway.'[4] In chameleon-like fashion, Merton responded quite differently in his letters to the theologian Rosemary Ruether, whose thinking was directly influenced by Bonhoeffer, Bultmann, and especially Gabriel Vahanian, who had first popularized the phrase 'God-is-dead' in its contemporary theological context. Naturally, Rosemary Ruether remained unsympathetic to the monastic project, referring to it disparagingly on one occasion as 'anti-matter theology' totally irrelevant to 'the arena of real historical action.' In an effort to tailor his responses to Ms Ruether's theological bearings, Merton experimented throughout his letters with a variety of self-labels: among others, 'Christian anarchist', 'anti-ascetic humanist', 'secularized hermit', non-monk', 'man as mere man', and so on, some of which might have made fine lapel buttons for the jacket of a new theologian.

Such ambivalences may only blunt Merton's public criticisms of the Death-of-God movement. At any rate, Merton's sharpest and most concentrated critical pronouncements came in a carefully edited cluster of six essays which comprise Part Four of *Faith and Violence,* culminating in the polemical pitch of the final two essays: 'The Death of God and the End of History' and 'Godless Christianity'. Merton most certainly had something in mind, incidentally, when he selected 'Apologies to an Unbeliever' to precede those essays. In that piece he adopted an epistolary style and engaged unbelievers in an intimate dialogue. His aim was not to justify his faith and belief to an audience of unbelievers nor to win their confidence. He chose instead to apologize for the penchant among Christian faithful to proselytize their message; he confessed that announcing the Good News with evangelical zeal only alienated unbelievers and shut down dialogue between Christians and atheists, thus breaching a 'compassionate respect for one another in their common predicament'. Most important, Merton did not characterize himself as the kind of believer whose tenacity of faith alone might prompt an up-coming attack on a new brand of Christian thinking that stressed the utility of unbelief and aimed to accommodate secular atheism. Rather, Merton characterized 'my own peculiar task in my Church [as] . . . that of the solitary explorer who . . . is bound to search the existential depths of faith in its silences, its ambiguities. . . .'⁵ In the course of that search Merton freely admitted that he had encountered his own faith 'mysteriously [taking] on the aspect of doubt'. He was fully prepared to accept, then, that 'the division between Believer and Unbeliever ceases to be so crystal clear', that both believer and unbeliever 'are bound to seek in honest perplexity', and that, ultimately, 'Everybody is an Unbeliever more or less'. By taking that sincere and egalitarian position in 'Apologies to an Unbeliever', Merton clearly intended an editorial maneuver designed to soften and qualify his disagreements with the Death-of-God theologians which would follow in the next essays. No sensitive reader would likely mistake such criticisms as issuing from the outrage of a famous Believer.

Although Merton may have characterized himself as the kind of believer not prone to reactionary bias when addressing the central question of God's existence and although he promises, in a headnote to 'The Death of God and the End of History', that his discussion of the death-of-God premise is reflective and not polemical, there is, even in the language of his summary descriptions, a touch of polemics which belies such evenhandedness. 'What is meant by the current solemnization of the "death-of-God"?' Merton asks wryly. 'It claims to be an act of fervent Christian iconoclasm which is vitally necessary both for Christianity and for the "world" since without it (so the argument runs) Christianity cannot recover any relevance at all in the modern world and the world itself cannot discover its own implicit and unrecognized potentialities . . .' (239). He viewed such a claim as nothing less than 'a declaration that the question of God's existence has now become irrelevant. An announcement of the "good news": God as a problem no longer requires our attention.'

> What is involved [in the Death-of-God movement] is a repudiation of *all* discussion of God, whether speculative or mystical: a repudiation of the very notion of God, even as 'unknowable'. Any claim whatever to know Him, or to know what one is talking about when discussing Him, is dismissed a priori as infected with mythology. [So] the language of theology and revelation has 'died' on us, so the argument runs. The words have lost their meaning. Or the meaning they have kept is purely formal, ritual, incantory, magic. . . .(240)
>
> The cornerstone of the whole . . . movement . . . is the formal belief that revelation itself is inconceivable. To say that God is dead is to say He is silent, that He cannot be conceived as speaking to man. . . . The whole concept of revelation has now become obsolete because modern man is simply incapable not only of grasping it but even of being interested in it at all. (260)

Obviously unimpressed by some of the theological issues raised by the movement, Merton seemed more interested in the phenomenon of the movement itself as signaling a revolutionary new stage in the history of human consciousness, what he called 'the expression of a "happening" in the consciousness of man,' a profound shift in 'psychological and epistemological assumption[s] about human consciousness in the modern age'. Beneath the popular rhetoric and the announced aims of the Death-of-God theologians to adapt theology to the collapse of Western Christendom and the advent of secular atheism, Merton sensed 'the epiphany of a new state of consciousness, a new mode of being in the world, a new relationship to the secular world'. With flashes of irony Merton caricatured that relationship as an Augustinianism in reverse, where the new Christian sings praises for secularity to the accompaniment of guitars while 'the sin which is confessed is the sin not of infidelity but of belief'.

Merton was not moved to such an unflattering and ironic treatment of the Death-of-God theologians because he interpreted their central injunction as mere atheism or apostasy. 'They are not "atheists,"' he explained, 'the old belligerent pseudoscientific militant atheists.' In fact, Merton entered the real paradox of the God-is-dead Christian for whom God remains immanent, Merton writes, 'empty and hidden in man and in the world', and 'present more especially in those who deny him and repudiate him and refuse to recognize him'. 'The basic dogma,' Merton then concludes, 'of the God-is-dead theology is that any claim to an experience of the reality of God and his relevance for life on earth today is bound to be fraudulent or at least illusory.' So the honest Christian has little choice except to confess to 'having sinned against the world, of having insulted the adulthood of man by having believed in a transcendent God.'

Summarizing briefly, Merton featured the death-of-God theology as radically *kenotic*. The God-is-dead Christian is emptied of the capacity to receive revelation, stripped of traditional metaphysical assumptions about Being or about God, and freed from traditional formalistic rituals of worship and the trappings of dysfunctional, archaic symbolisms. He is emptied especially of God-talk. He is liberated in his modernness. And the test of the authenticity of that liberation, Merton writes, is whether the new Christian's 'present subjective state of consciousness . . . corresponds to "the world of our time" in its historical, technological, political actuality.'

Merton would have much to say about that issue of historical, technological, political fidelity. But first he made a point to affirm certain aspects of the death-of-God theology before launching his critique. He noted, for example, that the claim made by certain radical Christian theologians that 'God-is-dead' is, in itself, of indisputable cultural and religious importance. It has 'special significance', he writes, as 'a critique of traditional Christian ideas' and because it preaches 'a radical "Christian worldliness"' at a time when relations between the church and the modern world were undergoing revolutionary changes. The movement ought not to be dismissed out of hand, for it reflects, Merton felt, an appropriate exasperation with an abstract and formal religiosity which carried on about a God in heaven while showing too little concern for human persons on earth. Aside from simply appealing to his antinomian, iconoclastic temperament, Merton argued that the radical theologians should be listened to, especially because they had addressed 'modern man's need for a religion he really feels to be authentic and not just a blend of pious imagination and submission to ethical and ritual prescriptions.'

Building from that foundation of affirmations, Merton then framed his critique. He was not convinced, first, that the 'god' which Radical Theology had interred was ever alive in the first place. He in fact concurred with the central premise of the Death-of-God theologians if the god they had in mind — and he suspected such was the case — was 'a God of hypothesis, a God of pious cliches, a God of formalistic ritual, a God invoked to make comfortable people more pleased themselves'. Also, and less significantly, Merton detected a Madison Avenue mentality arising from the movement. Ever-critical of fashion and especially intolerant of the modern phenomenon of marketing ideas like soft drinks, Merton trained that critical disposition, in particular (though perhaps not altogether fairly), on John A. T. Robinson and his enormously popular and successful book *Honest to God*. Merton wondered whether *Honest to God* was really little more than a sophisticated 'manual of Christian salesmanship', an attempt to pitch a 'reconditioned' Christianity — 'worldly', 'religionless', 'free of myths', and basically 'with it' — to a generation of disaffected believers who viewed Christianity as passe, unacceptable, unpopular. Merton dressed down Robinson for trying to make Christianity palatable to the tastes of a new generation, and Merton dismissed *Honest to God* as merely a more refined and intellectually respectable version of the guitar-playing parish hootenanny or the new phenomenon of corn flakes suddenly appearing on the abbey breakfast table.

In a similar vein, Merton could muster little tolerance for the note of fervent proselytizing he heard throughout the writings of the radicals. Just as he had little sympathy for zealous Christians who aimed to share personal experiences of salvation with captive and undissenting converts, so too did Merton criticize the post-Christian 'who is completely "hip" to the modern world and will not listen for a moment to anyone who he suspects does not experience the modern world exactly as he does'. Merton remained suspicious, in other words, of some of the radicals' pretense to open dialogue, especially those who, he felt, 'instinctively [regard] as suspect any tendency to question or criticize "the world". More precisely . . . any questioning of the pragmatic, technological, sociopolitical understanding of the world as autonomous and self-sufficient' (244).

Of greater trouble to Merton was the 'either/or' proposition he extrapolated from the logic of the radical theology, a proposition that moved him to question whether the movement was really as modern as it was cracked up to be. As noted earlier, Merton viewed the new choice being offered modern Christians—to choose the world and reject God—as an Augustinianism turned inside out: thus, in Merton's mind, not a modern liberation from the old dialectics of the sacred and the secular as much as a retooling of the old hierarchies. 'We can . . . easily understand,' he writes, 'a reaction against the stereotyped opposition by which traditional religion tended to set up God . . . over against . . . the secular, in a dualism that no longer seems valid or practical today. Unfortunately [he continues] it seems that the God-is-dead Christian has simply perpetuated this same dualism by turning it inside out.' He further questions whether 'the dialectic [is] really valid, the tension really operative? Or is it simply, once again, a 'four legs good two legs bad' argument, as in Orwell's *Animal Farm?*' No doubt Merton's intolerance for such dialectical constraints issued from the fact that he himself had struggled for years with the existential consequences of such tensions. The personal difficulties and self-doubts, the crises of self-contradictions and ambivalences caused by his decision, decades earlier, to reject the world left him naturally gunshy of the 'either/or' proposition, even when turned inside out.

The driving force behind Merton's critique hinged, above all, on his resolute rejection of an uncritical worship of the modern in its all-embracing modernness. Merton took careful aim at certain unnamed 'secular city theorists in America', no doubt Harvey Cox and other interdisciplinary intellectuals, who had borrowed elements from the radical theology and fashioned what Merton considered a pop ideology of secularism. He wondered whether such theorists had merely reshuffled old formulas and replaced 'metaphysics' and 'revelation' with 'history' and 'politics' —whether they had negotiated a change of venue from St Augustine's *City of God* to a new earthly city where, Merton wisecracked, Los Angeles becomes the New Jerusalem. That substitution, Merton feared, may only nourish a complacent praise of American affluence and encourage a drift into 'a quietism which simply celebrates and glorifies the muzak-supermarket complex'. Some of Merton's toughest language surfaced as he pondered the ramifications of an unchecked and frenzied contemporariness and as he pictured the modern person submerged in the flux of changing fashion, uprooted into the 'breathless dynamism of the ephemeral', and emboldened by 'a quasi-Christian mystique of technological man as the summit of the evolutionary process'. 'The enthusiasm for the secular city,' Merton warns, 'coincides with a fervent praise of American affluence, which is in fact rooted in the enormous military-industrial complex.' He further cautions: 'though the God-is-dead movement repudiates transcendence, mysticism, inwardness, divine law and so forth, turning to immanence, outgoing love and creative innovation in interpersonal relationships, its substitution of "history" and "politics" for metaphysics and religion may run the risk of ending in conformism, acquiesence, and passive approval of the American managerial society, affluent economy, and war-making power politics.'

Not only did Merton fear an uncritical glorification of pro-bourgeois American suburbansim, but he questioned the very efficacy of the historical/political consciousness itself. Merton cites Camus and Hannah Arendt in an effort to highlight the altogether indistinct relationship between historical fact and historical illusion, between political action and political manipulation.

. . . today, with the enormous amplification of news and of
opinion, we are suffering from more than acceptable distor-
tions of perspective. Our supposed historical consciousness,
over-informed and over-stimulated, is threatened with
death by bloating, and we are overcome with a political
elephantiasis which sometimes seems to make all actual forward motion useless if not impossible. But in addition to
the sheer volume of information there is the even more
portentous fact of falsification and misinformation by
which those in power are often completely intent not only
on misleading others but even on convincing themselves
that their own lies are 'historical truth'. (250)

It followed, in Merton's reasoning, that the historical/politi-
cal consciousness, allowed to evolve unchecked, will lead inevitably to 'the death of history': a situation in which, in the
name of political realism, 'we may altogether cease to know what
is happening let alone understand it'. He turned the axiom of the
radical theologians against radical theology through recourse to a
rugged Orwellian realism, claiming that just as God-is-dead so
too history-is-dead, 'for the idea of history . . . becomes fiction
which keeps one from being aware of what is going on and from
making decisions that are really capable of influencing man's
destiny in a free and constructive manner.' In short, Merton saw
no little naiveté as he looked beyond the bracing enthusiasms of
the God-is-dead Christian. Blinded by a passion for the modern,
intoxicated by 'the constant unpredicable flux of existence,' he
must, Merton persistently warned, 'be more aware of the
deviousness of his own heart and of his own propensity to justify
destructive tendencies with moral, religious, philosophical or
even scientific rationalizations'. Merton could find, in a word, little value in swapping a mystique of revelation for a mystique of
secular liberation.

Although Merton ultimately rejected the claims of the new
radicals, his reservations did not issue from a sense of insult to his
Christian beliefs and values, nor was his critique undertaken as
an apologetic counter-attack in defense of monasticism. He turned

against the New Theology because he viewed it as merely replacing old dysfunctional myths with a new secular mythology that did not promise, in his mind, human freedom and liberation from collective delusions. Above all, he may have detected in the all-embracing enthusiasm for the modern a violation of the balanced humanism he had struggled for years to attain: that amalgamation of traditional Christian compassion and a full, critical, responsible awareness of modern realities which formed the basis of Merton's radical humanism and inspired the best, I believe, of his social criticism. He articulated that sense of violation best by posing questions as he neared his final arguments in *Faith and Violence.*

> Does the New Theology simply 'liberate' the Christian from traditional Christianity in order to subject him to a ready-made political or a-political ideology of questionable worth? Or does it turn him loose in a world without values, to occupy himself with the infinite variety of possible metamorphoses in his own consciousness, his own awareness of himself in his self-creating milieu?
>
> Are we . . . drifting into a new world of total, predetermined necessity, a new 'system' entirely closed to liberty and impervious to revolutionary change (except for its own immanent technical revolutionsim, determined not by man's will but by technology's own capacity for self-perfection in its own realm, without consideration for man's real needs)? (252–253)

University of California
Santa Barbara

NOTES — Thomas Merton and the New Theology

*An expanded version of this article will appear in *Thomas Merton's Art of Denial: The Evolution of a Radical Humanist,* from the University of Georgia Press.

1. *Prisoner for God* (New York: Macmillian, 1954) p. 122.
2. *Honest to God* (Philadelphia: The Westminister Press, 1963) p. 17.
3. *Letters and Papers from Prison* (New York: Macmillian, 1972) p. 360.
4. Thomas Merton to Marco Pallis: 17 June 1965. *The Hidden Ground of Love: The Letters of Thomas Merton on Religious Experience and Social Concerns,* ed. William H. Shannon (New York: Farrar, Straus and Giroux, 1985) p. 471.
5. *Faith and Violence* (Notre Dame, Indiana: University of Notre Dame Press, 1968) p. 213. All further references in the text are to pages in this volume.

William H. Shannon

The Year of the 'Cold War Letters'

THIS PAPER IS INTENDED as an outline — and a kind of preview — of what I hope will be a section of a book on Merton's involvement in the issue of war and peace. Most people who want to study Merton's attitudes on the war-peace issue go to *The Non-Violent Alternative* edited by Gordon Zahn or, if they are fortunate enough to have a copy of it, to the unpublished volume of Merton's *Cold War Letters.*

Both the Zahn book and the *Cold War Letters* are very helpful in understanding Merton's stand on the war-peace issue. But the latter is largely unavailable and the Zahn book, valuable though it is, suffers from the fact that the articles in it are arranged according to Gordon's classifications, and not in terms of the way in which they are related to one another as Merton wrote them. Hence they do not show the development of Merton's thought. Further, the book does not make clear how Merton struggled with these articles, how one grows out of another as a correction or an expansion. Nor does this work show the unique concentration into a fairly short period of time of most of what Merton wrote on this issue. Neither does Zahn's book indicate what it was that catapulted Merton—very suddenly and abruptly, at least so it seemed—into the middle of the anti-war camp. In thus evaluating Zahn's book, I am not intending to be unduly critical. It would be unfair of me to blame him for not doing something that it was obviously not his intention to do when he published *The Non-Violent Alternative*. His purpose was to bring together in one convenient volume Merton's major writings on war and peace. This he did, using categories of his own choosing. And there is no doubt that the book has proved exceedingly valuable to many who have wanted to study Merton's writings on this issue.

I want to do something different from what Zahn has done. I am planning a book on Merton's involvement in the war-peace issue that I see divided into four sections:

1) The first section would attempt to discuss why and when Thomas Merton—the man who in 1941 entered the monastery in order to leave the world, irrevocably so it seemed at the time—actually did 'return to the world'—not, of course, by leaving the monastery, but by becoming involved as a monk in the affairs that touched so deeply the lives of the people of his time. [And they are issues that involve us also.] The 'why' of his return was, I believe, his deepening experience of contemplation and the movement toward a non-dualistic understanding of reality that grew out of his prayer-life. As regards the 'when' of his return, I believe for a number of reasons (which time and space prevent me from detailing here) that the year of the 'big transition' was 1958. And it is no mere coincidence that this year was also the year of Pope John XXIII's accession to the papal office.

2) The second section of this book—which will comprise several chapters—I intend to call 'The Year of the "Cold War Letters."' I will clarify in a moment what I mean by this title and what I would hope to include in this section. In fact, this will be my principal emphasis in this paper. But first—for the sake of completeness—I would like to mention very briefly the two other

sections of the book I am envisioning.

3) Section three will deal with what Merton wrote on the issue of war-peace after what I am calling 'The Year of the "Cold War Letters."'

4) The fourth and final section I shall devote to a synthesis of his position on the meaning and practice of non-violence.

To return to Section II: what I am calling 'the Year of the "Cold War Letters"' is not a calendar year. It covers a period in Merton's life which, with some slight overlapping, extends from October 1961 to October 1962. October 1961 represents his 'official entry into the war on war'. His first article explicitly on the topic appeared in the October, 1961 issue of *The Catholic Worker*. From October of 1961 till the end of April, 1962 he wrote a flurry of articles—plus one book—on the subject of the Christian's responsibility regarding the issues of war and peace. On April 26, 1962, he was informed by his abbot, Dom James Fox, that the Abbot General of the Cistercian Order, Dom Gabriel Sortais, had sent orders that he was no longer to publish articles or books on the subject of war and peace. In fact, he was not even to submit them for censorship.

Merton obeyed the prohibition against *publishing* anything on war and peace. Nonetheless, he continued to write articles that, while unpublished, were circulated privately in mimeographed form among his friends; he also continued to discuss the war-peace issue in letters to his many correspondents. He even ventured to write two articles in 1963 under a pen-name: a review of *The Christian Failure* by Ignace Lepp, carried by *The Catholic Worker* (January, 1963) under the name 'Benedict Monk' and in the July-August, 1963 issue of *The Catholic Worker* an article on 'Danish Non-Violent Resistance to Hitler' authored by 'Benedict Moore.' But these two articles were written outside the boundaries of what I have called 'The Year of the "Cold War Letters"'. Besides these two there were other articles, though much less frequent, after April 1963. This was the date of the publication of Pope John XXIII's encyclical, *Pacem in Terris*.

After the publication of this papal statement, which said so many of the things Merton had been trying to say, the prohibition of April 1962 was eased somewhat, though by no means completely. (Merton wrote to Dom Gabriel Sortais that it was a good thing that Pope John was not a Cistercian: he would never have been able to get *Pacem in Terris* past the censors of the Order.) But it still remains that the period from October 1961 to October 1962 was the most vigorous, concentrated and productive period of Merton's war-peace writings.

The reason why I have called this period 'The Year of the "Cold War Letters"' is that during it Merton's many articles on the war-peace issue were interlaced with a constant stream of letters that discuss the same issue. From the many letters he wrote during this period of time Merton himself chose first forty-nine and later sixty-two additional letters which he called 'The Cold War Letters'.

He conceived the idea of such a selection of letters very early in this 'year.' On December 21, 1961, writing to Dr Wilbur H. ('Ping') Ferry of the Santa Barbara Center for the Study of Democratic Institutions, he asked Ferry if he would be willing to circulate some of his material in mimeographed form. 'I am having a bit of censorship trouble', he remarked somewhat casually and indicated that getting his 'stuff' around in this way would not require prior censorship. He then mentions *The Cold War Letters* for the first time: 'I have, for instance, some copies of letters to people — to make up a book called *Cold War Letters*. Very unlikely to be published(!)'

The first edition of *The Cold War Letters* consisted of forty-nine letters (there were two letters numbered #24 [presumably by mistake] and there is no #30 [presumably to make up for the earlier mistake]). The letters are numbered consecutively and are arranged in chronological order. The person to whom the letter is addressed is not named, but identified only by initials and by the place where he or she happened to be at the time Merton wrote. The final letter (#49) is a letter to the editors of *Commonweal*, written early in March, 1962. The reason for giving this date is that the preceding letter (#48 to Dr Wilbur H. Ferry) is dated

March 6, 1962. Since the letters are in chronological order, that would make quite plausible an early March date for #49. The letter to the editors of *Commonweal* was actually a reply from Merton to a letter of criticism about an article of his in the February 9 (1962) issue of that journal. The letter of criticism together with Merton's reply (the reply being Cold War Letter #49) appeared in the April 20 (1962) issue of *Commonweal*.

I have not been able to ascertain the exact date of the mimeographing of the first (smaller) edition of the Cold War Letters. In Merton's letter of May 8, 1962 he presumes that 'Ping' Ferry has already received several copies. This would indicate that they were duplicated just before or just after Merton received word from Dom James of the Abbot General's prohibition. If they were published after the prohibition they may well have been a way of expressing his frustration over the prohibition— though, as I have indicated above, the notion of a volume of (unpublished) Cold War Letters had been on his mind for some months.

At any rate, the decision to reach people with his ideas of peace through the private distribution of his letters became a project that he embraced with enthusiasm. In fact he decided, probably sometime during that summer, to enlarge the volume of Cold War Letters and actually more than doubled them. On September 22, 1962 he wrote to James H. Forest that 'we are mimeographing an enlarged edition of *The Cold War Letters*.' Then, after promising to send some copies to Forest, he remarks: 'No objections to it going to Europe where people are more intelligent about the peace issue, generally, than here.'[1] This promise of an enlarged edition that would be sent soon proved to be premature. The work was not completed at that time. On January 17, 1963 he writes to Forest and again speaks of the Letters: 'We are mimeographing an enlarged edition of Cold War Letters so this will reach you some day but not soon. It is quite a lot bigger and fuller, and we are doing a lot of copies.'[2] The enlarged edition continued the first edition, adding to it letters fifty through 111 and also a six page preface by Merton.

What was Merton's reason for giving the Letters the name he did? 'The Cold War,' a term coined by Walter Lippman in 1947, is intended to describe the atmosphere of suspicion and mistrust between the two super-powers that followed rather soon after the treaties that concluded World War II. It indicates a condition in which war is waged, not with the physical armaments of the 'hot' war, but with psychological weapons that are rhetorical and confrontational. Merton in his preface to the Cold War Letters specifically relates them to what was a major confrontation of the Cold War between the United States and the Soviet Union, namely, the Cuban crisis over the presence in Cuba of Soviet missile launching sites. On October 22, 1962, President Kennedy ordered a blockade of Cuba and on October 28, Nikita Khrushchev agreed to withdraw the missles and to dismantle the missle sites. Relating the Letters to this incident Merton writes in the preface:

> These copies of letters written over a period of a little more than one year preceeding the Cuban Crisis of 1962, have been made for friends who might be expected to understand something of the writer's viewpoint, even when they might not agree with all he has said, still less with all that he may have unconsciously implied.

The Cuban Crisis, while it may have been the decisive factor in determining the choice of Merton's title for this collection of letters, obviously did not influence the actual writing of the letters, since practically all of them were written before that Crisis occurred. There is evidence, however, that the deterioration of relationships between the USA and the USSR, with the consequent mistrust and fear which it created, was very much on Merton's mind at the beginning of what I have called 'the Year of the "Cold War Letters." ' I want to cite three examples that illustrate his earliest concern. The first is the effective prose-poem about the dropping of the first atomic bombs. Entitled *Original Child Bomb,* it was written probably during the summer of 1961,[3] though it was not published till October. The second is the long letter-essay written to Antonio Pablo Cuadra, a Latin American poet whom Merton admired very much. The third would be his first article specifically addressing the Christian obligation to work for the abolition of war: the article which I have already mentioned and which appeared in the October, 1961 issue of *The Catholic Worker* with the title 'The Root of War is Fear.' That Merton was struggling in the summer of 1961 about his obligation to speak out on the issues of the day, especially the war-issue, is clear from a letter he wrote — on August 22, 1961 — to Dorothy Day. Speaking about the 'Auschwitz poem' ('Chants to be Used in Processions around a Site with Furnaces' — he had already sent it to *The Worker* for publication), he expresses his apprehension that the censors may not accept it, because 'Trappists should not know about these things, or should not write about them'. He tells Dorothy what a great problem this presents for him, because he feels 'obligated to take very seriously what is going on, and to say whatever my conscience seems to dictate'. He situates his problem in the context of obedience and puts — really to himself — the question as to what one should do in a situation 'where obedience would completely silence a person on some important issue on which others are also keeping silence — a crucial issue like nuclear war.' He wonders whether this would call a person to change his or her situation. As if answering his own question, he goes on to say that he has no thoughts of leaving the monastery and professes his belief that 'somehow God always makes it possible for me to say what seems to be necessary'. But his concern about the failure of churchmen to speak up is deeply felt: 'Why,' he asks, 'this awful silence and apathy on the part of catholics, clergy, hierarchy, lay people on this terrible issue on which the very continued existence of the human race depends?'[4] Merton realized that, if others were going to remain silent, he at least could no longer continue to do so. 'I don't feel,' he continues, 'that I can in conscience go on writing just about things like meditation, though that has its point. I cannot just bury my head in a lot of tiny and secondary monastic studies either. I think I have to face the big issues, the life-and-death issues . . ,'[5]

In *Original Child Bomb* Merton seems almost to distance himself from the problem and treat the nuclear holocaust as if he were simply reporting what a journalist might see as historical steps leading up to Hiroshima and Nagasaki. It is this sense of standing apart and putting together what appear to be simple newspaper clippings that gives this prose-poem its power. The seeming 'objectivity' of 'facts', while appearing to suppress feelings, actually draws readers into the emotions of the experience almost without their realizing it.

If *Original Child Bomb* is moving by its apparent 'objectivity', the long letter to Antonio Pablo Cuadra calls for immediate participation in the writer's indignation and passion. Merton describes this letter-essay as a letter 'concerning giants'. The two giants in question — the USA and the USSR — are described under the images of Magog and Gog, the two apocalyptic figures mysteriously depicted in the book of *Ezechiel*. Gog, (the Soviet Bloc) and Magog (the West) have much in common with one another.

> Gog is the lover of power, Magog is absorbed in the cult of money; their idols differ, and indeed their faces seem to be set against one another, but their madness is the same: they are the two faces of Janus looking inward, and dividing with critical fury the polluted sanctuary of dehumanized man.[6]

With Gog and Magog locked in mortal combat, Merton looks to the Third World for the salvation of the human race. The Letter is strong, biting, even violent (so much so that Merton himself felt it necessary to question why it had gotten 'so violent and unfair').[7] He writes on September 24, 1961 to Dona Luisa Coomaraswamy telling her that he is sending 'an indignant' letter that he had written to a friend. The letter, he says, while long and irate (more angry than it should be, he admits) is 'about the merciless stupidity of the Great Powers and power politicians'. He tells her that he shares her indignation about the Pharisaeism of the West along with the Russian variety of the same. Believing that the time has come in which 'something must be said', he makes the significant statement: 'I am starting in Latin America where it may still be listened to.' To Abdul Aziz, who lives in

Karachi, Pakistan, and who, therefore, lives in a country which, like Latin America, belongs to the Third World, Merton offers a fairly detailed summary of this 'open letter.' The theme of it, he says, is 'the international situation and the deplorable attempts of the great powers to threaten one another and the world with nuclear weapons.' He sees an evil force more than human operating in these maneuverings of Power and he looks to the Third World for the restoration of sanity to society. He writes:

It is my belief that all those in the world who have kept some vestige of sanity and spirituality should unite in firm resistance to the movements of power politics and the monster nations, resist the whole movement of war and aggression, resist the diplomatic overtures of power and develop a strong and coherent 'Third World' that can stand on its own feet and affirm the spiritual and human values which are cynically denied by the great powers . . . Naturally in the monastery I am not very well versed in politics, but I feel that a certain spiritual outlook does have some value after all. It gives a perspective which is not available to those who think only in terms of weapons and money and the manipulation of political groups.[8]

These two works, *Original Child Bomb* and *A Letter to Pablo Antonio Cuadra Concerning Giants,* were preliminary intimations of the third work whose importance I have already indicated above: the article published in *The Catholic Worker* in October, 1961, and bearing the title: 'The Cause of War is Fear.' This article speaks directly to the issue of nuclear war and drives home what was to be a firm conviction of Merton's, at least from this time on: that the most important task to which God is calling all Christians in our time is 'to work for the total abolition of war'.

This article, while prepared for by the other two, marks — as I have already mentioned — Merton's 'official' entrance into the peace movement. It was especially 'official', since the article appeared in a journal well known for its pacifism and commitment to non-violence.

It should be noted that this article was actually a chapter from a book of Merton's that was soon to be published by *New*

Directions. What makes the article particularly explosive is that Merton added to this chapter (which had been passed by the censors) three long paragraphs, which had not even been seen by them. Rather casually, he indicated to Dorothy Day that they were added just to 'situate these thoughts in the present crisis.'⁹ In actual fact, these 'situating' paragraphs were highly inflammatory (in a way that the book chapter was not) and summed up in brief fashion what could be taken as a whole program for opposing war and working for peace.

The uncensored paragraphs begin with the description of an illness — a 'war-fever' — that has swept through the world. He sees the wh le world plunging headlong into frightful destruction and 'doing so *with the purpose of avoiding war and preserving peace!*' Of all the sick countries of the world, he singles out his own adopted country, the United States, as the most grievously afflicted. In an imaginative picture he describes people building bomb shelters, where they will simply bake slowly instead of being blown out of existence in a flash. He fantasizes that people will even sit at the entrance to their shelters with machine guns to prevent their neighbor from entering. And this, he asks, is a nation that claims to be fighting for religious truth and freedom and other values of the spirit? 'Truly we have entered the "post-Christian era" with a vengeance.'

He goes on to discuss at some length the duty of Christians in the present situation. They must not embrace a fatalistic attitude, much less the madness of the warmongers who would calculate how by a first strike the glorious Christian West could eliminate atheistic communism for all time. This sabre-rattling attitude he sees as 'the great and not even subtle temptation of a Christianity that has grown rich and comfortable. . . .' In a more positive vein he suggests that the one duty that every Christian must assume in this crisis is the task of working for the total abolition of war. Otherwise the world will remain in a state of madness and desperation, in which 'because of the immense destructive power of modern weapons, the danger of catastrophe will be imminent. . . .' Addressing the responsibility of the Church, he says that, while the Church does not always have clear answers as to precise strategies, 'she must lead the way on the road toward the gradual abolition of war as the way of settling international or civil disputes'. There is also much that must be done by individual Christians: much to be studied, much to be learned. Peace is to be preached. Non-violence is to be explained as a practical method. There is need for prayer and sacrifice. We have to overcome the hidden aggressions that often express themselves in our relationships, and we must work for the truth and not just for results. 'We may never succeed in this campaign, but whether we succeed or not the duty is evident. It is the great Christian task of our time. Everything else is secondary, for the survival of the human race itself depends upon it. . . . .'

This article in *The Catholic Worker* was followed by a barrage of articles, most of them written during what I have called 'The Year of the Cold War Letters'—though some of this material, because of the disapproval of the censors, was actually published later. For example, large sections of the book *Peace in a Post-Christian Era,* completed in the spring of 1962, but not even allowed to be submitted to the censors, were eventually published in *Seeds of Destruction* in 1964.

It is not my intention in this brief paper to go through these articles individually in order to show how they relate to one another. This, I hope will be one of the principal thrusts of the book I intend to write on *Merton as Peacemaker.*

I should, however, make the point that it was precisely at this time—namely, the time of the first article that related him to the peace-movement—that Merton began writing the one hundred eleven letters that would eventually be known as *The Cold War Letters.* The first of the *Cold War Letters* was written to Etta Gullick. Though I do not have the exact date, I can, by relating her letters to his, pinpoint the date as being probably about October 25. Neither can I give the exact date for the last of the Letters, number 111 (since I have not yet identified the person—it is written to E. G., at Princeton), but I can approximate the date with some accuracy. I can verify the fact that Letter #110 was written on October 30, 1962. Letter #111 could well have been written on the same day or the next. Either alternative would fit well with Merton's statement linking the *Cold War Letters* with the Cuban Crisis.

I want to bring my remarks to a close by quoting Merton's words in the Introduction he wrote to the enlarged edition of *The Cold War Letters*. He discusses the political climate:

> There seems to me to be a general air of insanity about the whole conduct of public life today. . . . *it is taken for granted* that the mere idea of questioning recourse to war as a valid, rational and ethical means of settling problems is not only absurd but may even be treasonable.

He then touches on the mentality of Catholic theologians:

> There are not lacking moralists, Catholic theologians, who can argue that there exists a *moral obligation* to threaten Russia with nuclear destruction! In the opinion of the present writer such opinions are not only disgraceful, scandalous and unChristian, but also plainly idiotic. They make much less sense than the measured rumblings of the theological experts who, in Galileo's day, did not want the earth to turn about the sun.

Finally, Merton states his own stance on the issue and he suggests that it is very much in line with the teaching of the popes.

> The writer is a Catholic, devoted to his Church, to his faith and to his vocation. He does not believe that in differing from theologians like these, even when they may perhaps be bishops, he is turning against Christ or the Church. On the contrary, he believes himself obliged in conscience to follow the line of thought which has been made quite clear by the modern Popes, particularly Pius XII and John XXIII, who have repeatedly appealed for rational and peaceful ways of settling disputes, and who have forcefully declared that the uninhibited recourse to destructive violence in total war, nuclear or conventional, is " a sin, an offense and an outrage." (Pius XII).

Rochester, New York

NOTES – The Year of the Cold War Letters

1. William H. Shannon, ed., *The Hidden Ground of Love: The Letters of Thomas Merton on Religious Experience and Social Concerns* (New York: Farrar, Straus and Giroux, 1985) p. 271.
2. *Ibid.*, p. 273.
3. See *Ibid.*, 18.
4. *Ibid.*, p. 139.
5. *Ibid.*
6. Thomas Merton, *Emblems of a Season of Fury* (New York: New Directions, 1963) p. 73.
7. See Michael Mott, *The Seven Mountains of Thomas Merton* (Boston: Houghton Mifflin, 1986) p. 365.
8. September 24, 1961, *Hidden Ground*, p. 150.
9. September 22, 1961, *Void*. 140.

William H. Shannon

Christian Living
In An Age of Technology

AS HE ENTERED the decade of the 1960's, Thomas
Merton saw the world in a way that was radically different from the world view he had embraced when in 1941
he had entered the Abbey of Our Lady of Gethsemani. One way of
expressing his thinking at the beginning of the 1960's is to say that he
had moved away from the simplistic view of the world, so evident in
Seven Storey Mountain in which the world is divided into a monastic
and a secular world. Now what he saw was a world in which men and
women were faced with one of two choices: either a society of persons
conscious of community and communion or a society of isolated
individuals drowned in the nameless isolation and the unredeemed
alienation of the collectivity. And what was going on before people's
very eyes was the mighty pull of a technology drawing them relentlessly in the direction of the collectivity and away from the community.

More and more Merton comes to understand that the real
struggle in human life is the struggle to construct the human
community — with its values of human dignity, human freedom,

solitude and contemplation. The alternative to this struggle is to be absorbed almost helplessly into the collectivity, in which men and women give up their freedom of thought and action and become part of the system that controls them and all of human life.

This contrast between the community (the place of freedom) and the collectivity (the place of slavery) is, at least implicitly if not always explicitly, a constant theme in Merton's writings in the 1960's. Closely linked with this contrast is the difference between the person and the individual. Merton has much to say about this difference. The person is the man or woman who lives in community; the individual is the man or woman who is isolated in the collectivity. The individual is simply a unity divided off from all other units. He or she is a single separate being, definable only in a negative way: he or she is not 'someone else'. 'Individuals' live in isolation and alienation from one another. They are united only superficially by an external uniformity that has scarcely any relationship to the inner realities of the human spirit. The collectivity is the mass-society that is constructed out of these disconnected individuals or, to use Merton's words, 'out of empty and alienated human beings who have lost their center and extinguished their own inner light in order to depend in abject passivity upon the mass in which they cohere without affectivity or intelligent purpose'.[1]

Far different from the 'individual' is the 'person' who is a center of freedom and love, linked with his or her brothers and sisters in the unity of all that makes them human and in a sharing of all that makes them one in Christ. Whereas the individual is absorbed in the stereotype, the person is conformed to the archetype who is Christ. For Merton the fullness of personhood and the meaning of community is 'to be in Christ'. Merton would want to say with St Paul: 'Now it is not I (that is the isolated individual' but Christ (that is, the person linked together with other persons in the archetype of all humanity) who lives in me.'

Persons find in the community the place for solitude and therefore for contemplation. The collectivity, on the other hand, is the place of what Pascal calls *divertissement*, an untranslatable word which roughly means 'distraction' or 'diversion': it is the escape from life's problems, and also its invitations, into activities that in ultimate terms are meaningless. People whose lives are shaped by the collectivity are people who have lost their sense of transcendence. This means that they are deprived of their natural capacity for contemplation.

In an essay that has become something of a classic, 'Rain and the Rhinoceros,' Merton describes the sickness of this mass-society that has lost its sense of solitude and its capacity for contemplation. He calls it 'rhinoceritis'. He is drawing on Eugene Ionesco's powerful play *Rhinoceros* to illustrate what he means by the collectivity. In this play everyone, except Beranger, becomes a victim of 'rhinoceritis.' This is a disease which consists in compliance with whatever is the norm of the moment, no matter how absurd it may be. In the play everyone is swept into the collectivity and becomes a rhinoceros. Beranger is the last human being left on earth, the last person. He feels a strong urge to abandon his humanness and join the herd, but something deep in him prevents him from doing so. He persists in remaining human in what has become a non-human world.

One of the responsibilities that Merton sees for himself and other contemplatives in society is to call for more 'Berangers' to face up to the fatuity of the collectivity's illusory priorities and to renounce the 'mass mind' so that they may once again become true persons and be in touch with what is real. Merton quotes Ionesco as saying that there will always be a place 'for those isolated consciences which have stood up for the universal conscience' as against the 'mass mind'. Merton adds' 'But their place is solitude. They have no other. Hence it is the solitary person (whether in the city or in the desert) who does mankind the inestimable favor of reminding it of its true capacity for maturity, liberty and peace.'[2]

Ionesco himself has made the same point that only the solitude which is proper to the community can save people from the slavery of unthinking conformism. Thus he writes: 'Forms of rhinoceritis of every kind, from left and right, are there to threaten mankind when men [and women] have no time to think or collect themselves; and they lie in wait for mankind today, because we have lost all feeling and taste for genuine solitude. For solitude is not *separation* but *mediation*. . . .[3]

At this juncture I think that I ought to point out that it would surely be a misunderstanding to think that either the community or the collectivity exists in a pure state. There is a bit of each in all of us. This was also true of Merton and he would have been the first to admit it. Our Christian task is to expose — in ourselves as well as in our society — the illusions that the collectivity lives by and to work for the building up of the community.

The dialectic between the community and the collectivity has taken place within the context of an ever-escalating technology. This has been true certainly since the Industrial Revolution and probably to some extent through the whole of human history. Technology has had a strong voice in determining whether it will be the values of the community or the collectivity that will predominate in a particular society.

Merton did not write extensively about technology, though references, explicit or implicit, are not infrequent in his later writings especially, and in his letters. Technology he saw as a human art that has immense possibilities for building the human community; yet at the same time it is continually open to the temptation to cripple the community and move people more and more into the clutches of the collectivity. Considered in itself and apart from the circumstances in which it operates, it is neither good nor bad. Yet in the concrete it is never neutral; it either builds or destroys the commonweal; it either serves or exploits the human family. And consistently throughout history it would appear that technology tends to move in the direction of destructiveness and exploitation rather than toward building and service. At least this is true when technology has not been guided by wisdom; and it seems true to say that the grim reality of history is that technology has seldom been in the hands of the truly wise.

The reason that technology can easily become anti-community is that its general thrust is away from such things as human dignity and equality, neighborly love and compassion (the things that make for community) and toward those things that foster the mood of the collectivity. This is because the intrinsic goals of technology (namely, what it seems to tend toward of itself, apart from the human motivation that may direct particular technologists) are power and profit, with the means to those intrinsic goals being greater and greater efficiency. Great power and enormous profit tend to separate rather than unite people. Power almost of necessity tends to be concentrated in the hands of the few, often at the expense of the many; and profit-oriented endeavors tend to enrich even more the already wealthy and to increase the poverty of the already poor.

This of course is not to say that technology has not achieved many benefits that have improved the style of human living and made life more comfortable. But it is necessary to ask the question whether these undeniable material advantages have not been at the expense of true spiritual goods. Thus we have built fantastic ways of transportation which make it possible for people to go anywhere they want to; yet the irony is that we live in an age that has lost its sense of direction. Physically we can go wherever we want to, even to the moon, but spiritually we have no notion of where we really want to go.

Or think of the ever-increasing marvels of communication. Not more than a couple of generations ago, a person could not be heard beyond the range of his own voice. Now we have the technological capability of communicating with the entire globe. Yet we have to ask the question: 'Given the fact that we can speak to the whole world, do we have anything that is worth saying? Do we have the wisdom to say the things that will be for the peace and betterment of the world?' Henry David Thoreau (who was born in 1817 and died in 1862)—a person who took a rather dim view of technological advances—was told one day that inventors were on the verge of producing a technology that would eventually make it possible for people in New York City to speak with people in New Orleans. His response was: 'What if they don't have anything to say?'

His question still remains a valid one today. The miracle of modern communication systems has brought people together so that their destinies are intertwined. But have we yet learned to speak to one another? We have suddenly come to realize that the word 'communication' can mean two quite different things: it can mean being able physically to be in touch with others; or it can mean being able to reach their minds and hearts. The first has little human value without the second. There is no point in being able to get in touch with people all over the world, unless we can reach their inner spirits. And this we can do only if we believe that all men and women are brothers and sisters who are united to one another spiritually and ecologically in a fellowship that is global in its dimensions. It must be our common task to build that fellowship for the good of the whole human race. This calls for wisdom: the wisdom that alone can build community and expose the illusions of the collectivity.

Thomas Merton was not opposed to technology and the wondrous advances it has made. Thus, in early 1968, he welcomed the addition to his hermitage that included inside plumbing. He counted it a distinct advantage that he no longer had to face regular encounters with 'the Bastard' — as he had 'affectionately' named the snake who had staked equal claims to the outhouse that had served Merton's needs in his first years in the hermitage. It is equally true to say that Merton enjoyed his typewriter for writing and his refrigerator for keeping his beer cool.

The Merton book that has the most references to 'technology' is the kind of summary journal that was published in 1966 called *Conjectures of a Guilty Bystander.* You will not find there any lengthy or exhaustive study of technology, but a number of significant references — a few of them fairly extensive. Some of the reviewers and readers of this book criticized him for what they described as an overly negative attitude toward technology. In a circular letter sent to his many friends in mimeographed form during Lent of 1967, Merton replied to this criticism. 'I got a letter from a Holy Cross Brother in Brazil taking me to task, as many critics have done, for what seems to be a negative attitude on technology in *Conjectures.* I might as well try to dot the i's and cross the t's on this point. Am I against technology?' He answers:

Obviously I am not maintaining that we ought to get rid of matches and go back to the making fires by rubbing sticks together . . . Nor am I maintaining that modern transportation, medicine, methods of production and so on are 'bad'. I am glad to have a gas heater this winter since I can't cut wood. Yet I am not saying that I am a better human being this winter, when I have more 'leisure', than I was last winter when I did a lot of chopping. Nothing wrong with chopping either. What I question is the universal myth that technology infallibly makes everything in everyway better for everybody. It does not.

He goes on to discuss how technological advance can be used to help people or destroy them. 'Thank God,' he says, 'for the fact that penicillin saves thousands of lives. But let's face the fact that penicillin saves lives for people whom society then allows to starve because it is not set up to feed them. If it used its technological resources well, society certainly could feed them. In fact it doesn't.'

He speaks too of what technology has done in the underdeveloped countries of the world. Multi-national corporations have gone into financially backward countries with technological skills that may work fine in affluent countries, but can be disastrous in countries that are poor. What happens is that these corporations bring huge profits back to their own country but often bring about the dislocation of the people of the 'backward country'—many of whom move to the city seeking work and soon find themselves living in abject poverty. Why? Because technology, by developing labor-saving methods of production, has reduced instead of increased the number of jobs available to them. This, Merton says, is a technology that is in the service of profit, not of people.

If I were asked to list the faults that Merton felt all too often dogged the path of technology, I would list five:

1. A faulty choice of goals. Technology all too frequently is afflicted by a false ethic that gives priority to material progress over moral growth and to efficiency in getting things done over social

responsibility. The overriding imperative of technology is: what can be done must be done. All too often it ignores the wisdom which would teach us that the fact that we are able to do something does not by itself mean that we should do it or even have the right to do it. Human values which technology simply as technology cannot know may offer compelling reasons for not doing something that we have the power to do. This drive to make the possible real can threaten the values of the community, even as it helps to construct the illusions of the collectivity.

2. The second fault Merton would find with technology is a more specific form of the first: namely, the lack of a proper balance or sense of hierarchy in choosing its goals. There are many worthwhile goals that technology may work toward. Granted that it cannot do everything — because time, energy and funds are limited, it must decide priorities among the possible goods it can work to accomplish. Too often basic human needs are ignored for the sake of scientific accomplishments. Too often the exotic is preferred to the ordinary. It is all very exciting (though with repetition the excitement quickly begins to wear off) to put satellites in space or even dramatically to repair those that have broken down. There is a sense of acting like God when He made the stars and put them in the heavens. Yet is peopling the heavens our most pressing task? Do we not have a greater responsibility to feed those who people the earth? In 1961 President John F. Kennedy promised that by the end of the decade the United States would put a man on the moon. And on July 20, 1969 it happened: Neil Armstrong stepped out of his Apollo spaceship onto the moon. A marvelous accomplishment indeed. It was science-fiction come true.

Yet one cannot help but think. Suppose President Kennedy in 1961 had set a different priority and said: 'By the end of this decade we shall eliminate starvation from the face of the earth?' Could we have done it? The answer, of course, we do not know. But should we have tried? Did the choice to put people on another planet prevent us from making the choice to put food in the mouths of all the men, women and children on our own planet? In our technological choices does the service of people often yield place to scientific achievement?

3. A third fault of technology is a false actionism that is obsessed with the need to get things done and as quickly and efficiently as possible. Such a mentality is fatal to the spirit of solitude and the love for quiet that are characteristic of the community.

4. A fourth problem Merton would see in technology is that for vast numbers of people it has dulled the creativity of the human spirit. For it has made work boring, routine, monotonous—so much so that the worker's sense of his own worth and of his own creative powers has been diminished by the very work he does. Work becomes something to escape from as quickly and as often as possible. Workers are thus drawn into the vortex of *divertissement* or 'distraction', where they lose themselves in activities that are mindless and without any real human significance. The soap opera of television has become the stereotype of this kind of soporific activity. Such *divertissement* moves people in the direction of the collectivity rather than the community.

5. A final fault that Merton would point to in modern technology is what might be called its Pelagian tendencies. Pelagianism was the heresy that said we could save ourselves: our own efforts were all that we needed; we did not need the grace of God. The myth of the 'Omnipotence' of technology is the Pelagianism of the twentieth century. We can run our own universe: we have the technological skill. Merton published in 1967 in a small magazine called *Season* an article that appears to be whimsical enough, but actually is in deadly earnest. Entitled 'The Angel and the Machine', it shows how the angels once thought to be our helpers in carrying out God's plans have been replaced by the machine. He writes:

Technological civilization is . . . a civilization without angels . . . in which we have chosen the machine instead of the angel: that is to say we have placed the machine where the angel used to be: at the limits of our own strength, at the frontier of our natural capacity.

More than that, Merton points out, 'the machines are "our angels"'. We made them, not they themselves. They are, we think, entirely in our own power. They become extensions of our own intelligence, our own strength.' 'They form part of our own enclosed and comfortable world, they stand between us and nature. They form a "room" in which we are isolated from the rest of material creation, and therefore all the more from spiritual beings. They create our weather for us and even abolish day and night, as we dwell in our windowless buildings surrounded by angels of chromium and steel.'

Merton goes on:

> In our folly we have tried to convince ourselves that our machinery is sufficient for all our needs and that there is nothing that science cannot do for us. It is in our anxiety to make our machine world completely self-sufficient and autonomous [something which is no fault of the innocent machine!] that we render it spiritually unlivable for ourselves.

He suggests that we need the angels: not to replace our machines, but to teach us how to live with them.

> For the angels come to us to teach us how to rest, to forget useless care, to relax, in silence, to 'let go,' to abandon ourselves not in self-conscious fun but in self-forgetful faith. We need the angels to remind us that we can get along without so many superfluous goods and satisfactions which instead of lightening our existence weigh it down. May they come back into our world and deliver it from its massive boredom, its metaphysical fatigue.

What he is saying is that we must and we can live in the world of the machine, the world of technology, and still build the community. But we need the wisdom that comes from God: a wisdom that earlier ages personified in the form of super-human beings. Without needing to explain what precisely earlier ages meant by these angelic beings, we need the wisdom they personified, the wisdom that was their message from God.

Almost all societies have recognized the 'way of wisdom.' It has been respected, not as a flight into illusion, but as a return to realtiy in its hidden ground and roots. Indeed special homage has been paid to those people who have attained to the inner meaning of life and being, who have expressed this meaning for their brothers and sisters and who have been able to unite in themselves the divisions and complications that confuse the lives of their fellow men and women. This can also be true of a technological society, but only if it is ready to renounce its obsession with the triumph of the isolated individual and the collective will to power — in order to adopt a different view of reality that springs from solitude and contemplation and is able to build the life of the community. The fundamental question posed by the contrast of community and collectivity is: 'Do we mechanize the person or do we personalize the machine?'

I have tried to suggest in a brief way that the way to build the community and overcome the pull of the collectivity is the way of contemplation and solitude. Yet, I need to point out, that — even when we have a commitment to solitude and contemplative living — we may not always be in agreement as to what is best for the community — whether that community be the family, the parish, the religious community, the national community, the community of nations, the community of the Church. Thus, for example, what the Church in Latin America has learned through its solitude and reflection may not agree with what Vatican officials have concluded from their own prayerful reflection. We cannot but feel, when we think, e.g., regarding the recent confrontation between Father Leonardo Boff and Cardinal Joseph Ratzinger: that each believes that the position he is taking is the one that will best help to build the community of the Church. Inevitably we are going to take sides in these issues; yet it would be sad if we did not talk with one another and through further solitude and reflection let the Spirit of God, Who is the Spirit of unity, help us to work out the tensions that inevitably arise.

Meanwhile, we have to live with tension: not just that which exists between the community and the collectivity, but also that which is within the community itself. Helpful in understanding this tension within the community is a text from Thomas Merton that I discovered in the unpublished typescript of the *Sign of Jonas*. In this passage, which never made it into the published version of *The Sign of Jonas*, Merton distinguishes true solitude from a 'narcissistic solitude' on the one hand and a 'crass activism' on the other. Both these extremes Merton sees as forms of escape, though they move in opposite directions. It is then that he makes the very significant statement:

> Our whole life must be a dialectic between community and solitude. Both are tremendously important, and our contemplative life subsists in the *fruitful antagonism* between these two terms.

It may seem surprising—though perhaps it ought not—to speak of antagonism within the Community itself. "Antagonism" is a strong word. Yet I am sure we all feel it—at times in our own personal dialectic between the demands of community and those of solitude, as well as in the dialectic of the Church. The important thing is that we let that 'antagonism' be 'fruitful'.

Rochester, New York

NOTES — Christian Living in an Age of Technology

1. Thomas Merton, *Disputed Questions* (New York: Farrar, Straus and Cudahy, 1960) p. x.

2. Id., *Raids on the Unspeakable* (New York: New Directions, 1966) p. 22.

3. Eugene Ionesco, *Notes and Counternotes* (New York: Grove Press, 1964) p. 151.

Lawrence S. Cunningham

Crossing Over in the Late Writings of Thomas Merton

AFEW YEARS AGO I happened on a review of Monica Furlong's biography of Thomas Merton in, of all places, *The Village Voice*. The reviewer was the feminist critic, Vivian Gornick, a writer who gives new depth of meaning to Schleiermacher's category of the 'cultured despiser' of religion. Gornick's main point, if I remember correctly, was that Thomas Merton's later years—the years of peace activism, the turn to the East, the pilgrimage to the Dalai Lama,—indicate that Merton may well have had a radical turn of mind but it was a mind, not saturated in religion, but trying to free itself from religion.

My intention here is not to answer Gornick's vulgar reductionism but simply to recall it in tandem with a remark made casually to me by a very bright undergraduate student who had just read *The Asian Journal*. Her point was that there were very few clues in the book, if one knew only that book, that Merton was a Christian believer, let alone a Christian monk. She cited, to prove her point, the capacious index with its many references to Krishna, Buddha, and the very meagre entries under the heading 'Jesus Christ'. My response to her observation—an observation that was not, by the bye, a hostile one— was to note what Merton did say in his entries about Christ and, further, to note that his observations about Asian religions were framed within his many references to his monastic exercises of recitation of the Office and celebration of Mass. I am not sure that I was convincing.

From these two very brief and quite disparate vignettes we might frame the issue which will be the subject of these reflections: What was the *Christian core* of that Thomas Merton who, in his last years, danced to Dylan records in the hermitage, constructed long poems of Chinese puzzle like complexity, drenched himself in studies of Asian religious experiences, fretted and carped about monastic life, raged against war and racism, dreamed, implausibly, of Alaskan hermitages, being a forest dweller amid the Redwoods of California, or, most notoriously of all, of bolting with a student nurse for God knows what kind of life? Was Thomas Merton simple a microcosm of that collective nervous breakdown that threatened all of us who were awake and over twenty-one in the late 1960s? In that cultural chaos, did his center hold?

Let me say, at the offset, that my purpose is neither to argue that Merton was moving beyond Christian faith nor to construct an apologia establishing him as an orthodox Christian and exemplary monk. It so happens that I believe him to be an exemplary, indeed, paradigmatic, monk but my purpose is not apologia; it is to seek understanding. In fact, to phrase it more positively, what I believe about Thomas Merton is this: that he is one of the very few public persons of our time who exhibited a genuinely Catholic mind, which is to say, that he was one of those exemplary figures who shows us what it means to be a Christian believer *in profundis* while, at the same time, being unflinchingly open, to everything that might enlarge, give texture to, and deepen the existential choice of being a Christian. I think that this openness is akin to what David Steindl-Rast calls 'exposure' as he looks at Merton's pilgrimage to the East.[1]

It is even more useful, I think, to turn to a concept developed by the Notre Dame theologian, John Dunne. Dunne has argued in a series of books that a person can 'pass over' or 'cross over' to other religious experiences (and traditions) in such a way that one learns from, and experiences, those traditions in a genuinely empathetic manner, and then return again to one's tradition enriched and deepened by that experience. In *The Way of All the Earth* (1972) Dunne invites the reader to cross over to Eastern religions and to take a return trip to one's own tradition; in *The Reasons of the Heart* (1978) the 'crossing over' becomes a 'journey' into solitude and back again to the human circle; in *The House of Wisdom* (1985) the 'crossing over' and the 'journey' is now a pilgrimage to places redolent of the sophianic tradition: Hagia Sophia, the Mark Rothko Chapel in Houston, and the Meditation Room at the United Nations building in New York.

These transits are not exercises in information gathering as if one wanted to 'store up' knowledge or experiences to enrich the cultural and intellectual horizons of a person. They take the form of Buberian dialogues by which one becomes open and vulnerable to the hiddenness and mystery of the other (person, place, or experience) so that the other, as it were speaks back. In that intimate dialogue the hiddenness of God, hiddenly, is also revealed:

> In every sphere, through everything that becomes present to us, we gaze towards the train of the Eternal You; in each we perceive a breath of it, in every you we address the Eternal You, in every sphere, according to its manner.[2]

The attractiveness of Dunne's paradigm is that it combines fidelity to a tradition with an openness that is catholic in the deepest sense of the term. It also strikes me that one cannot 'pass over' or 'journey' or make a 'pilgrimage' in Dunne's sense of the term unless one has a deep experiential center that serves as an anchored *terminus a quo*. Otherwise 'passing over' loses the sense in which Dunne intends for it and becomes a kind of dabbling in religious experience(s); a kind of spiritual tourism.

There is a paradox in Thomas Merton. His writing was, from

beginning to end, autobiographical to the degree that, as Elena Malits has noted in her study,[3] he made the personal pronoun 'I' respectable for the theologian to use. Yet, and here is the paradox, this autobiographical writer was notoriously reticent about his own spiritual life. The recent volume of his letters is all the more appreciated because they begin to provide glimpses into the 'hidden' Merton of prayer. I refer not only to the already famous passage describing his sense of prayer but the compellingly beautiful confessions of his sense of the presence of Christ. As early as 1959 Merton was writing to D. T. Suzuki about the Christ who is unknown and unseen; the One who is lost but becomes like our own true self.[4] In 1968, the year of his death, he writes to June Youngblut, in a brilliant discussion of the meaning of icons, of the Christ who is in us and in being in us becomes the One 'in whom and by whom one is illuminated'.[5]

I wish that I could trace out Merton's christology in greater detail here (there is yet to be written a satisfactory study of that crucial subject) but time and space forbid it. This much needs be said. From his earliest writings, the christology of Merton was, with very rare exceptions, a high one. Merton's fascination was with the divine enfleshed but it was the fact of divinity that compelled him. Christ transforms the contemplative person of prayer: he does not stand apart as an object of contemplation. This losing of Christ in contemplation which he alludes to in his letters to Suzuki is paralleled in his brief but compelling remarks in *New Seeds of Contemplation* about Christ coming to us but not necessarily as we may picture him in the imagination:

> The 'what' may or may not be imaginable, but we reach the 'Who'—the mysterious ineffable divine Person—*directly and immediately* through grace and love without images (or *with* them if you like, but this is less direct) and without rationalization. The real mystery of Christian *agape* (charity) is this power that the Person of the Word, in coming to us, has given to us. The power of a direct and simple contact with Him, not as with an object only, a 'thing' seen or imagined, but in the transsubjective union of love which does

not unite an object with a subject but *two subjects in one af-
fective union.*[6]

That passage, written early in Merton's career, reflects a continuing theme in his writings even though it takes different forms
and mutations. That passage reflects his convictions about the
reality of Christ, transcendent in his divinity but immanent in
the world and in the believer as *sophia* and grace and love. That
theme runs like a leitmotif detectable in his essay on Pasternak,
in 'Barth's Dream of Mozart' in *Conjectures;* in his tightly allusive
reflections in *Raids on the Unspeakable.* It is christology that pro-
poses a Christ who is hidden but radiant. Christ, to use a powerful image from *The Sign of Jonas* is the 'hermit who is at the
center of history'.[7]

With that in mind we can now turn once again to our question: what was the Christian core of Merton's pilgrimage to the
East and, more generally, what was his Christian core in those
last, frenetic, years of his life?

At one, more obvious level, the answer is simple. He was a
Christian monk who identified himself as such and who lived as
one until the day of his death at a monastic conference in
Thailand. It is true that in those last few years of his life Merton
thought long and hard about what it meant to be a monk in the
tumultous days of the 1960s and how to establish a more authentic monastic identity but that he was a monk and saw himself as
such is beyond dispute. It is also worthwhile noting that for all of
his thinking about the radical changes that were ahead for the
monastic life in the West there was also a deep sense of tradition
and continuity in his approach to monasticism. The
posthumously published essays in his book *Contemplation in a
World of Action* and his notes in *The Asian Journal* not infre-
quently flash with that sense of continuity and tradition. Here is
Merton speaking a month before his death:

. . . In the West there is now going on a great upheaval in
monasticism, and much that is of undying value is being
thrown away irresponsibly, foolishly, in favor of things that

are superficial and showy, that have no ultimate value. I do not know the situation in the East but I will say as a brother from the West to Eastern monks, be a little careful. The time is coming when you may have to face the same situation and your fidelity to your ancient traditions will stand you in good stead. Do not be afraid of that fidelity.[8]

It is at a far deeper level, however, that we reach the Christian core of Thomas Merton. It would be otiose to demonstrate that Merton was interested in the pursuit of contemplative consciousness; that, after all, is the given, the *telos,* of monastic life. What is crucial is to grasp that this consciousness is not to be construed as the individual ego in relation to an object as one object confronting another; this consciousness is not, as Bernard Lonergan says of insight, simply 'taking a look'.

The key text for understanding Merton's approach to contemplative consciousness is one of his most philosophical and theological essays entitled 'New Consciousness'. Written in 1967 and published in its definitive form in 1968 [9] Merton is at pains first to establish the legitimacy of the contemplative life against those critics who (a) view it as a hellenic aberration in Christianity and (b) charge that it is a quietistic retreat from the activisim of prophetic life and secondly to show that a cultivation of the insights of Buddhism can help in the growth and appreciation of this new Christian consciousness.

This new consciousness, appropriate for the needs of this period of our human and religious history has four aims: to develop and sustain a profound sense of human community and solidarity; to provide a context for giving deep meaning to the everyday aspects of human life; to provide a holistic sense of human existence while overcoming any false dichotomy between nature and supernature; and, most importantly, freeing people from an excessive reliance on self reliance, self awareness, self consciousness, and self fulfillment. Immediately after Merton outlines these four goals of the new consciousness he adds two short paragraphs that I think fairly well sum up the deep Christian center of Thomas Merton as he prepares to 'cross over' to the world of Asian religions:

For all these needs, but especially the last, the Christian would do well to return to the simple lessons of the Gospel and understand them, if he can, not in terms of an imminent second coming, but certainly in terms of a new and liberated creation 'in the Spirit'. Then he can be delivered from the obsessions of a culture that thrives on the stimulation and exploitation of egocentric desire.

But he will also do well, perhaps, to turn to Asian religion and acquire a more accurate understanding of its 'unworldliness'. Is the basic teaching of Buddhism — on ignorance, deliverance, and enlightenment — really life denying, or is it rather the same kind of life-affirming liberation that we find in the Good News of Redemption, the Gift of the Spirit, and the New Creation?[10]

It is my conviction that over his long years of monastic life Merton attempted to live in that spirit of Christ who was not an object in his imagination to be 'looked at' nor an idea in his head to be 'thought about' but a presence to be lived with. It is living in that presence that is Merton's mature Christian core and it is that core that Merton refers to in *The Asian Journal* when he juxtaposes fragments of the New Testament with his 'crossing over' into the world of Asian religions. They are the 'Christian mantras' that he says he uttered as his plane took off from the United States as he began his final earthly pilgrimage. Here are a few of them:

In ipso omnia constant . . . All is in Him, from Him, for Him, for the Father through Him. (p. 38)

A Christ mandala, in St Paul's 'to understand the length and the breadth, the height and the depth . . .' (p. 99)

The Risen Christ, suffering, compassion for all creatures, motives for 'helping others'. (p. 143)

I am the opening, the shewing, the revelation, the door of light, the Light itself. 'I am the Light' and the light is in the world from the beginning (It seemed like darkness.) (p. 155)

For Merton, as for all the great mystics of the church, Christ is discovered in the Void/Plenum and accompanies one in the pilgrimage to that discovery. An analogy, imperfect to be sure, might help. Ad Reinhardt, Merton's old friend from his days at Columbia University, gave Merton one of his black paintings for his hermitage. I have not seen that particular work but I have seen some other black paintings that Reinhardt did. He was a most spare and minimalist painter. A Reinhardt canvas would be painted totally black. There was no color, line, or break in the canvas to detract from the essential and textured blackness. Only by a careful and studied scrutiny of the surface of the canvas did one discover that there was yet another surface of blackness on the black ground. Slowly, out of that ground emerged another shape (a cross; a square) that gave complexity and provided complementarity to the seemingly unremitting sameness of the canvas.

That dialectic of seeing, perceiving, and deepening in the face of the Void/Plenum is not unlike the presence of Christ in the mature Merton. He looked into the Void/Plenum and found simplicity and quiet in the presence of Christ and that presence came again, almost wraith like, fully present to him and in all things. That is the Christ, I think, that he addressed in *Cables to the Ace:*

> Slowly slowly
> Comes Christ through the garden
> Speaking to the sacred trees
> Their branches bear his light
> Without harm
>
> Slowly slowly
> Comes Christ through the ruins
> Seeking the lost disciple
> A timid one
> Too literate
> To believe words
> So he hides

Slowly slowly
Christ rises on the cornfields
It is only the harvest moon
The disciple
Turns over in his sleep
And murmurs:
'My regret!'

The disciple will awaken
When he knows history
But slowly slowly
The Lord of history
Weeps into the fire.[11]

What, then, is the core of the Christian contemplative life? It comes when, to quote Merton, 'God Himself, bearing in Himself the secret of who I am, begins to live in me not only as my creator but as my other and true self.'[12] To say it another way: The authentically transformed contemplative is not one who addresses Christ as 'other' but who takes on, becomes conformed to, and is in tandem with Christ in absolute openness before God. The abolition of the false self, so much a project of Zen Buddhism, was, for Merton, the stage at which one could be free to be naked before God; when that illusory self is gone we are ready for that 'loving consent to the purely gratuitous mercy of God'.[13]

Like all things of the contemplative life, there is a paradox here: the paradox of the Christ who is absent in image and as object so as to become the Christ who shapes and molds the true self in its nakedness before God. In a powerful analysis of the conversion(s) of Thomas Merton, Walter Conn, using Merton as a paradigm of Christian conversion, outlines the steps by which a person reaches that level where, at the same time, a person is fully open to God and fully compassionate towards the world as a result of the shaping force of the life of Christ. For Conn Merton stands as a model of *Christian* conversion. He writes, in words which can stand as a final coda to this paper, that:

In Merton's life we discovered again the fundamental Gospel truth that lies at the heart of the Christian tradition: the radical religious conversion of Christian conscience finds its fullest realization in loving compassion—the self-transcending perfection of human empathy and justice.[14]

The Florida State University
Tallahassee

NOTES — Crossing Over in the Late Writings of Thomas Merton

1. David Steindl-Rast, 'Exposure: Key to Thomas Merton's *Asian Journal?'*, *Monastic Studies* 10 (1974) 181–204.
2. Martin Buber, *I and Thou*, trans. Walter Kaufmann (New York: Scribners, 1970) p. 57.
3. Elena Malits, *The Solitary Explorer: Thomas Merton's Transforming Journey* (San Francisco: Harper and Row, 1980).
4. William H. Shannon, ed. *The Hidden Ground of Love: The Letters of Thomas Merton* (New York: Farrar, Straus, and Giroux, 1985) p. 564.
5. *Ibid.*, p. 643.
6. Thomas Merton, *New Seeds of Contemplation* (New York: New Directions, 1961) p. 153. The mature thinking of Merton on this whole issue can be found in his essay, 'The Humanity of Christ in Monastic Prayer', *The Monastic Journey*, ed. Patrick Hart (Garden City: Doubleday, 1978) pp. 121–44.
7. Thomas Merton, *The Sign of Jonas* (Garden City: Doubleday Image, 1956) p. 251.
8. Naomi Burton, *et al.*, eds. *The Asian Journal of Thomas Merton* (New York: New Directions, 1973) p. 307.
9. Thomas Merton's *Zen and the Birds of Appetite* (New York: New Directions, 1968 pp. 15–32.
10. *Zen and the Birds of Appetite*, p. 31.
11. *The Collected Poems of Thomas Merton* (New York: New Directions, 1977) p. 449.
12. *New Seeds of Contemplation*, p. 41.

13. *Ibid.*
14. Walter Conn, *Christian Conversion: A Developmental Interpretation of Autonomy and Surrender* (New York/Mahwah: Paulist, 1986) p. 268.

Roger Corless

Fire on The Seven Storey Mountain
Why are Catholics Looking East?

ONCE WHEN THOMAS Merton consulted the *I Ching*
he received the hexagram *Lü* 'The Wanderer', the components of which are interpreted as 'fire' over
'mountain'. He said that he thought this represented his relationship with the rest of the community of Gethsemani Abbey:
he was a 'fire' on their 'mountain'. But he was persuaded to think
that it might refer entirely to himself. He was a pilgrim, but not
to any known goal, a wanderer at war with himself.[1]

In this essay I wish to ask the question why Catholicism is
looking outside itself for answers, specifically why Catholics are
looking to 'eastern mystical traditions' (the vagueness of the term
is intentional) as if they could gain something. Not so long ago
such a search would have been unthinkable. The pagans might
have a good idea here and there, but Catholicism had the fullness
of what the pagans dimly sought. But for some years now,
Catholicism seems to have become unsure of itself. It has become
a wanderer, a pilgrim to an unknown goal.

In asking why this could be I have found it helpful to use the life of Thomas Merton as an allegory of the Wandering Church. Anthony Padovano has already suggested that Merton's life can be seen as an allegory of the human condition, specifically of the twentieth-century American human condition,[2] but I want to use his life here a little more mythologically. During his fifty-three years, Merton passed from worldliness to monasticism to an attempt to move beyond them both. I wish to characterise his life in four stages which I suggest are also the stages of the Wandering Church: alienation, medievalism, orientalism, and an open future. The fascination of Merton's life is, I believe, due to his passing through these stages in step with the Wandering Church and being its voice to itself as each new stage was entered.

MODERNITY AS ALIENATION

It is almost a truism that the present age is the age of alienation, and it is well-known that Merton's pre-monastic life was one of dissipation, a wild searching through alcohol and sex for some feeling of connectedness.[3] What is important for an understanding of the Wandering Church is that this alienation can be seen as a fragmentation of the unified cosmos of medieval Christendom, a rending of the Seamless Robe.

Henry Adams suggests this in his interpretation of the addition of the fifteenth-century *châtelet* (fortification) to the medieval architecture of Mont-Saint-Michel. In its original structure

> The whole Mount . . . expressed the unity of Church and State, God and Man, Peace and War, Life and Death, Good and Bad; it solved the problem of the universe . . . God reconciles all. The world is an evident, obvious, sacred harmony.[4]

But the addition of the defensive châtelet by Abbot Pierre

> . . . forebodes wars of religion; dissolution of society; loss of unity; the end of the world.[5]

Joseph Hillis Miller finds that by the nineteenth-century this loss of unity is complete. In the Middle Ages

> The Eucharist was the archetype of the divine analogy whereby created things participated in the supernatural reality they signified. Poetry was . . . modelled on sacramental or scriptural language. The words of the poem incarnated the things they named, just as the words of the Mass shared in the transformation they invoked.[6]

Miller claims that

> The history of modern literature is in part the history of the splitting apart of this communion. This splitting apart has been matched by a similar dispersal of the cultural unity of man, God, nature and language.[7]

To-day, instead of feeling at one with nature, we find ourselves in an artificial, that is to say self-made, environment.

> Everywhere the world mirrors back to man his own image . . . Even the fog is not natural fog . . . but is half soot and smoke.[8]

What has died out, says Miller, is a sense of the Incarnation as a continuing event. The Reformers made of it a historical event, something which had once happened, and then ceased.[9]

Catholicism has tried to hold on to the sacramental view of life so that, as Archbishop Fulton Sheen put it, 'Christmas is not something which happened, like the Battle of Waterloo, it is something which is *always happening*.' However, it has had a problem maintaining its view against prevailing modernity. The myth of our times, that is, the story that seems true to us, is history. The Myth of History, or historicism, is essentially the Myth of Relativity.[10] This means that what I really am is a lonely, alienated, merely witnessing consciousness lost in a directionless world of endlessly hurrying matter.[11] I am alienated from myself, a schizophrenic in a schizoid world.[12]

Descartes has triumphed. The Absolute exists only if I believe in It. I am condemned to radical subjectivism wherein anything can be just as true or false as anything else.

ROMANTIC MEDIEVALISM

We could escape from this nightmare of radical subjectivism and relativism if we could convince ourselves that modernity is a temporary lapse, a collective sin of which we can repent. Perhaps the Middle Ages can be rebuilt, or at any rate preserved, against the time when the secular world will see the error of its ways.

Merton's entry into the Trappists was a move back into the Middle Ages. Gethsemani Abbey in 1941 was being run as Saint Bernard might have run it,[13] with the cautious addition of electricity and soap. The photograph of Merton's ordination in 1949 could almost have been taken in 1149, had the camera been invented then. Most telling was an experience which Merton had, just prior to his entrance into Gethesmani, of God as incarnate definitely, and in some sense exclusively, in the Mass. The hierophany closes his worldly period and ushers in his monastic period.

In 1940, in the Church of Saint Francis in Havana, during Mass,

> . . . I knew with the most absolute and unquestionable certainty that before me, between me and the altar, somewhere in the center of the chruch . . . directly before my eyes . . . was . . . God in all His essence . . .[14]

This is a very othodox, very straightforward, experience of the eucharistic Real Presence. It is thoroughly medieval. It has nothing whatever to do with modernity, alienation and the loss of symbol, with what Miller calls *The Disappearance of God.*,[15] God is real, he is incarnate, and he is incarnate here and now in this very Mass.

I can readily sympathise with Merton's Havana vision, for I had something similar myself. In 1958, in the Anglo-Catholic parish of Saint Mellitus, Hanwell, West London, I was attending

Mass out of curiosity. I was a Buddhist, or at least I called myself one, and I wondered what these Christians meant by God. I was intrigued to be visited with the inescapable feeling that, between the consecration and the putting away of the elements in the tabernacle, some powerful Life Force was concretely present. It made me, to cut a long story short, become first a High Anglican and then a Roman Catholic. I sensed that God was *present at Mass,* but was somehow *otherwise absent.* Had I sensed this as powerfully as Merton did, I might have become a monk in order to live perpetually close to God, cut off from the secular world.

This cutting off was vital to Merton at the time:

> So Brother Matthew locked the gate behind me and I was enclosed in the four walls of my new freedom.[16]

Padovano claims that Merton needed the rigid structure to enforce simplicity, reduce his drives, and thus bring freedom.[17] He calls his entry into Gethsemani a homecoming.[18]

The Gethsemani of the 'forties, however, was a kind of stage set of the Middle Ages, not the Middle Ages itself. The monastary was not the high point of culture, triumphant like Michael on his island mount, but a backwater within it. We have a sense of quaintness when we see those photographs of the old abbey church, as if we had wandered into the medieval sector of Disneyland. It is the resuscitated Gothic of Sir George Gilbert Scott (1811–78), painstakingly recreating the Way It Must Have Been. With the most modest of shoves, it topples over into the harmless idiocy of the Society for Creative Anachronism. How could anyone, especially one so intelligent as Merton, take it seriously?

I believe it is Charles Williams who gives us our answer. Williams (1886–1945) was the 'sleeper' of the Inklings, that informal club that gave us T. S. Elliot, C. S. Lewis and J. R. R. Tolkien, but whereas Eliot and Lewis tried to be ahead of their times, and Tolkien tried to be behind them, Williams assayed the difficult task of *re-creating* the Middle Ages in nineteenth-century Britain. His attempt is still too little studied, and even not very well known, but he was as literary as Eliot, as Christian as Lewis, and as mythologicaly compelling as Tolkien. His unfinished cycle of Arthurian poems, *Taliessin through Logres* and *The Region of the Summer Stars*[19] is far from a pastiche of Malory and is never in danger of reminding us of *Monty Python and the Holy Grail.* It is true re-creation.

The heart of what Williams is doing is explicating what he called co-inherence. This word, taken from incarnational theology, he used to mean the mutual enclosure of this world in the next and the next in this. This is surely the 'evident, obvious, sacred harmony' noticed by Henry Adams on Mont-Saint-Michel.[20] Williams also called co-inherence the Doctrine of Exchange, and he taught it as being the essence of the Christian message. As God and man abide each in the other in Christ, so

. . . the everlasting house the soul discovers
is always another's; we must lost our own ends;
we must always live in the habitation of our lovers,
my friend's shelter for me, mine for him.[21]

Glen Cavaliero explains Williams' method on the basis of the standard medieval theory of Biblical interpretation: the four 'senses' known as the historical (or literal), the allegorical, the tropological (or moral) and the anagogical (or eschatological) and then says

If Britain, the literal meaning, is to come to Sarras, the eschatalogical one, it can only be through acceptance of its nature as Logres, and through the dedication in personal action which is summoned up in Carbonek, the castle of the Hallows. Thus the poems' methodology itself dramatises the hierarchical mode of poetic interpretation, and re-creates it for the more personal idiom of to-day.[22]

That is (I think!) there is, in the literal sense, Britain, that is, the world as an actual location, which for Williams meant especially London, in all its everyday banality and tedium. In his poems,

Britain is called Logres and the Castle Carbonek is the earthly gate of heaven, in which confession and repentance is made, and through which Sarras, the heavenly city, is approached. The poems do not mention Britain explicitly: we are supposed to use our imaginations and intuit that Logres stands for it. However, Logres is in trouble, which means that Britain sees itself as merely Britain (the loss of symbol) and it can only come alive if it moves towards Sarras through Carbonek (towards the sacred through repentance) so that it can see itself as *always having been* Logres. Logres is the point of the co-inherence of Sarras and Britain, that is, the secular is precisely where the sacred is, if and when the incarnation is seen not only as a historical fact but also as a timeless mythological reality co-inhering in historical fact.

> The Incarnation and the Mass have as their logical end the transubstantiation, the inclusion within the Divine Humanity, of the whole creation.[23]

The words are those of Alan Watts, describing what Christian mysticism should be all about, at least, what it should be all about if Christian mysticism is to be recognisably medieval.

The trouble is, it can't be. Charles Williams is, after all, an anachronism. Sir George Scott's churches are unsuitable for the revised liturgy. Trappists no longer keep silence, pray in Latin, and wear habits inappropriate for the climate. Merton moved towards Asia and Watts decided definitely for it. I myself can no longer understand what it was I felt in the Church of Saint Mellitus.

The problem is, as J. Hillis Miller has suggested, progress. Although the Middle Ages of course changed, it was possessed of the myth that it did not, and that was the myth that the nineteenth-century recreated and into which Merton entered. But this 'iconographical, static'[24] myth is incredible to us. Whether we like it or not, we believe in progress. Progress, or at any rate, process, is 'true' for us even though, as historicism, it seems to relativise and therefore trivialise all truths. We *must* move on.

Merton moved on in 1958 as a result of another hierophany, this time not in a church but on a street corner:

> In Louisville, at the corner of Fourth and Walnut, in the center of the shopping district, I was suddenly overwhelmed with a realization that I loved all these people, that they were mine and I theirs, that we could not be alien to one another even though we were total strangers. It was like waking from a dream of separateness, of spurious self-isolation in a special world, the world of renunciation and supposed holiness.[25]

Merton now saw the containment of holiness within the Church, the ideal of monastic withdrawal from the wicked world and the 'prisoner of the tabernacle' spirituality, which had so overwhelmed him at Mass in Havana, as 'pure illusion'.[26] The Middle Ages, for Merton, were dead. The châtelet had at last been built onto the entrance of Mont-Saint-Michel and recovery of the Grand Harmony was impossible. His romance with Medievalism was at an end.

ROMANTIC ORIENTALISM

The fire now began to burn on the seven storey mountain. *Lü*, the Wanderer, began to move away from traditional Catholicism without becoming separated from it. The attempt was still to find a unity, or a utopia,[27] but now it had to be sought *beyond* the medieval ecclesial structure which, even up to the present day, is the only unity Catholicism has known.

The difficulty which is apparently felt in the classical (i.e., medieval) Christian unity is that it is not, after all, really a unity. For all the talk of co-inherence of equals with equals, it is fundamentally hierarchical. The Great Chain of Being is just the way things *are*. The lord has more *ens* than his serfs, and God, being Lord of All, has so much *ens* that he actually is *ens* Itself, the aseity who, being Being, overflows himself to create all beings, who are therefore in some sense 'not' being, 'always on the edge of the void of non-being' as Aquinas says.

The Great Chain of Being lends itself, in fact sells itself
outright, to the Sky Father *leitmotif* of God as 'a transcendental
monarch modelled on the Pharaohs and Cyruses'.[28] No matter what
the theologians tell us in their carefully worded treatises about God
being sexless and placeless, still when they get into a church and start
praying, their 'liturgies consist almost entirely of telling God what to
do and the people how to behave'.[29] It is almost as if we *have* to have
an alienated and alienating divine puppet-master for a Deity, even
though we do not want one and say we do not mean what we
evidently do say. Paul Knitter has called this 'Anonymous Dualism'
and has suggested that Merton's turn towards the east was an attempt
to remedy this theological defect.[30]

Knitter's suggestion becomes even more convincing when
we look at the sort of 'eastern mysticism' which attracted Alan
Watts, Timothy Leary, various and sundry flower children of the
Haight-Ashbury era, and Merton. It is pretty solidly monistic. Interest centers on Vedanta and various Indian and other systems
which either are, or can be interpreted as, monistic. The heritage
is a long one, by American standards. It goes back to Emerson's
brahmanic Oversoul, to Thoreau's quasi-Taoist nature musings
and to Mary Baker Eddy's panpsychic re-interpretation of Christianity. The 'Bible' of the flower children was perhaps *Be Here
Now* by Richard Alpert/Baba Ram Dass.[31] It explicitly favours
Vivekānanda, and therefore Vedānta, but recommends a
meditation practice that cannot be identified except as 'basic Indian.' Systems which had, and in some places still have,
alternative-tradition popularity are the monistically inclined
aspects of Judaism (Hasidism divorced from the Talmudic
mitzvôth), Islām (Sūfism divorced from the *sharī a*), Taoism
(concentrating on the *hsien* rather than the *fang-shih*) and even
something called Esoteric Christianity[32] which turns out to be the
underlying monism which the saints really experienced but could
not or would not proclaim openly.

When Merton 'looked east' he gathered to himself Taoism,
Hinduism and Buddhism without clearly distinguishing them.
He quotes Chuang Tzŭ, Ramakrishna and Hui-nêng as if they
might have agreed with each other. He makes Hui-nêng speak of

'ultimate mind' which is 'the "Unconscious" (*wu nien*). (This is equivalent to the Sanskrit *prajna* or Wisdom).'[33] This allows Merton to say that

> . . . the 'light which enlightens every man coming into this world' (John 1:9), seems to correspond pretty closely to the idea of *prajna* and of Hui Neng's 'Unconscious'.[34]

That is, the Logos, the Word of God, is the same as Sanskrit (Hindu or Buddhist? And which system of either?) *prajñā*, which is the same as 'The Unconscious' of 'Zen Buddhism.' This reminds me of the time when, as an undergraduate, I informed a lady at the Buddhist Society in London that the Logos and Buddhist Enlightenment were *exactly* the same. She smiled patiently and said that in Buddhism everything changes so nothing could be *exactly* the same as anything else. I was peeved.

Merton was confirmed in his confusion when he discovered that the Chinese translation of John 1:1 is 'In the beginning was the Tao' and the remark by the Chinese convert to Christianity, John C. H. Wu, that *'The Tao Incarnate* is absolutely the *Same Tao* who was from the beginning with God and is God. Before Lao Tzu was, He is'.[35]

It is clear that Dr. Wu is writing theology, not history of religions, and this gives us the clue to what is going on in so much of this 'looking east'. We so desperately want to find a new unity beyond the medieval ecclesial structure that we will read it into anything that doesn't fight back. D. T. Suzuki gently criticised Merton for reifying Buddhist Emptiness (which is an assertion about the incomprehensibility of any reification, including monism and dualism) as a kind of monism within a dualism:

> Father Merton's emptiness . . . does not go far and deep enough, I am afraid . . . Zen emptiness is not the emptiness of nothingness . . .[36]

Emptiness is not 'The Unconscious' nor is it the Logos. And yet, Dr Suzuki then goes on to say

. . . but [Zen emptiness is] the emptiness of fullness . . .
in which this equation takes place: zero = infinity.[37]

With all due respect to the late Dr Suzuki, I am bound to say, as a
Buddhologist, that this definition of Emptiness is not a definition at all, it is nonsense. And, unfortunately, it is the kind of
nonsense that eager seekers-after-unity can misinterpret as 'All Is
One And One Is All', that is, as some species of monism.
Logical and philosophical rigour has never been much
favoured in Japan. Arguments are found persuasive if they are
aesthetically pleasing or if they contribute to social cohesion and
harmony.[38] Dr Suzuki was at his best when he was discussing art
or promoting cordial relations between Christians and Buddhists. If we want a *logical* demonstration of Emptiness, we must
go elsewhere, preferably to the Gelugpa lineage of Tibetan
Buddhism, which specialises in logic and debate. Therein we
find that Emptiness is taught as neither a thing, a no-thing, both
or neither, but as the lack of inherent thing-ness (or quiddity, in
medieval terms) in any thing or no-thing. So then, the question
of how Emptiness relates to the Tao or the Logos or the Brahman
cannot even begin to be raised.[39]

When Merton and others 'look east' and see only monism, par-
ticularly when they confuse Buddhist Emptiness with Upanishadic
Brahman, they are saying more about their problem of Anonymous
Dualism than they are about any answer they are finding in 'the east.'
They are trying to do theology, but they are not doing it well, for they
are not controlling their sources in a respectable manner.

Towards the end of his life Merton began to realise this —
significantly, as he came into contact with Tibetan Buddhists —
and his romance with Orientalism ended with another
hierophany, this time at the Buddhist site of Polonnaruwa, Sri
Lanka. Standing before the gigantic rock-hewn figures of Buddha Sākyamuni and his disciple Venerable Ānanda in 1968 he
had a moment of clarity when *the questioning dropped away.*

The thing about all this is that there is no puzzle, no problem, and really no 'mystery'.[40]

In his description of his experience, the word 'clarity' occurs three times and 'clear' twice. This experience of *citta-prabhāsa*, 'shining mind', which in some Buddhist schools is taught as Emptiness and in others as a close approximation to Emptiness, seems to be the closest Merton ever came to understanding Emptiness. Emptiness is not an answer, not a 'no' or a 'nothing', it is how *reality appears* when *questions disappear*, and the principal question which disappears when Emptiness appears is the vexing old western conundrum of choosing between absolute objectivity and absolute subjectivity.

NO RELIANCE ON STRUCTURES

On December 10, 1968, in Bangkok, Merton gave us what was to become his last will and testament in his speech 'Marxism and Monastic Perspectives'. He spoke as a Wanderer with the clarity of the Polonnaruwa hierophany still shining in him. He told us what he thought Buddhism and Christianity are all about — no reliance on structures.

. . . we can no longer rely on being supported by structures . . . You cannot rely on structures. The time for relying on structures has disappeared.[41]

This is certainly the voice of modernity. The Communist Manifesto says

All that is solid melts into air, all that is holy is profaned, and man is at last compelled to face with sober senses, his real conditions of life, and his relations with his kind.[42]

The châtelet in front of the original entrance to Mont-Saint-Michel is now itself a museum piece. Modernity demands that we stand on the corner of Fourth and Walnut and feel the holiness of our communion with our fellow humans in the secular city. Compassion is primary. God is in our neighbour.

. . . His name . . . is like a pure diamond, blazing with the invisible light of heaven. It is in everybody . . .[43]

But how do we see this? If we cannot retreat into a medieval fantasy nor mellow out in an oriental fantasy, are we left with diabolical materialism, pie in the sweet by and by? 'Jam tomorrow, jam yesterday, but never jam *to-day*'? In 1958, Merton said, 'I have no program for this seeing.'[44] Does he, in his last address, begin to point us towards one?

In a long and difficult cycle of poems, sent to the publisher just before his death as a work in progress and given the mysterious title *The Geography of Lograire* he throws together in strange, Micawberesque strophes, sacred and secular images:

The sacred books are confiscated by police to keep eyes under sightless dome. Study famous text in court. Sacred words kept shut in horny room . . . Fulltime work for Monsignori canonizing randy films. Keep sacred religious motions private . . . Sacred ideas confiscated by eminent machine . . . Sacred books confined to ecclesiastical pen . . . Lost his glasses reading books in sacred buildings. Never found again . . .[45]

He seems to be saying that mysticism and pornography are alike banned by authorities who themselves delight in them, and that there is some connection here. What the connection is is not stated, although the strophes occur in a section called 'Queens Tunnel', which suggests a continual process of exchange.

Exchange is the principle of Incarnation. Both Charles Williams and Karl Marx (no doubt to their mutual surprise) lament that Exchange is now debased to its medium:

Money is the medium of exchange . . .
When the means are autonomous, they are deadly; . . .[46]

The bourgeoisie . . . has put an end to all . . .idyllic relations . . . and has left remaining no other nexus between man and man than . . . callous 'cash payment.'[47]

We cannot reverse our economic system. The Marxian economic arrow is temporally asymmetric, but perhaps we can 'go beyond the thesis and the antithesis, this and that, black and white, East and West. We accept the division, we work with the division, and we go beyond the division'.[48]

Merton had wished to do this for divided Christendom:

If I can unite *in myself* the thought and devotion of Eastern and Western Christendom . . . I can prepare in myself the reunion of divided Christians . . . We must contain all divided worlds in ourselves and transcend them in Christ.[49]

In medieval Christianity, divided worlds were resolved by being put securely in the grand divine-human harmony of the Chain of Being. In Monism, divided worlds are merged into a single triumphant sameness. As Ram Dass' Hindu guru said, when Christ meditated, 'He lost himself in the ocean of Love'.[50] In Marxism, divided worlds breed their own destruction and self transcendence. All of these unities are in one way or another the victory of something over something else. In all of them variety is lost or minimised. But the world now seems to us, biologically, socially and ideologically, to be deeply, and possibly irreducibly, pluralistic.[51] We call this relativism, but that is a back-door way of minimising the pluralism. Suppose there were to exist a plurality of *Absolutes?*

Buddhism and Christianity say that such is the case. Co-inherence is a true plurality: the divinity wholly in the humanity and the humanity wholly in the divinity, not hierarchically nor monistically nor by a Hegelian-Marxist synthesis. Emptiness is likewise a true plurality: saṃsāra is wholly in nirvana and nirvana is wholly in saṃsāra, not hierarchically, monistically nor synthetically.

Catholics are looking east, I submit, in order to understand Emptiness. Having understood it, they will be able to understand Co-Inherence, or the Incarnation as a cosmic spirituality, a *sacramentum mundi* in a true *coincidentia oppositorum*, without the dubious aid of the hierarchical four senses of Scripture. In this context, there is neither cloister nor world without also a world-in-the-cloister and a cloister-in-the-world.

The monk belongs to the world, but the world belongs to him insofar as he has dedicated himself totally to liberation from it in order to liberate it.[52]

Which is also to say, the layperson in the world and the monk or nun in the cloister each belongs to and exists in the other insofar as each is dedicated to liberation from the world in order to liberate it.

The locus of this co-inherence is the human person, the individual mind or soul. A new unity which genuinely respects our recently perceived pluralities can be sought by means of a spirituality of containing all divided worlds in ourselves and allowing them to co-inhere as the divinity and the humanity co-inhere in Christ and as our liberation from the world (nirvana) co-inheres with our activity to liberate the world (the bodhisattvic return to samsara). I am experimenting with this spirituality myself as I try to be faithful both to Catholic Christianity and Gelugpa Buddhism. This spirituality of co-inherence of cleric and lay, liberated and liberator, is also, I believe, what Liberation Theology is all about, and it is therefore no accident that one of Merton's novices should have been Ernesto Cardenal.

Duke University
Durham, North Carolina

NOTES — Fire on The Seven Storey Mountain

1. This is my recollection of the incident as reported to me by Father John Eudes Bamberger while he was on retreat at the Monastery of the Holy Mother of God, Oxford, North Carolina, just prior to taking up his post as Abbot of Our Lady of the Genesee. My apologies to Dom John Eudes if my recollection is in any way faulty.

2. Anthony E. Padovano, *The Human Journey. Thomas Merton: Symbol of a Century* (Garden City, NY: Doubleday, 1982).

3. The standard biography would appear now to be *The Seven Mountains of Thomas Merton* by Michael Mott (Boston: Houghton Mifflin, 1984). Mott treats Merton's life as a symbolic pilgrimage, seeing it as a progress across seven mountains, from Canigou to Kanchenjunga.

4. Henry Adams, *Mont-Saint-Michel and Chartres* (Princeton: University Press, Paperback edition, 1981) p. 44f.

5. *Ibid.*, p.45.

6. J. Hillis Miller, *The Disappearance of God. Five Nineteenth-Century Writers* (Cambridge MA: Belknap Press/Harvard, 1975) p. 3.

7. idem.

8. *Ibid.*, p.5.

9. *Ibid.*, p. 6.

10. *Ibid.*, p. 9.

11. The images are drawn from Soren Kierkegaard and Alfred North Whitehead.

12. R. D. Laing's model of the Divided Self shows a striking structural similarity to Descartes' model of reality. Morris Berman, *The Reenchantment of the World* (Bantam Books, 1984), figures 2 and 3 with appropriate accompanying text.

13. More precisely, it was being run in the way Abbot de Rancé thought Saint Bernard should have run it. Mott, p. 209.

14. Quoted in Mott, p. 151.

15. See note 6 above.

16. *The Seven Storey Mountain* (New York: Harcourt, Brace and World, 1948) p. 372.

17. Padovano, p. 86.

18. *Ibid.,* p. 22.

19. Published with a commentary by C. S. Lewis and an introduction by Mary McDermott Shideler (Grand Rapids MI: Eerdmans, 1974).

20. See note 4.

21. 'Bors to Elayne: On the King's Coins,' *Taliessin through Logres*, p. 62f.

22. Glen Cavaliero, *Charles Williams: Poet of Theology* (Grand Rapids MI: Eerdmans, 1983) p. 172.

23. Alan Watts, *Behold the Spirit: A Study in the Necessity of Mystical Religion* (New York: Vintage Books, new edition, 1971) p. 113.

24. Cavaliero, p. 169.

25. *Conjectures of a Guilty Bystander,* (Garden City, NY: Doubleday, 1968) p. 156.

26. *Ibid.,* p. 157.

27. The suggestive word is offered by Alexander Lipski in *Thomas Merton and Asia: His Quest for Utopia* (Cistercian Publications, 1983).

28. Watts, p. xiii.

29. *Ibid.,* p. xii.

30. Paul F. Knitter, 'Thomas Merton's Eastern Remedy for Christianity's "Anonymous Dualism,"' *Cross Currents* 31:3 (1981) 285–295.

31. It is really a good joke to footnote this anti-academic item (sometimes it came out as a book and sometimes as a box of leaves) in an academic paper. Goodness knows who might have published various versions. The one I have is in book format and is labelled 'Lama Foundation, 1971, Year of the Earth Monkey, Box 444, San Cristobal, New Mexico'.

32. Jacob Needleman has kindly recovered this for us in *Lost Christianity: A Journy to the Center of the Christian Experience* (New York: Doubleday, 1980). The theosophist (or rather, Fourth Way Movement) presuppositions of Needleman's book are not explicated and it is helpful to read it in the light of Annie Besant's openly Theosophical *Esoteric Christianity,* published in 1902.

33. *Mystics and Zen Masters* (New York: Farrar, Straus and Giroux, 1967) p. 24. Parentheses original.

34. *Ibid.,* p. 25.

35. Quoted in Lipski, p. 11. Italics original.

36. *Zen and the Birds of Appetite* (New York: New Directions, 1968) p. 133f.

37. *Ibid.,* p. 134.

38. This point is made more politely, and with logical and philosophical rigour, by the eminent Japanese Buddhologist Hajime Nakamura in his *Ways of Thinking of Eastern Peoples* (University of Hawaii Press, 1964), chapter 36.

39. The most extensive treatment of Emptiness from the Gelugpa standpoint is *Meditation on Emptiness* by Jeffrey Hopkins (London: Wisdom, 1983). Its length, 1017 pages, indicates the inadequacy of catchy little definitions of Emptiness.

40. *The Asian Journal of Thomas Merton* (New York: New Directions, 1973) p. 235.

41. *Ibid.,* p. 338.

42. *The Marx-Engels Reader,* edited by Robert C. Tucker (New York: Norton, 2nd. ed., 1978) p. 476.

43. *Conjectures of a Guilty Bystander,* p. 158.

44. *Idem.*

45. *The Geography of Lograire* (New York: New Directions, 1968) p. 49f.

46. 'On the King's Coins,' *Taliessin through Loogres,* p. 62.

47. *Marx-Engels Reader,* cit. p. 475.

48. *Asian Journal,* p. 340f.

49. *Conjectures of a Guilty Bystander,* p. 21. Italics original.

50. Correspondence of Ram Dass to the author, December 1971.

51. The world may also be irreducibly plural even at the *physical* level. This is the position of the Copenhagen School, who follow Niels Bohr in maintaining that although physics may have a single nature at the macroscopic level, at the microscopic level events possess a dual nature of irreducible 'complementaries.' Einstein and his school reply that with more data we will be able to solve such puzzles and show the single nature of microscopic events. The advantage has recently passed into the Copenhagen court with the demonstration that some *macroscopic* events are quantised, that is, are not 'either-or'; D. E. Thomsen, 'Quanta at Large: 101 Things to do with Schrödinger's Cat.' *Science News* 129:6 (February 8, 1986) pp 87, 90.

52. *Asian Journal,* p. 341.

Joachim Viens

Thomas Merton's Final Journey Outline for a Contemporary Adult Spirituality

W HEN I BEGAN a series of talks on 'Spirituality and Process' recently, I could think of no better illustration of my themes than the life journey of Thomas Merton. Twenty years after his death in Bangkok, there are Thomas Merton Centers and Thomas Merton students everywhere; he lives in the minds and hearts of many of us. Why? Merton is intriguing because he successfully negotiated the spiritual journey which characterizes our age. That is the theme of these reflections. Anthony Padovano spelled it out in *The Human Journey: Thomas Merton Symbol of a Century:*

> Thomas Merton summed up an era. If one wishes to know where the Western World was in the second half of the Twentieth Century, Thomas Merton offers considerable enlightenment. He showed us our spiritual potential in the midst of our secular endeavors. He made holiness equivalent with a life that seeks to be whole, honest and

222

free. He taught us that it was possible to be truly religious without being formally religious. He proved that contemplation could occur in the throes of restlessness and that it was permissible to be fully human.[1]

On an even deeper level, we could say that Merton is intriguing because he expresses dramatically something that wants to live in all of us. Raimundo Panikkar has called it the monastic archetype. I do not mean archetype in the sense that a person like Merton expresses some ideal form more perfectly than the rest of us, but archetype in the sense that Merton expresses in his own way something that wants to live in each of us. 'Monkhood represents the search for the center. Inasmuch as we try to unify our lives around the center, all of us have something of the monk in us.'[2]

The following reflections are a dialogue on the meaning of Merton between Sister Luke Tobin, S.L. and Padovano's *The Human Journey* and myself. Sister Luke Tobin was a friend of Merton's whose name occurs frequently in the official biography. A couple of years ago, Sister Luke presented a film of Merton's last talk and commented on it. Whereas Merton's life had been a dark mystery to me, that last talk somehow made his death seem less tragic. Sister Luke asked me to speak in a local series, 'Thomas Merton As We Knew Him'. Since then, I have tried to rethink the real nature of my own relationship to Merton. Hence, the rather personal nature of these reflections. What follows is narrative theology. There will be no further apologies for the use of the first person!

In a first stage of reflection on Merton, I jogged my memory and filled in the details by reading Monica Furlong's *Thomas Merton: A Biography*,[3] Anthony Padovano's, *The Human Journey*, and the authorized Merton biography, Michael Mott's *The Seven Mountains of Thomas Merton*.[4] Reviewing Merton's life in such detail was a reliving of my own life in the fifties and sixties. At first this was quite painful. I knew so many of the actors personally as friends and I suffered through many of the struggles that Thomas Merton suffered through. During the past year, with the themes of this present paper in mind, I have been working through Merton's literary corpus directly. The work has confirmed and enriched the beginning intuitions.

My present view of spirituality parallels what Merton articulated in the sixties. I consider Merton prophetic because he lived a process spirituality before many others were able to speak about it. In this essay then, I wish to share my own struggle to understand Merton, the parallels in my own life and the kind of spirituality which has emerged in the process. I believe with Padovano that, 'Merton's life is a preface to our own'.[5]

I have chosen to express the stages of my own struggle with Merton by two words which may need some explanation: koan and parable. *Koan* is a Zen term for a mind-breaking riddle or question that a spiritual master gives to the disciple. It is a paradox designed to stop analytical thinking in its tracks. *Parable* is a similar Christian term. Parable is a story and it, too, is designed to put a crack in one's world view, but it is less esoteric and more easily available than a koan. My reflections on Merton have gone from koan to parable to koan.

1. KOAN: MERTON AS I KNEW HIM

When I knew Merton in my younger days, I did not know him; his life was a koan to me.

Thomas Merton is a truly modern man. He was born in 1915 in the south of France of a New Zealand artist father and an American mother who was very well read, well traveled, especially in Europe, and who loved to paint and write. Merton's mother, Ruth, died when he was six. He attended an English school and was separated from his only brother, John Paul. John Paul was killed in a bombing raid over Germany in 1943. Merton was also mostly separated from his father who died when Merton was sixteen. His godfather became his guardian. Merton studied at Cambridge, but apparently, when a young woman became pregnant by him her family was paid off and Merton was encouraged by his guardian to return to the United States.[6] He studied

English at Columbia writing his M.A. thesis on Blake, went on to teach at St Bonaventure's College in Olean, New York and then joined the Trappists in 1941.

The monk became the famour writer with a long succession of books, *The Seven Storey Mountain, Seeds of Contemplation, The Sign of Jonas, Conjectures of a Guilty Bystander,* and many more. Padovano lists Merton's writings under sixteen categories. Merton was restless and in continual search for the ideal monastic life. His writing became literary and cultural critique. He was a major force in the movement to accept hermits in the Trappist Order. After twenty-six years he was allowed to travel, but was electrocuted on his first major trip, December 10, 1968. The parallel to the Master of the Last Bead Game in Hermann Hesse's novel is eerie. *The Magister Ludi* is the story of a man who takes a lifetime to evolve out of a kind of monastic life. On his first weekend in the mountains where Joseph Knect is to be tutor, he plunges into the lake at dawn and dies! A koan surely. In *Magister Ludi,* however, there are a series of other incarnations where Knect fills out neglected aspects of his personality. Merton, I believe, was allowed these integrations in the one lifetime we know about. There are some 1800 folders of letters in the correspondence section of the Thomas Merton Studies Center, some containing as many as two hundred letters (well over 3,500 letters to a thousand correspondents).[7] Before Merton died his list of correspondents read like a Who's Who of the sixties; Boris Pasternack, Joan Baez, Abraham Heschel, Daniel Berrigan, to name only some obvious ones.

If these personal reflections are to make sense, I must refer at least briefly to the parallels in my own life. As a young man I had read all I could find on monks and monasticism, including the books emanating from the Abbey of Gethsemani in Kentucky, Merton's monastery. In 1950 I joined the Trappists at Spencer, Massachusetts, was ordained in 1956, studied theology in Rome, and spent the remainder of my twenty-two years in the Order between teaching theology and filling the office of religious superior at Snowmass, Colorado.

During my years at Snowmass I had many occasions to travel and I met Thomas Merton on various visits to Gethsemani. I was struck by his cordial manner and sophisticated intelligence. Merton showed me his hermitage and its many cherished mementos. I recall walking in the woods and talking about Saint Anselm and the origins of Scholastic Theology.

I had asked Merton to write a postulants' guide for our monastery in Snowmass. In the course of our correspondence, Dom James Fox, Merton's superior, read Merton's letters, and even sent me a letter of cautious commentary. This little incident, taken as normal at the time, is indicative of the structures which caused the alienation Merton spoke of in his last lecture.

In the early seventies, I left the Trappist Order. I felt that alienation described by Merton on the day he died as, 'the end result of a life lived according to conditions someone else determines'.[8]

The paradox of those years was that I did not know Merton when I knew him, when I had the opportunity to write to him and speak with him. There were many reasons for this. To begin with, Gethsemani in the forties and early fifties, especially to an outsider, seemed to portray what the old latin called a 'rude' or peasant's life. There was an extreme asceticism, described in the books of Father Raymond and in Merton's own *The Waters of Siloe* and *The Sign of Jonas,* for example. Some Trappists of that time gloried in being peasants. They slept in their day clothes, they did not take showers very often, the monastery was not adequately heated, the soup was an accumulation of leftovers. By contrast, the monastery I entered in 1950 in Spencer, Massachusetts was humanistic, under the leadership of Dom Edmund Futterer, with a penchant for architecture, liturgy and gregorian chant, and theology, my own first love. The abbot of Spencer brought in Dominican priests to teach theology, Benedictine monks from France to teach gregorian chant, and architects to build the beautiful stone monastery which graces Spencer's hills today. In 1950, Merton and I were living in very different Trappist worlds.

Another point of contrast. Padovano suggests that Merton was not an encyclopedist but an essayist. He was not setting out to synthesize; rather, he would eventually produce brilliant essays. On the other hand, my Dominican professors were teaching me to synthesize and to fit everything into cathedral-like intellectual pyramids.

Finally, it must be said that, in many ways, the early writings of Merton reinforce the stereotype of the triumphalist, chauvinistic convert. This is especially true of *The Seven Storey Mountain,* where Merton consistently identifies grace and salvation with the Catholic Church, and 'the world' and 'the merely natural' and sin with all that is not the Catholic Church. Merton is equally chauvinistic in speaking of monasticism. In this case, his words are a naive idealization of the monastery as The Promised Land and the world as the biblical 'land of garlic and onions'.[9] The same pure mythology enshrines his references to priesthood and ordination in *The Sign of Jonas.* For example, 'Everybody in the Universe is tongue-tied, except the priest, who is able to speak for them all'.[10] For all these reasons, it is now clear to me why I stopped reading Merton shortly after I myself joined the monastery in 1950.

Nonetheless, because of the life we had chosen, there were significant parallels in our lives which I am only now coming to recognize and appreciate. Merton became whole through writing. I have become whole through study and teaching. These other vocations, in each case deeper than the monastic vocation, —Merton chose monasticism, he *was* a writer,[11]—were not always appreciated by 'the powers'! In addition, we both owed to monastic life our opportunity to search out and experience the great Catholic Christian religious tradition and the opportunity to live a rich contemplative life of silence and liturgy.

To return to Merton. From the perspective of the brute facts, the mere facts, which you can find in Furlong and Mott, Merton's life may look sad, restless, misunderstood, filled with psychosomatic illnesses and the absence of human love. You might feel that you understand why an Abbot felt constrained to sit on Merton because he had all these wild ideas and plans. Merton was kept under wraps by this Abbot, never allowed to accept speaking engagements that involved serious travel. At last, a new Abbot came along, after twenty-six years, and allowed Merton to travel. He made a couple of short trips in the U.S. and then a major trip to Asia, where he gave an important talk. He was recognized, finally, as an international figure, he was coming into his own, had all sorts of plans. On this first major trip, after giving the talk, he went back to his cottage, took a shower, stepped out of the shower and somehow or other grabbed a floor fan, and was electrocuted. That is a koan! It had been a hard year for Merton, several of his close friends had died. It was also my nemesis; my year in rainy Belgium. Karl Barth died, Martin Luther King and Robert F. Kennedy were assassinated. It seemed to me, with all these deaths, that the world was coming to an end.

II. FROM KOAN TO PARABLE: THOMAS MERTON AS I KNOW HIM

Thomas Merton is a story told by God to shake us out of our complacency.

The more pertinent question is how do I now know Thomas Merton? When I viewed the film clip of Merton's last talk the koan moved a little toward parable. This process continued as I worked through Furlong, Mott and Padovano. Each of these biographies is worth reading but they operate on two levels. Parable, as extended metaphor, is a story to be understood on two levels. Furlong and Mott give you all of the brute facts but not so much understanding. Mott mentions the death of Merton's father in a sentence or two and then moves on without comment. In contrast, Padovano's, *The Human Journey*, gets to the heart of the meaning. As I perceive these deeper meanings they resonate in my soul, and that is what I now wish to share with you; four themes from the life of Thomas Merton, themes for a contemporary spirituality.

Meditation as Mediation

The first theme I would like to identify is 'Meditation as Mediation'. It is an example of Merton's ability to work out for *chose? where is call?*

himself ideas which have later been systematized and refined. I noted earlier that Merton *chose* monasticism but that he *was* a writer. He struggled all his life with the conflict between chosen vocation and his inner essence as writer. I experienced a similar dilemma in my struggle with monasticism and theology. Merton was a compulsive writer. We can reconstruct almost every day of his life from his journals and letters. I find it intriguing that it was especially in his journals, that Merton worked out this conflict between his monastic vocation and his desire, his need to be a writer. Padovano notes,

> *The Secular Journal* settles for him the question about whether he should enter the monastery. *The Sign of Jonas* resolves the problem about the compatibility of a career as a writer and his Trappist vocation. *Conjectures of a Guilty Bystander* moves him into the radical social commitments of the last decade of his life. In the *Asian Journal,* he becomes convinced that oriental religion and culture are not only genuine in themselves, but indispensable to Christianity and the West.[12]

In the past several years I have studied, practiced and taught Ira Progoff's *Intensive Journal Method.* In his writing, Ira Progoff elaborates a notion of 'meditation as mediation'. which throws light on Merton's story.

In the first part of our life, our psychic energy flows outward in the construction of our social role or persona. The more rigid the society, the stronger the mask — till we get so far out of touch with our true self that a neurosis may develop which stops the outward flow of energy. Our psychic energy then seems to be damned up, it returns to us and often we find a reintegration more in tune with our deepest selves.

The successful fine artist is the model of the ability to preclude the crisis I have spoken of by learning to go back and forth between the inner life and the outer life.[13] The fine artist starts out with an inner vision and works at incarnating that vision externally. When such artists come up against a block, they know how to go back to the sources of their inspiration to get started again. A successful life is like this, it demands an ability to go back and forth between the outer world of work and the inner world of inspiration. That is precisely what meditation should do for us, mediate between work and inspiration. If there should be a divorce between our inner self and our external life, we will not produce fruit. Now the monastic theory of the fifties and sixties didn't allow for this moving back and forth. The monastic theory did speak of incarnation; the liturgy, the asceticism, the rule were all incarnations or sacramentalizations of what was thought to be the essence of Christianity. But one's personal work life, one's own personal projects were not valued. The Trappist life as imposed on us in the fifties and sixties in America, was an attempt to live only one side of that inner-outer cycle.

This is the significance of Merton's great struggle with the conflict between monastic vocation and writer's vocation. Meditation as mediation, as practiced in his journals allowed him to break through this dilemma. But at times it must have seemed to Merton that he had to break through that rigidity violently, all by himself. For example, Merton's exasperation is evidenced in a letter to June Yungblut, Jan. 2, 1968.

> About the other letter: of course we are available any time to any one wanting to make a retreat, and if Dr. King prefers to come before the march, well and good, fine with us. The only thing was that from the long term viewpoint, since the new Abbot opened our first official conversation in his new capacity by saying he wanted me to stick to my bloody mysticism and not get involved in all them outward works, it might be well to go a little bit slow on anything that might signify a tie in with some onslaughts on the bastions of squaredom. He is essentially open, just inexperienced and still a little closed in on set positions, but I think he can learn, given time. To have Dr. King, Vincent Harding and others later in the year for a quiet, informal, deeply reflective session would probably get the Abbot to see where I really do belong, half way between in and out of action. Not just all the way out.[14]

Because of the importance I attach to this need for a method of integration, I now devote part of my professional life to teaching the art of journaling and meditation as mediation.

Life as Process

The second theme I wish to explore is life as process; I mean that life is developmental and that it goes through stages. A few summers ago I spent a week at the Trappist monastery in Snowmass with my former colleagues and spent the time reviewing the major religious experiences — in terms of the Intensive Journal, the moments of connection — in my life. The major experience which seems to overshadow and shape all the others was the transition from a static world view to a processive one. The symbol of that transition remains a day spent driving through the mountains to Colorado's Western Slope, to St Benedict's Abbey in fact, listening to a lecture on the world view of Teilhard de Chardin. My whole world, paradigm, was ready for this, and like a *gestalt* shift, my life moved!

Let me characterize this process view of life. In a static world view one assumes that things have always been as they are now and the burden of proof is on the one who would challenge that understanding. This is delightfully exemplified by the remark made when the New English Bible came out, 'If the King James Version was good enough for Our Lord, it should be good enough for us'! In a processive world view, on the other hand, the omnipresence of change is acknowledged and the burden of proof is on the person who would challenge it. In a static world view history is seen as archetype and we are always longing for the good old days. In a processive view, history is viewed as prototype, a rough draft of our task.[15] In a static world precedent is law, whereas in a processive world view, the imagined future and its demands become the norm. In addition to memory we need imagination.

Here too, Merton seems to have found out about process for himself before it was really fashionable. My first recollection of a process view involves Merton at Gethsemani. He was speaking to a gathering of abbots and novice masters and noted that the constitutions of the order assumed that the novice and the twenty-year veteran were in the same place. Given the fact of slow gradual growth and maturity, this state of affairs placed great stress on both novice and veteran. In this talk, Merton was making a plea for new rules and constitutions which would recognize the processive nature of monastic life. As for Merton himself, in the middle sixties, he set out to bury any number of old Thomas Mertons.

> As you say, I represent my own life, but not as I ought to. I have still too much reflected the kind of person others have assumed I ought to be. I am reaching a happy and dangerous stage, when I want to smash that image above all. But that is not the kind of thing that is likely to be viewed with favor by the superiors. Nor do I have any idea of what way the road will take.[16]

Merton was a process person who had to work his way through a static world view to his own process spirituality. Padovano shows how the 'return journeys' to New York, to Japan (metaphorically in his writings), show the enormous change in his life. Compare, for example, *Exile Ends In Glory* with *Zen and the Birds of Appetite*. Enormous change, yet he remained deeply faithful to the originating religious experiences and conversion.[17] Padovano paraphrases *Seeds of Contemplation*, 'To be holy is a question of appreciating where one is in life and learning to foster the vital connections that are already operative.'[18] Here again, Merton has almost described what later became a popular method of spirituality – an extension of the Intensive Journal called 'Process Meditation'. But twenty years in advance!

People who have learned of identity, fidelity, commitment and discernment in terms shaped by a static philosophy are ill-equipped to live in a world of change. Because of the value I place on this process view of spirituality, it too has become a focus of my professional life. I teach Progoff's 'Process Meditation' and am particularly interested in restating the Christian symbols in a language available to persons who absorb the process worldview by osmosis if not by formal training. An adequately articulated process spirituality will be an asset to people who are trying to be faithful in an ever changing world. Padovano's thesis rings true over and over: Merton is intriguing because he successfully negotiated the journey which characterizes our age.[19]

Where is God's Word?

I would like to discuss two other themes in Merton's life which symbolize our age and outline a contemporary spirituality. The themes concern the opening of the Church to the world, what has been called a Copernican revolution in our self-understanding as Church. The Church's center of consciousness has shifted outward toward the world. This has involved a similar shift in where we are to look for God's word.

Reflect for a moment on seeing one's life and world as a parable told by God. When we see our life and our world as a parable told by God — revelation in its most fundamental sense happens. If we can say yes to that revelation, then faith in its most fundamental sense happens.[20] Merton seems to have reached this point in his last lecture. He exudes a peace, even on videotape, which turned his life for me from koan to parable. This was the peace-giving insight which came to me as I viewed his last talk.

Let me expand that last statement. From experiences in his own life he came to a deeper knowledge of God and the world. He began to find God's Word beyond the Scriptures and the Fathers of the Church. 'Merton's answer to a disappointing experience in prayer is more expansive human experience rather than greater effort or new technique.'[21] Such a spirituality was, of course, the result of an evolution in Merton's consciousness. In *The Sign of Jonas* Merton tells us how excited he was to wear the priestly vestments in his early days. But he had a seemingly mystical experience downtown one day which changed him profoundly. In Louisville, on the corner of Fourth and Walnut, Merton realizes to

his joy that he is a man, only a man. From then on he seems to take
pride in not wearing the habit more than necessary.[22] In this too he
is a symbol of our age. He realizes that to be merely a man is God's
gift to him. Merton accepts his own life as God's gift and revelation.

The point I am making is exemplified dramatically in Merton's final work and poem, *The Geography of Lograire*. In this
exceedingly rich work, Merton contemplates his own life and the
world—South, North, East and West. The work combines a
global meditation with all of the personal and spiritual themes in
Merton's life and reading. Merton reflects on his total life experience, on the Third World, on East and West, on racial tensions and cultural conflicts. The work shows the enormous
breadth of Merton's interests and insights. In this last great work,
which is not even a final draft, Merton gathers together
everything he had read and experienced.[23]

During this last period in his life Merton struggled to experience all that he could. He was restless. Here especially, one
must see the two levels of his life as metaphor or one might be
scandalized by this monk. He became a hermit, but as he became
a hermit he became much more active in reaching out. He needed
people in his life. He enjoyed going into Bardstown to meet people. He needed music. He read voraciously; he was making all
kinds of plans to travel, and finally, he fell in love with a nurse he
met in the hospital. But the paradox in all this, as I have already
noted, is that his prayer life deepened according to the authorized
biographer[24] and that Merton's answer to problems in prayer was
more expansive human experience.[25] Not everyone will believe the
biographers on this point; I happen to believe them.

Where is God's Word? By the time of his death, the traditional doctrines and the Bible are still there, but they are now but
the keys to God's word everywhere calling out to us. God's word
is embedded is one's life and world. This is a shift that may look
like secularization, in fact, it is the final maturing of faith in God
the Creator of all. The final great poem, *The Geography of
Lograire,* is an attempt to synthesize and meditate on the meaning of all of his life and experience. How fitting that this should
be the project he accomplishes as he dies.

What is God's Word?

Our last theme concerns the meaning of God's Word, and this too has undergone considerable change in the twentieth century. Raymond E. Brown remarked once that many Christians do not really know what the Bible is about, and when some of them find out they may not like it!

Merton, like several other great people of our age, notably Dietrich Bonhoeffer and Abraham Heschel, underwent a journey from a life totally dedicated to biblical contemplation to a life of social activism. Why? Because of what he and they found when they read the Bible. Heschel's understanding of the Jewish prophetic tradition explains how such a journey comes about.

For Heschel, the prophet is a person who resonates with God — and what the prophet senses about God is His Pathos — his vulnerability, his passionate concern for the world which is His creation, His artwork. The prophet is convulsed by this sense of God's care, and it causes the prophet to cry out in the night.

Like a scream in the night is the prophet's word. The world is at ease and asleep, while the prophet is hit by a blast from heaven. No one seems to hear the distress in the world; no one seems to care when the poor is suppressed. But God is distressed, and *the prophet has pity for God who cares for the distressed*. . . . Prophetic sympathy is no delight; unlike ecstasy it is not a goal but a sense of challenge and a commitment.[26]

From this point of view the closer one comes to God, the more passionate one becomes for the world. This is a paradox, but it explains Merton's growing preoccupation with social issues, and his expanding geography. Tertullian said, 'Nothing is more foreign to us than the State, for there is only one State we recognize and that is the world'. Merton grew impatient with institutions, such as his country and his church and his monastic order because he had grown beyond parochial and nationalistic concerns. What the Bible is about, the meaning of God's Word,

finally, is this: God's desire for the world is that it be a global
community of peace and justice. This very desire is the animating
force of *The Geography of Lograire*. This global consciousness is
also evident throughout *The Asian Journal* and all of Merton's
later writings.

As I reflect on these themes from the life of Merton—Meditation as Mediation, Life as Process, God's Word Embedded in
Our Own Lives and Worlds and the Call of God to Global Community—I find an outline for a contemporary adult spirituality.
Merton is a parable of the human journey. He is a story told by
God to shake us out of our complacency. His life says, 'To be holy
is a question of appreciating where one is in life and learning to
foster the vital connections that are already operative'.[27] And yet,
there is one final koan as I contemplate the life of Thomas Merton.

FINAL KOAN: AM I NOT A MAN?

Dom Jean Leclerq, who himself is a monastic figure much
like Merton, summed up Merton's life by saying, 'Merton's
humanism explains why his message . . . found so great an audience'.[28] Merton would have loved the comment. I believe this
to be the final koan: *the ascetic is ultimately the humanist.* For
many people, I am thinking, for example, of Francis Schaeffer
the evangelical writer, Christian spirituality and humanism are
antithetical. But here we have Merton who joined this most
'rude' of monasteries, and lived a peasant's life. He surely is a
monk—still, at the end of his life, someone who really knows
says, what made Merton so available to the world was his
humanism.

Let me quote here the passage from *Conjectures of a Guilty
Bystander* about the experience in Bardstown:

> In Louisville, at the corner of Fourth and Walnut, in the
> center of the shopping district, I was suddenly overwhelmed
> with the realization that I loved all those people, that they
> were mine and I theirs, that we could not be alien to one
> another even though we were total strangers . . . this sense

of liberation from the illusory difference was such a relief and such a joy to me that I almost laughed out loud . . . thank God, thank God, that I am only a man among others.[29]

The parallel with Zorba is irresistible. The Boss asks Zorba:

Are you married? Zorba answers, Am I not a man? And is not a man stupid?
I'm a man! So, I'm married—wife, children, house, everything . . . the full catastrophe![30]

The climax of Zorba the Greek—Zorba who is flesh and the Boss who is logic and mind—is when Zorba hands the Boss a flower and says, 'I have never loved a man as much as I have loved you'. In their embrace, flesh and spirit are reconciled. So it was with Merton's final journey:

The East was his Beatrice. In it he found a light that burned brightly, a light not necessarily better than that of the West but different enough to allow new things to be seen . . . no journey had more meaning for him than his journey to get beyond the duality of Western thought.[31]

As he, too, overcomes the separation of self and persona, inner and outer, fidelity and process, sacred and profane, solitude and love, East and West, Merton seems to say, 'Am I not human? Are not humans restless, in process, psychosomatic, in need of love? I'm human.'

Colorado State University
Fort Collins

NOTES — Thomas Merton's Final Journey

1. Anthony Padovano. *The Human Journey: Thomas Merton Symbol of a Century* (New York: Doubleday, 1982) p. 170.

2. Raimundo Panikkar. *Blessed Simplicity: The Monk as Universal Archetype* (New York: Seabury Press, 1982) p. 15.

3. Monica Furlong. *Thomas Merton: A Biography* (San Francisco: Harper and Row, 1980).

4. Michael Mott. *The Seven Mountains of Thomas Merton* (Boston: Houghton Mifflin Company, 1984).

5. Padovano, p. xvi.

6. This piece of information is taken as true by Furlong, p. 59, Padovano, p. 9, p. 113 and Mott, p. 84. The source for each seems to be a cryptic passage in Ed Rice. *The Man in the Sycamore Tree* (New York: Doubleday, Image Books, 1972) pp. 22, 23.

7. Mott, p. 347.

8. *The Asian Journal of Thomas Merton*, ed. by Naomi Burton, et al. (New York: New Directions, 1973) p. 335.

9. Thomas Merton. *The Seven Storey Mountain*. pp. 316–17; pp. 369–378.

10. Merton, *The Sign of Jonas*, pp. 186; 260–66. The citation is from p. 266.

11. Padovano, p. 50.

12. *Ibid.*, pp. 50, 51.

13. Ira Progoff, *At a Journal Workshop* (New York: Dialogue House Associates, 1975) ch. 13.

14. Mott, p. 511.

15. Elisabeth Schussler Fiorenza. *In Memory of Her: A Feminist Critical Reconstruction of Christian Origins* (New York: Crossroad), p. 33.

16. Mott, pp. 355 and 371.

17. Merton's abiding dedication to the monastic ideal is clear in the latter parts of *The Asian Journal*. Notice, for example, his talks in Calcutta and Bangkok.

18. Padovano, p. 83.

19. Padovano, pp. 22 and 144.

20. Joseph Powers. 'Faith, Morality, Creativity: Toward the Art of Believing', *Theological Studies* 39 (Dec. 1978).

21. Padovano, p. 84.

22. Merton, *The Asian Journal*, p. 305.

23. Padovano's commentary on this poem opened its richness to me, pp. 136–165.

24. Mott, p. 527.

25. Padovano, p. 84.

26. Abraham Heschel. *Between God and Man* (New York: Macmillan, 1959) p. 125–26.

27. Padovano, p. 83.

28. Padovano, p. 173.

29. Merton, *Conjectures of a Guilty Bystander* (Garden City, NY: Doubleday) pp. 156–57.

30. *Zorba the Greek*, Original Soundtrack Album, Twentieth Century Fox Record Corp., 1966.

31. Padovano, pp. 74 and 88.

Scott Nelson

Three Decades of Poetry
Merton's Spiritual Maturation

DIVERSITY MARKED the life of Thomas Merton. He was a virtual chameleon as he shared different aspects of himself with the many he came to know throughout his lifetime. As Michael Mott observes, Merton had the rare gift of making a person feel that for a time he was on the most intimate and open terms with Merton; but such a rapport could create the problem of having 'many people thinking that they alone knew what Merton thought or planned'.[1] Some of these people insist to this day that they knew Merton better than anyone, and then they launch into a description of the man they knew, emphasizing the elements of political activist, peacenik, writer, artist, radical Catholic, disillusioned Christian, poet, Zenman, contemplative, young father, middle-aged lover, and whatever else, perhaps highlighting one or two primarily and paying a lip service to the other facets. Merton was indeed all of these things; but the most neglected side of the man is central to all of his endeavors. For as varied and wide ranging as he was, Merton was continually and consistently sourced from the center of the mystical realm (sometimes called God) throughout his entire life. This concept, while hardly new, is what this short paper will attempt to clarify through the examination of some randomly selected poems written by Merton at ten year spans thus comprising his monastic life.

'A Letter to My Friends' was published in *A Man in the Divided Sea,* but as the subtitle suggests, was written in 1941 upon 'entering the Monastery of Our Lady of Gethsemani'.[2] Full of pious romanticism and naiveté, this poem is a didactic representation of *contemptio mundi* and the reaching out of man towards the divine (*kopos*). On the former pole the young novice Merton seeks haven from the world, his past (his future), and his guilt by entering,

> This holy House of God,
> Nazareth, where Christ lived as a boy,
> These sheds and cloisters,
> The very stones and beams are all befriended
> By cleaner sun, by rarer birds, by lovelier flowers.[3]

Such an idyllic setting is misleading in the sense that the monastery threshhold does not serve to keep out the grime and dirt of humanity. The sun, birds and flowers are the same on both sides of the abbey wall; but greater acuity is afforded to the cloistered monk. Yet it is not the peaceful appearances or the false hope of simple security that leads men inward,

> Lost in the tigers' and the lions' wilderness,
> More than we fear, we love these holy stones,
> These thorns, the phoenix's sweet and spikey tree.

> More than we fear, we love the holy desert,
> Where separate strangers, hid in their disguises,
> Have come to meet, by night, the quiet Christ.[4]

In his tradition of the earliest Desert Fathers, Merton paints a scene of entering the untamed regions, where aridity and hence certain death exist, and where man alone would perish without the divine assistance. Fear is natural in such a portrait, yet the 'holy stones' are 'loved' as are the 'thorns'. In this love is the acceptance of the same suffering of Christ which is to share simultaneously in his resurrection; for as the mythical phoenix sacrificed itself on a funeral pyre in the desert only to assume a new life, so too is the desire of the monk. This desire is not born out of the perverse grasping for nonexistence. It is the hope that, like the phoenix, like Christ, the monk will arise to a new life. It is in this beloved desert that individuals, hidden in their cowls, are brought together on an intrinsic level to await in silent expectation and darkness (as at the Office of Vigils) for Christ. These stanzas expose the often neglected side of monastic life and, at times, of Christian life in general. Yet the seeming sense of escapism and piteous contempt creeps back into the poem as Merton continues,

> We who have some time wandered in those crowded ruins,
> (Farewell, you woebegone, sad towns)
> We who have wandered like (the one I hear) the moaning trains,
> (Begone, sad towns!)
> We'll live it over for you here.
>
> Here all your ruins are rebuilt as fast as you destroy yourselves,
> In your unlucky wisdom,
> Here in the House of God
> And on the holy hill,
> Where fields are the friends of plenteous heaven,
> While starlight, as bright as manna,
> All our rough earth with wakeful grace.[5]

As they too are men, monks have all once lived among the world's and their own failings; but the monk takes the radical stance and assumes responsibility for his life by sacrificing it, by renouncing his past, and laying his future on the highest altar. Inseparable from this offering is the elemental commitment to all people as Christ's sacrifice is for all generations even though the historical event occured some time in the past. In this sense, the monastic vocation becomes a living sacrifice that is not merely a metaphor, or simply a reminder of a perfect way of life. It is a life in which the suffering and rising of Jesus Christ is embodied for all, so that the monk can state that he will 'live it over for you here'. Even in a world where self destruction and ignorance marry, where the towns have become sad, this sacrificial action of the monastic community serves to bolster and shore up the earth, or if you will, the mystical body of Christ (*koinonia*); for the 'ruins are rebuilt as fast as you destroy yourselves.' While this notion could have a broader meaning in terms of the instrumental position of the monastery versus the entire Church, it is clear that at the time of his writing this poem Merton was thinking strictly in the light of his vocation. He most readily identifies the physical domain of the monastery as he alludes to the trains he hears in the distance (which one could in fact hear from Gethsemani at that time), the expanse of farmland (the match mates of 'plenteous' skies), and like many novices who find novelty in the early morning rising, he remembers the starlight of the Office of Vigils.

The 'desert's' hope materializes and is fostered by the monastery as Merton sketches further the grounds and architecture of Gethsemani in the final stanza:

> And look, the ruins have become Jerusalems,
> And the sick cities re-arise, like shining Sions!
> Jerusalems, these walls and rooves,
> These bowers and fragrant sheds,
> Our desert's wooden door,
> The arches, and the windows, and the tower![6]

This early poem reflects Merton's total immersion within the novitiate. His consistent referral to the stillness of the night serves to 'record the poet's love of nature, of solitude, and the contemplative vocation'[7] as do many of the other pieces included in *A Man in the Divided Sea*. 'A Letter To My Friends' is Merton consciously identifying with his contemplative vocation and it simultaneously exhibits his deep association with the world and

its inhabitants. Yet both of these elements await clearer definition through the goal of his calling, and consequently the crux of
this poem, which is God, Christ, the Sublime.

Nearly ten years later Merton was still writing as a contemplative, a monk; however there is no longer the robust
romanticism through superfluous words. *The Strange Islands*
(1957) found him writing about the initial sense of his calling in a
greatly matured fashion as exhibited by 'In Silence'.

> Be still
> Listen to the stones of the wall.
> Be silent, they try
> To speak your
> Name.
> Listen
> To the living walls.
> Who are you?
> Who
> Are you? Whose
> Silence are you?[8]

In this unusual syncretism of animism and quietude, the
'poet's rare vision is toward a profound experience and the reader
must be prepared to extend himself to meet it'.[9] That the stones
are alive represents his intuitive experience of all the world as being infused with the spirit of God. One must be still, however, to
listen, to feel the earth's pulse asking the angst sustaining, 'Who
are you?' A step further is the question, 'Whose silence are you?'
In another way, one might ask when all is still, when the mind is
silent, when the heart is calm, and hence the ego quieted to the
point where it seems that there is no room for the self, then what
are you? More acutely, since 'you' are no longer and silence per-
vades, whose essence, 'whose silence' have you become?

> Who (be quiet)
> Are you (as these stones
> Are quiet). Do not

Think of what you are
Still less of
What you may one day be.
Rather
Be what you are (but who?) be
The unthinkable one
You do not know.[10]

Amidst the longing, almost painful desire to confront and push through the 'Who are you?' of the mind, the heart reveals the advice to be quiet, still. It is the same heart that reiterates the fundamental question of the mind further into the poem — and it is at this deeper, more intrinsic level that the self is compelled to a leap of consciousness and of faith. Merton recognizes here that to be still is to fall from time into timelessness through transcending, even suspending, one's thoughts of what the ego is and may become in the future. It is in this void (this desert) that the self unites with God, 'the unthinkable one', who is unknowable outside of this condition.

O be still, while
You are still alive,
And all things around you
Speaking (I do not hear)
To your own being,
Speaking by the Unknown
That is in you and in themselves.[11]

Exemplified here is Duns Scotus' influence upon Merton, as God, the 'Unknown,' is recognized, if not always acknowledged ('I do not hear'), as permeating all that exists. The pleading voice which opens the stanza is rooted in the fleeting reality of life. At this point the poem is less dispersed in its thrust so that now it verges upon the passionate and ceases to be a purely cognitive function of man. Rather, having fed upon the spiritual desperation of inner blindness wrought by empiricism, it has become a paean to truly live.

> I will try, like them
> To be my own silence:
> And this is difficult. The whole
> World is secretly on fire. The stones
> Burn, even the stones
> They burn me. How can a man be still or
> Listen to all things burning? How can he dare
> To sit with them when All their silence
> Is on fire?[12]

Man, Merton, accepts the challenge to live. More particularly, he assumes the task in the same way as the stones are their own
silence. The irony and difficulty lie in the fact that one cannot be
silent alone, by oneself, when all things burn. Yet one must
become still to be a part of life at this level. This silence is not a
simple quietude expressed through a nihilistic violation of life. It
is the affirmation of existence on the most vibrant plane, that of
the Creator himself. In this realm of silence, the acceptance of
one's life is at the same time to be consumed totally, as by fire, in
the experience of tapping into this sublime mystery of God. Yet,
both the doubt and confusion of rational man surfaces naturally
at the contrary state of these affairs; for 'How can a man be still or
listen to all things burning?' With the further realization of the
magnitude of this dilemma it becomes inconceivable and
audacious for man to know God when even 'silence is on fire'; but
it is in the flames of all things burning that one sacrifices
everything (foremostly the ego) to the Unknown, to God, and
then becomes silently alive or, as the poem suggests, 'secretly on
fire'.

Finally, in *Sensation Time at the Home,* written in the last
years of his life but not published until 1977 in the *Collected
Poems,* 'the old quiet Merton of the desert'[13] reemerges after par-
tially disappearing in *The Geography of Lograire* and *Cables to
the Ace.* 'The Secret' is an unusual piece in that it lacks both the
piety and levity of the other examples examined in this paper. It
is almost childlike, yet there are contianed in its simple lines
qualities of the shamanisticly arcane. Written in the early hours

of the morning, the poem 'occured all of a sudden'[14] and its
magic springs forth in like manner.

> Since I am
> Somebody's dream,
> I have a good life.

> Sometimes I go away in my sailboat on a cloud
> and take a quiet little trip.

> I have a secret
> which I have learned how to read inside myself;
> if I told it to you,
> it would make you laugh.[15]

Life is good for the poet. It is not a dream, nor he merely
part of one either. He is a dream belonging to 'Someone' other
than himself. As a dream, it is his nature to go on 'quiet little'
trips. Who owns this dream? Where does it go when partaking of
its gentle excursions? Alas, it is a secret understandable within
poet's spirit — the dream. It is a secret that could elicit derisive
laughter; but would most likely encourage a loving smile. It
depends not upon the dream, or the dreamer (God); but upon
the sharer of this secret as to how it is received.

> My heart is naked
> and no one can put clothes on it,
> and nothing can be put on
> that will not immediately fall off.

> My secret is ignorant,
> it doesn't sing songs,
> no lie,
> it has nothing to tell you.[16]

Boldly the dream is so pure that it stands as Adam stood, innocent in the light of the Creator. This dream's innocence cannot

be lost and nothing can alter its intrinsic quality of goodness as it is indivisible from the Creator. It is here that the dream's secret is revealed as it stands unhidden in its nakedness. Paradoxically, this obvious state 'has nothing to tell anyone, it is 'no lie', and it is dumbly 'ignorant', yet by its elemental purity it doesn't need to 'sing songs' to be heard.

> My two eyes
> are maps of the planet —
> I see everything
> and nothing upsets me.
>
> Just now
> I was in China
> and saw there a great peace of happiness
> that belonged to one man.
>
> And I have been to the center of the earth,
> where there is no suffering.[17]

Eyes have become mirrors, calm topographical settings, upon which is reflected and observed the life throes of creation. The sight penetrates into the deepest finality, seeing 'everything' in its wholeness through the purity of the dream so that nothing 'upsets' the viewer. It is the power of the dream, or rather its nature, that allows it to travel the distances to China (in a 'sailboat on a cloud'), and certainly beyond in order to see so much happiness in one man. This vision is in part a continuation of the dream's secret: that suchness abides in the world if one could but become the dream of the dreamer. As dream is inseparable from the dreamer, so man is inseparable from God and in this realization is the secret's other part: that man need not strive on his own, indeed he cannot, in order to live in bliss. Further defining and affirming this revelation is the poet's journey where there is found no suffering at the center or *axis mundi*.

> If on your loneliest nights,
> I visit other planets
> and the most secret stars of all,

besides being no one,
know that I am you
everybody.[18]

Merton reminds his reader: Even in his solitary escapades to
the soul's furthest reaches, he is not to despair though he
becomes dissolved in the dreamer's dream. For it is here that man
becomes wholly one through God.

But if I go away
without giving you a name to remember me
with,
how will I find
the right dream to return to?

You won't have to mark down
on your calendar that I am coming back;
don't bother to write me into your notebooks.
I will be around
when you aren't thinking about me,
without hair or a neck,
without a nose and cheeks
no reputation —
there won't be anything.[19]

The body is not lasting, names are not for remembering,
and there is no right dream. For there is only 'Somebody's dream'
in which there is no departure and no returning and hence where
one's travels are timeless. Consequently, there is no need to mark
and set aside days for ourselves in this reality as God is always,
and what is and was oneself that was and is not God 'won't be
anything.' What then was Thomas Merton, this dream of the
divine dreamer?

I am a bird
which God made.[20]

Troy, New York

NOTES — Three Decades of Poetry

1. Mott, Michael, *The Seven Mountains of Thomas Merton* (Boston: Houghton Mifflin, 1984) p. xxvi.
2. Merton, Thomas, *Collected Poems of Thomas Merton* (New York: New Directions, 1977) p. 90.
3. *Ibid.*
4. *Ibid.*, p. 91.
5. *Ibid.*
6. *Ibid.*, 91f.
7. Kramer, Victor A., *Thomas Merton* (Boston: G. K. Hall, 1984) p. 49.
8. *Collected Poems*, p. 280.
9. Lentfoehr, Thérèse, *Words and Silence* (New York: New Directions, 1979) p. 28.
10. *Collected Poems*, pp. 280f.
11. *Ibid.*
12. *Ibid.*
13. Woodcock, George, *Thomas Merton: Monk and Poet* (Vancouver: Douglas and McIntyre, 1978) p. 182.
14. Lentfoehr, p. 72.
15. *Collected Poems*, pp. 827f. It should be noted that this is a translation by William Davis of Merton's original French in *Sensation Time at Home*, pp. 635ff.
16. *Collected Poems*, p. 828.
17. *Ibid.*
18. *Ibid.*
19. *Ibid.*, p. 828f.
20. *Ibid.*, p. 829.

Thomas P. McDonnell

The Trouble With Thomas Merton

T
HE TITLE, of course, requires an immediate explanation. I do not mean to imply by it that I am about to deal here with anything particularly flawed, say, in the writings of that most remarkable Cistercian monk, Thomas Merton, who died suddenly by an electrical accident (December 10, 1968) while attending a spiritual conference in the Far East nearly two decades ago. If you were to ask me parenthetically, however, whether there are indeed any aspects of his work which may now be called into question, I should have to answer in all candor, yes, of course; for all his great achievement, Merton does not remain everywhere above question.

I happen to believe that a number of Merton's major attitudes were seriously flawed, though he seemed always to be left off lightly by others, I think, because of the almost untouchably high esteem in which he was held — especially by his earliest admirers. I thoroughly shared that high regard as well. But when I use the unlikely phrase 'the trouble with Merton', I mean this in

251

a more or less sardonic sense — as derived, perhaps, from an old spiritual tune — that nobody knows the trouble I've seen in having worked both with and without Merton himself on projects having to do with his literary output and general reputation.

So for what it may be worth, and I must admit that it may be of hardly any worth at all, I'd like to tell you about this so-called trouble if only to keep the record straight. Michael Mott, who wrote the official biography of the monk in *The Seven Mountains of Thomas Merton*,[1] did not get it quite straight insofar as the production of the anthology *A Thomas Merton Reader* (1962) is concerned. As editor of the *Reader,* I said as much in a review of Mott's biography in the Winter 1986 issue of the quarterly *This World*.[2] I promised there to give my own account of the 'trouble' in due time, and I reckon that this may just as well be it.

I want to say at once on Michael Mott's behalf, however, that it is nearly impossible to write any kind of serious biography which will not sooner or later reveal a few minor deficiencies of one kind or another — or even a major one. For example, there exists an overwhelming consensus on the excellence of Leon Edel's *Henry James: A Life*[3] in which Edel states that 'through the Edwardian years, Wells and James were excellent friends'. But now, in *H. G. Wells: Aspects of a Life*,[4] the author Anthony West — who is Wells's son by the late Rebecca West — comes along to say that, on the contrary, 'They were never friends', and then proceeds to demonstrate his case rather conclusively.

The point is: How could so thorough a biographer as Leon Edel have been that far off the mark? More or less easily, I'm afraid, insofar as he did not apparently go to primary sources. Well, neither did Michael Mott go to one of the primary sources relating to the production of *A Thomas Merton Reader* — namely, myself. I can only conclude, therefore, that he went instead to someone who would give him one side of the story only. Too, in Mott's biography, I am referred to as 'the designated editor of the *Reader*'. But, frankly, I don't know what a designated editor may be in this particular instance. Certainly, I was not designated in the sense of someone who came along after the idea for a *Reader* had already been hatched.

The fact is I hatched the idea itself, in the latter part of the fifties, and proposed it directly to the publisher then known as Harcourt Brace and World (Jovanovich now replacing the last term). At that time I was a night watchman in a papermill in Hyde Park, Mass., writing in my spare time. I freelanced in such periodicals as *America, Commonweal, Catholic World,* and contributed poetry to *Spirit* magazine. I was, therefore, to coin an oxymoron, slightly stunned when invited by Harcourt Brace to visit their offices in New York for a discussion on the idea which I had proposed: the making of *A Thomas Merton Reader.*

At this point, I must emphasize the conception of the *Reader* itself, because it was—and, of course, remains—so essential to the form of the anthology as a unified whole. The idea was to project the seven storeys, or levels, in Thomas Merton's career from its worldly origins to the spiritual ascent itself in his role as contemplative monk *par excellence.* A similar notion, incidentally, is used by Michael Mott in his present structure for the official biography. In any case, the idea was found to be agreeable with Merton himself; and so I commenced to assemble the various materials. In due time, Harcourt Brace sent me down to the Abbey of Gethsemani, nestled among the knobs of Kentucky, near Bardstown, for two working sessions of one week each. The first session was during a particularly beautiful portion of May, 1961, and the second in an equally beautiful October week of that same year.

I shall always be grateful for the experience of meeting and working with Thomas Merton there and for gathering, as best I could, some remote notions of the Cistercian way of life. I must add at this point, however, that a subsidiary idea of the *Reader* was based on my privately held view that Merton had reached a plateau in his career where a selection drawn from the writings was now feasible—that is, if only as a way of looking back on what he had accomplished so far. I had half hoped as well, I think, that this kind of publication would give Merton pause to stop and take some serious inventory of his works and to determine what he had in mind for the future. I learned that I was not the only one who had reached the conclusion, by the end of the

fifties, that Merton was simply publishing too much. I envision-
ed that he might settle down to produce one book which would
be a really serious and substantial work of spirituality for the
twentieth century.

In the meantime, the idea for a *Reader* was not lightly
taken. I never considered it as a kind of scissors-and-paste job
with its designated editor set to handle the tedious end of the
project. Mostly through a tangle of correpsondence which now
looks like an effort to crack the Japanese code before Pearl Har-
bor, Thomas Merton and I went through a grueling process of
selection and rejection of the various materials at hand. So, yes,
the work was difficult but bearable and eventually fruitful. What
proved to be not so very nice was an incredible situation which involved the withholding of reprint rights by one of the major
publisher of Merton's books. This was Farrar, Straus & Cudahy
(now Farrar, Straus & Giroux). The situation was at an impasse.

'In the end', writes Michael Mott in the official biography, 'a
compromise had to be reached, and the first edition of *A Thomas
Merton Reader* came out in October 1962, without much of the
material Merton had hoped to include.' To me, as editor, Mott's
statement about a compromise having been reached does not
make any sense at all. The fact is that there was no compromise to
be reached in the first place. It was not a question of compromise,
indeed, but of outright exclusion. We were simply denied access
to materials under the Farrar, Straus imprint. In view of this, I
then prepared an alternative version of the *Reader* without
benefit of the withheld materials. In other words, literally speaking, I prepared two versions of the *Reader,* and of course we ended up with the one that was eventually published by Harcourt
Brace in the autumn of 1962, with a view to the Christmas shopping season just ahead.

Talk about trouble, however, for as soon as the advertising
copy had been prepared for a full-page announcement of the anthology in the Sunday book review section of *The New York
Times,* a city-wide newspaper strike occurred and left us high and
dry, the fruits of our labors still hanging on the vine. The politics
of book publishing notwithstanding, the *Reader* proved to be

negotiable without Farrar, Straus materials, which, on the whole, do not seem to be as important as those produced by Harcourt Brace, Doubleday, and New Directions. The book most sorely missed, perhaps, was Merton's minor classic, *Thoughts in Solitude* (1958).

In any case, the machinations involved in this whole situation were both nasty and childish, in my opinion, and reflect no honor upon those at the center of it all. At a soiree following a talk by the late James T. Farrell on the campus of Boston College, in 1961, I was told by one of the principals in the above-mentioned dealings that the *Reader* would never see the black of print, let alone the light of day. This was said to me in a tone which I could only interpret as benign contempt; but with the alternative version already in hand, I was not intimidated — as, of course, Merton himself had not been. All this folly went so far as to suggest the trading off of several major authors under the imprints of two of the publishers involved and which would have been conditioned, in turn, on the release of the Merton materials, etc. I later joked with Merton that he and Robert Lowell, apparently, were not worth one T. S. Eliot. So much, then, for the impure joys of bookmaking.

In the end, it was nevertheless encouraging to find that Merton's summing-up of the matter was both philosophical and therefore resigned. I found his attitude also extremely touching in its admonition to be very wise and patient and to watch one's step in these matters. He told me not to worry about the difficulties that might arise in the political hassle of getting the *Reader* through, as he said with such precise penetration, the Scylla and Charybdis of his publishers. I have some seventy letters and cards which document this excruciating experience, from beginning to end, and Michael Mott could have had access to them simply for the asking.

I was invited some years ago to place my Merton letters with the many that are housed in a collection chiefly for research and academic purposes. I declined on the grounds that (1) I am generally disinclined to violate matters of privacy, and (2) I'd have wanted reasonable assurance, from any future biographer, that he clearly understood, in this particular case, the situation in question. Instead, like Leon Edel stating casually that Henry James and H. G. Wells were the best of friends, Michael Mott was just as casual in concluding that, in the matter of the *Reader,* a compromise had been reached. This remains absolute nonsense.

But that's not the end of the trouble with Merton. Though I loved the man dearly, I never touched any project having to do with his writing which did not end up in some kind of trouble — meaning difficulty of a seemingly unwarranted nature. For example, having prepared an 'Editor's Note' for the Doubleday Image Books revised edition of *A Thomas Merton Reader* (1974), I was later rather testily informed that I should have cleared this with The Merton Legacy Trust. It was the first intimation I had experienced, in my own career as a writer, that I could not write freely about Merton in a free land.

Shortly after that, I started selecting and editing materials for a yearbook of daily meditations drawn from the full range of Merton's writings, which was eventually published in a hardcover edition under the title *Blaze of Recognition.*[5] I say eventually published, because it was in fact held up for a good number of years on rather obscure reasons. It has since been reissued as a paperback in Doubleday's Image Books series, under the title *Through the Year With Thomas Merton* (1985). I still find unbelievable that the ostensible reason for delaying publication of the book had to do with the opinion of one of the members of the Legacy Trust that, incredibly enough, there was thought to be too much of *me* in it. This in itself I found amazing because, aside from the selection and introduction, the book is of course all Thomas Merton's.

I readily admit that any anthologist will necessarily leave the mark of his own taste and acumen — or lack of it — on any selection of writings which he or she happens to edit, for such indeed is the very nature of the form itself. I have never known it to be otherwise. But, in sum, the trouble with Thomas Merton was a fair, certainly memorable, and thoroughly redeemable exchange for the privilege of having known so exceptional a man of our time. It only remains to add that I had indeed been somewhat troubled by the prospect of publishing this brief account at all. But, however minor such a footnote may appear to be, perhaps it is something which the field of Merton studies may now tolerate.

Stoughton, Massachusetts

NOTES — The Trouble With Thomas Merton

1. Mott, Michael, *The Seven Mountains of Thomas Merton* (Boston: Houghton Mifflin, 1984).

2. Washington, DC: Institute for Educational Affairs.

3. Edel, Leon, *Henry James: A Life* (New York: Harper and Row, 1985).

4. West, Anthony, *H. G. Wells: Aspects of a Life* (New York: Random House, 1984).

5. McDonnell, Thomas P., ed., *Blaze of Recognition* (New York: Doubleday, 1983).

Paul Wilkes

Merton In These Places
Early Days in Europe—
Final Days in the East

My Lord God, I have no idea where I am going. I do not see the road ahead of me.
I cannot know for certain where it will end. Nor do I really know myself, and the
fact that I think that I am following your will does not mean that I am actually do-
ing so. But I believe that the desire to please you does in fact please you. And I
hope I have that desire in all that I am doing.

PRAYER OF THOMAS MERTON

MILLIONS OF READERS of Thomas Merton had felt his
loneliness as a child in France, his self-hatred as a
hedonist during the Cambridge days, his exhilaration at
the transcendence of Tre Fontane and Sts Cosmas and Damian in
Rome. They could almost shiver with him at the coldness of the
school in Montauban and bristle at the 'muscular Christianity' of
Oakham. Their chests loosened, with Merton's at the time-ravaged
beauty of St Michel de Cuxa near his birthplace in France.

Then, near the end of his life—after those many fruitful
years at Gethsemani—when he was again back in the world, Merton made it so vividly possible for us to experience with him the
overpowering presence both of the stone figures at Polonnaruwa
and in the human form of the Dalai Lama. And who can forget
the final days in Bangkok; noisy, bustling and religious Bangkok? Wasn't it possible to smell the food cooking on the streets,
gape at the splendor of the Temple of the Emerald Buddha and

259

with him, approach that fateful Red Cross Center on the out-
skirts of the city, the place that would be the last stop on his
earthly journey?

Many have been to Gethsemani, seen the fields he walked,
the abbey church where he worshipped, his beloved hermitage.
Still others have had the opportunity to visit some of the places
Merton wrote about so evocatively in his books. Fewer people
still, I would imagine, have visited all the foreign locations, done
it within a month and for no other reason than Merton had been
there.

The making of the PBS documentary, MERTON, allowed
such an opportunity for me.

From the beginning of the making of this film, it was apparent to me that the people who knew him best should be heard
and the far-flung places that formed Merton be shown. And furthermore that Merton's own words about these places should be
the guide. I felt it was important to depict those places accurately
and artfully, but far more important to try to see them as Merton
did — in a sense, to enter into his spirit as much as that is humanly
possible.

In May, 1983, with most of the domestic filming and at least
half of the interviews for MERTON completed, a two-person film
crew — Tom Hurwitz, the cinematographer and Barbara Zahm,
the soundwoman — and I set out for what would be a 40,000 mile
around the world trip to find what there was of Merton in these
places. At least whatever this one man could find.

EARLY DAYS IN EUROPE

Prades

The crew and I had planned to rest after arriving in Toulouse
via Paris, but the sunny skies bid us to go on. Heading south, the
relentless tide of development, of factories and rows of new
houses that Merton would never have known — and might easily
have scorned as he was no fan of modernism — gently gives way to
the rolling foothills of the Pyrenees. Now there are precise

vineyard rows, the brown, claylike soil neatly devoid of weeds. Wheat waves in the breeze, heavy heads nearly ready for harvest. The fine, ancient grey Pyrenees, shrouded in the remnants of the cloudy, damp spring, look down serenely upon all matter of worldly pursuit as they always have.

Blink and the time is 1915.

On the narrow and bumpy cobblestone streets of Prades, constructed centuries before with no motorized conveyance in mind, I do not even have to blink, the city is so well preserved and similar to Merton's time. Most of the houses are alike with sandstone cement finish over stone, usually accented by red shutters and just as predictably, an earthen pot or two gushing opulent chrysanthemums. In the small courtyards at the rear of the buildings, vegetables and flowers grow in embarrassing abundance; the weather of this southernmost part of France is temperate and most kind to growing things.

In the house on the corner of Rue du 4 Septembre and Rue du Palais du Justice, I am led by the current owners, a French woman and her British husband, up a steep stairway to the room where Merton was born.

For some reason, my first impression is that is is a room of death and not life. There was always melancholy in Merton about his earliest years, in Prades, and I can feel it in this room. Here he began a life's journey that, until he found what his true calling was, would be restless, unhappy, confused, unfulfilled.

A white chenille bedspread covers a firm double bed, perhaps—although the current residents are not sure—the one in which Merton was born. At the head of the bed is a matching stand, with an austere Norman cross. The hardwood floor glistens. White, almost brittley clean curtains move ever so slightly in the late afternoon breeze.

No, for sure the spirit of Merton is not here. It is time to go on.

My mother and father came from the ends of the earth, to Prades, and though they came to stay, they stayed there barely long enough for me to be born and get on my small feet, and then they left again. And they continued and I

began a somewhat long journey: for all three of us, one way
or another, it is now ended.

The Seven Storey Mountain

St Michel de Cuxa

The winding narrow road from Prades to the medieval
monastery of St Michel de Cuxa takes the traveler even further
back, to another era. Here, off the oft-traveled roads of France,
time moves as slowly as the old man walking along his village
street, cane in hand, jacket over his shoulders. Fields reclaimed
from the woods once covering the Pyrenees foothills are green
with rich grass, sprouting after the first cutting. And there are
even more vineyeards, neat parcels of land which clearly and pro-
udly display the age of the vines — the older, the fuller they climb
and sprawl over wire and post.

On this hot morning, the monastery's cloister walls at first
could be taken for those of a landowner's estate. But beyond, as the
rugged, time-worn rock buildings come into view, the dull red tile
roofs and the tiny windows — allowing the occupants neither too
much sun, nor the option to see very much of the world outside — it
is apparent that this is a place both holy and serious.

Restoration work is underway today to keep St Michel de
Cuxa from crumbling entirely, but the place looks little different
from the day Thomas Merton, a boy of perhaps ten or twelve,
climbed the huge stone steps to spend the first of many days
wandering about this bare, ruined monastery.

The countryside is quiet, only the sounds of birds and in-
sects are heard, but once within the walls there is an absolute lack
of noise. The days' heat is immediately muted. The interior
cloister is a riot of stone carvings atop Roman pillars, menacing
gargoyles, agonizing man and beatific angels. It must have been
a fairy tale to Merton, where his young, fertile mind could begin
to wrestle with these forces that war within every person's soul.

Walking these well-known stone paths, it is easy to see why this
place meant so much to the young Merton, why the first stirrings of

transcendence came to him here. How a lonely, introspective boy—seemingly out of place both in France and in America—could come here time and again for an afternoon of peace. He was drawn again and again to a structure at once so beautiful and so ravaged by age, representing a timeless and heroic persuit that was surely beyond his comprehension. But perhaps not outside his youthful imagination.

> My mind goes back with great reverence to the thought of those clean, ancient stone cloisters, those low and mighty rounded arches hewn and set in place by monks who have perhaps prayed me where I now am.
>
> *The Seven Storey Mountain*

St Antonin

This old, old town, which dates back to Roman days, caressed so tenderly by the Bonnette and the larger, Aveyron River, its streets a maddening labyrinth, seems to breathe in a way Prades does not. Brilliantly whitewashed stucco homes and centuries-old guild halls stand shoulder to shoulder. Bicycles whiz by; overhead a network of electric and telephone cables draw a pattern of black streaks across the cloudless blue sky.

It is more crowded, more alive and perhaps its vigor overwhelmed the monk Merton as he tried to recall this town from within the Gethsemani walls as he wrote *The Seven Storey Mountain*. In his mind, every street in the town led to the church of St Antonin, but in trying to recreate this for the film, it was soon apparent that it was not exactly so.

But, what magnetism that church must have had for the tow-headed boy in his short pants, running through alleyways and under merchant's signs. For him, every way he turned, the church was there. Beckoning, inviting, but standing in place and waiting for him to approach.

Oh, what a thing it is, to live in a place that is so constructed

that you are forced, in spite of yourself, to be at least a virtual contemplative!

The Seven Storey Mountain

Montauban

For Merton, who was boarded at Escole Ingres when his
father went off to paint, Moutauban marked one of the lowest
periods of his young life. He talked often about being sick at the
school and hating the arrogant, cynical attitude of the students.

Approaching the high wrought iron gates with the
prepossessing relief sculpture of the great French painter, Jean
Auguste Ingres, I can at once feel with Merton. There is nothing
inviting about the school. It could easily pass for a private
sanitarium. I open the gate and walk into the yard.

Seated on a bench under one of the trees is a man who turns
out to be the school's bursar, a cheery Frenchman who quickly
brings out cold bottles of beer. He speaks with nothing but enthusiasm about the school, its largely French, but international
student body, the high standards, good education and fine
preparation for some of the best upper schools and colleges in
Europe.

But, walking about, hearing my own solitary footsteps on the
cement and not the laughter or jibes of children, Escole Ingres
becomes the dark, forbidding place that it was for Merton. Outside
the infirmary where, stricken with tuberculosis, he looked longingly
out the windows, a half dozen stretchers on wheels stand in the
hallway, as if anticipating a catastrophe. The sun disappears behind
clouds, casting a grey pall over the courtyard, its grass pounded to
death by so many young feet, moving from class to class.

A young boy, a brilliant student torn between two countries,
speaking each of their languages fluently, had seen no sunlight here
either. His mother was dead, his father away; he felt a lonesome
pilgrim on the face of this earth with no real home to call his own.

The experience of living with the kind of people I found in
the Lycée was something new to me, but in degree rather

than in kind. There was the same animality and toughness and insensitivity and lack of conscience that existed to some extent in my own character, and which I found more or less everywhere.

The Seven Storey Mountain

Oakham

With its wide expanse of rugby and cricket fields, a well-preserved and lovely town nearby, building after building of English grace and beauty, Oakham would seemingly have been the antidote Merton needed after Montauban and Escole Ingres. The chapel is a monument to God and good taste and, with such amicable school chums as John Barber, who, after attending both Oakham and Cambridge with Merton, returned to teach and be the headmaster here, it gives the idea today of being an altogether enjoyable place.

Barber's rememberances of both 'Merty' and the way the school was in the 1930's tell another story. It was not the relaxed country school it is today, but rather a rather rigid boarding school of not great standing where the sons of rural British merchants and farmers would be sent to have as much education and civility pounded into them as a few years would allow before going back to take up the family business.

Merton was a precocious, continental, bilingual young man. His classmates had rarely ventured further than a few hundred miles from home. The religious thrust, popular at the time, was 'muscular Christianity', which called for impeccable manners, the ability to endure suffering, but said nothing about grace, forgiveness and love, the very qualities Merton was desperately seeking.

But, in this paneled library, in these well-scarred classrooms, on these stone benches beneath flowering apple and cherry trees, Merton began to come alive. At least intellectually. Certainly not spiritually. There were a few faculty members in whom he could sense the quest and hunger for knowledge. His own reading increased enormously. Although the school had been founded on religious principles and chapel attendance was required, the life of the spirit was of yet no concern to Thomas Merton.

> . . . I think St. Peter and the other Apostles would have been rather surprised at the concept that Christ had been scourged and beaten by soldiers, cursed and crowned with thorns and subjected to unutterable contempt and finally nailed to the Cross and left to bleed to death in order that we might all become gentleman.
>
> *The Seven Storey Mountain*

Rome

Merton was, at a young age, already well traveled and well read. At seventeen, when he came to Rome, he was pulsing with energy, eager to touch and taste, feel and see the Eternal City. He had a passion for everything it seems: architecture, history, art . . . girls and drinking.

He came by his own admission, as a tourist.

Today's Rome is still the Rome of Merton, a maze of narrow streets that skirt fine piazzas and end abruptly at the site of an ancient church or some fenced off ruins under excavation. There are few and begrudging concessions to the twentieth century; Rome is a city that worships its past, choosing inconvenience over ease, excess over restraint, beauty—albeit it tarnished, worn or eroded—over comfort.

It was perfect for Merton.

Guidebook in hand, he wandered through the streets gawking at buildings and statues. It was a feast for him as it is for most travelers. Rome is a city of such brilliant abundance and vibrancy that it can tend to overwhelm. But then, just as a person approaches exhaustion, it demands still more of its succulence be experienced.

The church of Sts Cosmas and Damian is such a place, its ceilings covered with glittering frescoes; its walls graced with beautifully detailed stations of the cross, each a precious work of art; its confessionals marked by life-like bleeding hands of the crucified Christ. Here is art in unparalleled abundance.

And so it the Trappist monastery of Tre Fontaine outside Rome a place of imposing beauty. Here, a cool roadway, shaded by enormous trees, leads past the statue of St Benedict, finger pressed to his stone lips to admonish silence, and on to a church reminiscent of St Michel de Cuxa in its stark monastic simplicity.

Outside the church, a monk in tattered overalls tends to the flower beds. Yes, indeed he knows of Thomas Merton and knew that he had visited this church. Yes, indeed, he will show where Merton knelt. His accent is strangely un-Italian. He smiles. He is from the Abbey of New Melleray. In Iowa.

Sts Cosmas and Damian, Tre Fontaine. The first, where Byzantine mosaics and statuary leapt off the pages of the books he had seen, no longer works of art but pathways of praise. Here he began to sense that the One to whom all this art was dedicated and the One artists struggled so hard to represent and make clear was someone he wanted to understand. Someone he had to know.

And Tre Fontaine. Within those simple, high walls, in a church that was designed not to somehow illustrate God, but to give him honor with space, simplicity and humility, Merton began to sense a way to know him.

And now for the first time in my life I began to find out something of Who this Person was that men called Christ.
. . . I walked up and down in the silent afternoon, under the eucalyptus trees, and the thought grew on me: 'I should like to become a Trappist monk.'
There was very little danger of my doing so, then. The thought was only a daydream.
The Seven Storey Mountain

Cambridge

Here, where thought is revered, knowledge is coveted, where academic giants have walked, the sky is brittle with blueness, the air, even though summer air, crisp and bracing. It is impossible to wander leisurely along the walkways, beneath carved stone arches streaked black with age. Everyone moves with great intentionality, as if earthly moments were too few to partake of all the knowledge available within these imposing buildings, from these dons scurrying around on their old, rusty bikes.

Here Merton was finally introduced to minds as formidable as his own. And here, free of boarding school discipline, Merton gave way to his hunger for experience. All kinds of experience.

Which of the tiny pubs just off the Cambridge commons did he favor for his rowdy drinking bouts? And where did he meet that young girl who would bear the child that would cause him pain and remorse all his life? And in which room, or on what grassy glen, did they make love?

The high-ceilinged dining halls, with formal settings and coats of arms on the walls ring hollow with the sound of footsteps. On the Cam River, students glide their punts through still, amber water, silent with the beauty about them; for a few hours off the fast paths they must follow at this legendary institution.

And overlooking the River Cam in the courtyard of one of the halls, a party begins. Wine punch is poured into pewter mugs for the gentlemen and fine crystal glasses for the ladies present. A new literary magazine is launched. Laughter and witty remarks drift over the Cam.

In their midst is a young blond boy with a terribly engaging smile and an ingenuous way of cocking his head to the side in a way at once boyish and yet most seductive. His eyes never leave the pretty young woman in the pink silk dress. His blue blazer and white trousers is uniform, but that embracing look is not. He is a young man of uncommon charm and intelligence.

The girl touches his hand. He lays his hand upon hers.

Ah, Thomas, are you still here?

Perhaps to you the atmosphere of Cambridge is neither dark nor sinister. . . . I am even willing to admit that some people might live there for three years, or even a lifetime, so protected that they never sense the sweet stench of corruption that is all around them. . . . But for me, with my blind appetites, it was impossible that I should not rush in and take a huge bite of this rotten fruit. The bitter taste is with me after not a few years.

The Seven Storey Mountain

FINAL DAYS IN THE EAST

As Merton had been thoroughly immersed in European culture, history and art before he ever saw her cities firsthand, he was also well versed as anyone from the West could have been when he finally made his trip to the East. Merton had been attracted to things European primarily on aesthetic grounds. His were the eyes and soul of an artist. It was only later that he could unite the physical beauty of the objects and buildings with the divine power that called them into being.

His trip to the East was one infused with a hunger to see and sense the religious heritage he had been studying for perhaps fifteen years (It is humorous to look back at how easily and arrogantly Merton dismissed Eastern spirituality during his Columbia days and even during his first years at Gethesemani.), to see some of the great holy men, and to look upon religious art and artifact with eyes made clear by twenty-seven years of rigorous Trappist discipline and personal contemplation.

He knew that the twentieth century was overtaking the ancient cultures of the East and he wanted to go there before radical and unalterable changes occurred. He went to the East, not as a tourist, as he had gone to Rome, but as a pilgrim. He was a man whose capacious mind embraced much of what was happening in the world, but only through letters and publications and the visits of his many and diverse friends. Now, with an almost childlike openness, he would be able to experience them himself.

That Merton died on this, his first real journey from Gethsemani after twenty-seven years of cloistered life (enforced strenuously—and probably for Merton's good—by his abbot for most of that time, James Fox) gives it a special poignancy. There is a quality about the trip and his diary, so aptly put together after his death as *The Asian Journal of Thomas Merton*, that makes the death less of a shock than an inspired conclusion to a long, honest and excruciatingly personal quest for God.

In filming MERTON, I was able to visit, and within the same general time span as Merton, the key places of that fateful trip. And again, I sought to find what there was of him that was still there.

Polonnaruwa

The port of entry to Sri Lanka (known as Ceylon in Merton's day) is the city of Colombo, which sprawls along the Indian ocean coast. From the air, the countryside is divided into neat dark green blocks and those of a lighter, almost lime color. These are coconut groves and rice paddies, which produce two of Sri Lanka's most dependable and needed crops.

The road from the airport, the same that Merton would have taken, is an immediate shock to the Western eye. Not so much for the shacks of palm fronds and corrugated metal, but for the plethora of animals — from water buffalo to elephant — lumbering along with their various loads. The hot, muggy tropical air tends to take the new arrivee's breath away; cook fires and the smell of food wafts over the roadway where cars, trucks and buses often move no more quickly than the animals who have trod this path for centuries.

Heading north, toward the city of Kandy, famous for its plantations which produce the Ceylon teas so popular around the world, the road climbs and winds through verdant fields, far more infused with color than they appear from the air. At every rest stop, children come out to greet the visitor, beautiful fine-featured, dark-skinned children with luminous eyes and shining straight black hair. In the rice paddies, men call out in their ancient chant to their water buffaloes, as they plow the mucky soil in readiness for planting. The air is moist but cooler now in the higher altitude.

In the distance, a drum beat summons worshippers to the Buddhist temple. On the road, girls in blue jumpers and boys in blue slacks return home from school. These are the offspring of the town's more wealthy families, who can forgo the use of the children's labor and afford them the luxury of an education.

Outside Kandy, enormous mountain lakes provide water for drinking, bathing and the washing of clothes. Merton saw a lovely woman taking a bath on this very road. There are many of them, one after another, shy, smiling teenage girls, older sisters, mothers, unaware of their native beauty, bathing along the shoreline.

What did Merton think about when he saw that particular young girl, of whom he wrote so rhapsodically in the poem, *Kandy Express*? The woman who bore him a child in England? The young nurse he met in Louisville, loved so desperately yet who he decided never to see again? Were his thoughts on what earthly pleasures he had forgone in his monastic life? What was his state of mind right then? It is most important.

Monkeys scurry over ruins of another Buddhist temple and macaws call out their irritation at being disturbed. The jungle is quiet as the sun rises further into the sky. The morning breeze is gone. The heat rises from the ground. A burning sun in a cloudless sky beats down on sparse grass, eaten to its roots by wandering water buffalo.

Up ahead there is a huge rock outcropping. The sun's rays outline in searing white the shape of a head. There are but a dozen people about. All is silent.

Buddha sits cross-legged. Ananda stands beside still another Buddha, who lays his huge stone head on his hand. And sleeps.

The imposing statutes at Polonnaruwa, carved many centuries ago from the hillside, each some thirty feet in height, are all the more remarkable for the dark veins present in the rock that infuse their faces and bodies with life, as if blood were still coursing through them. But then again, these are statues beyond life, still, and made of rock, but emanating power and peace and, and —what?

Four women in saris pass before Ananda, their hands clasped in prayer, finger tips pressed to their foreheads.

It was here, on such a quiet day that Merton approached the mammoth statues at Polonnaruwa and experienced one of the most transcendent moments of his life. He had left the world, become a Christian monk, only to travel half way around the world to feel the presence of the God he so unswervingly sought here in a Buddhist holy place.

The statues appear to grow as you look at them, their blazing faces, turned white by the sun, relax still more. Yes, as Merton said, it is the look of acceptance, of embrace. Here, a weary pilgrim could rest, saying nothing, doing nothing. There are human footprints in the sand, a pair of sandals. To whom do they belong?

Surely . . . my Asian pilgrimage has come clear and purified itself. I know and have seen what I was obscurely looking for. I don't know what else remains but I have now seen and have pierced through the surface and have got beyond the shadow and the disguise.

                              The Asian Journal of Thomas Merton

Dharamsala

I travel to old section of Delhi to bargain with the one man in the city who has a van big enough for my crew and our equipment. He operates out of a stall no larger than a walk-in closet and it seems that at least six or seven of his friends have to be present as we talk. Over endless bottles of Coke Cola, the deal is struck and we set out just at sundown for the grueling sixteen hour trip north. Our driver is a lean, Hindi-speaking man perhaps sixty years old with many missing teeth and a ready smile.

India by day is a fascination, by night, it is a harrowing adventure. Cars and trucks whiz along the narrow highway as if it had six lanes and no ox carts. Most turn off their lights except when they see or sense an approaching vehicle. The road from Delhi to Dharamsala claims two or three lives a week. Casualties are mourned but expected.

Our driver goes through the night with no sleep and only two stops at roadside truck stops. Open air kitchens serve pooris and dal.

With the morning light comes a view of the Himalayas, awesome, snow-capped mountains in the distance. In their foothills lives one of the world's most respected holy men and religious leaders. The Dalai Lama.

His home in exile, the city of Dharamsala itself, is a strange mixture of East and East—and East and West. Tibetans with wrinkled, smiling faces make their way through the dirt streets, rosaries in hands, their lips whispering an unending prayer. These are people who fled with the Dalai Lama, or joined him in the ensuing years after China took over his kingdom. Huts climb the steep hills and prayer flags flutter in the mid morning breeze.

Also, on the streets, is a mixture of Indians, who lived here before the Dalai Lama and his people came, and a strange international amalgam of Europeans and Australians and Americans. The Westerners have come, it appears, for one of two reasons. To see and be close to the Dalai Lama. Or for a ready and inexpensive supply of drugs. Dozens of emaciated, vacant-eyed hippies, who seem left over from the 1960s and 1970s, wander about the streets, lining the road that leads to the Dalai Lama's compound high above the city, begging rupees from the pilgrims who have come to see him.

This is a holy city where Buddhist monks pray and chant long hours each morning and the towns' people spin prayer wheels and make endless trips about the great brass prayer cylinders, twirling them again and again, intoning their invocations. The sound of om-chanting drifts over the narrow, dusty streets; gongs punctuate the air.

Dharamsala is probably little changed from Merton's day and the man with whom he posed in one of the last pictures we have of him, has grown thicker of girth and rounder of face. But the warm smile and liquid eyes brimming with life have not changed at all.

Yes, he remembers him well. He was a Christian monk who knew deeply about Buddhism. He had a kind face and a deep spirit. If Merton were still alive, yes, they would be great comrades in trying to bring mental peace to people and world peace to our globe.

The Dalai Lama pushes his outer saffron robe aside to reveal a thick leather belt. Merton introduced him to the belt and he throws his head back in laughter. No more sashes for him. The belt never slips.

Is Merton here?

It was a very warm and cordial discussion and at the end I felt we had become very good friends and were somehow close to each other . . . and I believe too that there is a real spiritual bond between us.

The Asian Journal of Thomas Merton

Bangkok

After living at Gethsemani, with its bleak architecture, austere even by Cistercian standards, and worshipping for twenty-seven years in an abbey church unadorned by any religious art that might even tend to excite the senses, Bangkok must have been a delicious treat to Thomas Merton. In his heart he was a sensualist and this city, with its rich amalgam of religion and visual delights, certainly was a fitting place for him to spend the last days of his life.

The air, even in the middle of the night is moist, heavy and warm, scented with gardenias and rare tropical flowers unknown in the West. The traffic is a nightmare—albeit somehow good natured—of cars and taxis, motorbikes and people, each of which struggles for the little space on streets narrowed still further by vendors and carts. Moving from one part of the city to another is never easy, but the richness of street life and the serene faces of the Thai people make each outing a strange but exhausting pleasure.

The Temple of the Emerald Buddha rises up in the midst of the city like some glittering religious Disneyland: shimmering gilded forms and exquisite porcelain, a wonderland of huge statuary, murals and ornate porticos all perfectly restored and spotlessly clean.

And there is another place that Merton visited, Wat Bovoranives, a Buddhist monastery with filthy, polluted klongs running through the grounds and dozens of stray dogs, malformed and diseased, who have found a home where thy know they will not be harmed. Except perhaps by the boa constrictor who slithers out of the klong for a meal as the need arises.

A long, winding stone path to the Golden Mount yields a breathtaking view of the Bangkok skyline, which shows impressive skyscrapers as well as an amazing number of monastery compounds within the city. Saffron-robed monks sit along the path, one with a pack of Marlboros sticking out of his sock. They shyly look up at the Westerners and smile. 'Pretty lady', they offer as their tribute to my soundwoman, Barbara.

Religion mixes easily with everyday life in Bangkok; here monks are not sequestered as in American monasteries, but each dawn go out with their begging bowls. They never ask, just keep walking until a stall owner or a passerby places a bunch of flowers or cupsful of rice or a packet of spice in their wooden bowl. It is a wonderful sight and witness every day.

On the busy street corner outside our hotel is one of the most revered Buddhist shrines in Thailand. The pedestrian traffic is as thick as that downtown in any major city. People enter the tiny compound to lay a garland or food or to burn incense and candles before the Buddha, or rub their paper-thin swatch of gold leaf onto one of the idols. Hands clasped in front of them, the worshippers at Tao Maha Prom humbly and patiently ask that their earthly wishes be granted before they take to the sidewalk and are swept up in traffic and the immediacy of their own lives.

Bangkok is a naturally religious city inhabited by a remarkably centered and calm people, the Thais, and Merton embraced them immediately. Although the speech he was to give at the Red Cross center some thirty-five miles out of the city was the reason for his Asian journey in the first place, he was not eager to leave this crowded, throbbing city.

Sawang Kaniwat (Red Cross Center)

Along the dusty road leading from Bangkok, huge nets suspended on bamboo frames rise out of the river, dripping with water, flashes of silver showing fish have been caught. Rural Thais need not leave their homes to fish, for the nets are situated right out the front door of the houses built on stilts near the river's edge. An ingenious and convenient device, undoubtedly centuries old.

The further from Bangkok, the more primitive and poorer the people become, far cries from the city folk in their modern clothes and air conditioned cars. It was a country at war when Merton traveled along this route, so he probably saw even more signs of marginal living than exists today.

After a journey of an hour and a half, a neat sign on the right and a Thai flag whipped by a strong breeze announce the entrance of the Red Cross Center. It was here that the AIM meeting took place, a historic and hopeful gathering of Eastern and Western monks, who had just begun to learn in depth about each other's religious traditions and practices.

A group of earth-colored buildings and low bungalows with red tile roofs, the center is a home for convalescents as well as a conference center. There is ample space for groups to gather and simple living accommodations.

The directress, a stern-faced woman with dark penciled eyebrows, to whom the center's employees relate with obvious deference, says, yes, she remembers this man Merton and indeed, yes, people from time to time want to see the place where he died. She is quick to add that the cause of his death was a heart attack. She repeats: a heart attack.

The directress is too ill to accompany us, but her assistant, a young girl in the pictures taken at the time of the AIM conference and now in her late 30s, takes us to the cavernous hall where Merton gave his last talk. Merton hated television and movie cameras, but for some reason, he allowed the talk to be filmed and recorded. The first and last time in his life.

In that film, the hall gives the feeling of being much smaller than it actually is. It is a huge space and stiflingly hot. No wonder the audience looked so logy at Merton's talk. His quip about 'getting a Coke' at the conclusion must have made both Merton and those present quite happy.

It is a walk of two or three minutes to bungalow #11, one of the identical stucco buildings bleached almost white by the sun.

It is somehow touching that the room in which Merton died not only has no marking or plaque, but in a sense does not exist anymore. The partition on the right side of the first floor of bungalow #11, which had made it into private quarters, has been removed. Chairs and a table, sitting out in the center of the area, now form a sitting area.

Why does it seem like a sitting area no one uses?

The bathroom at the rear contains a toilet and in one corner, a squared off area of ceramic tile forms the equivalent of a sink or small tub. Water from a spigot above fills the tub. With a pan, a person can bathe themselves — as Merton did — taking a sort of a shower. The water drains through an opening in the wall to a klong at the rear.

The spigot has a faulty washer and drips constantly.

I walk out of the bathroom, tracing Merton's steps, across the dustless terrazzo floor and stand in the middle of the room. Here, this man, at once a never satisfied wanderer, but also the most stationary of men, had died. This orphan, who had found a home at Gethsemani and, for the first time having left it, would return in a simple sealed coffin.

Thomas Merton I had first read when I was a high school boy, needing both an anchor in my faith and a spirited inspiration to sustain it. Merton, who stayed with me throughout my lifetime, always struggling, always forthright, never satisfied with himself. Merton, who I sought to find so as to portray him on film.

The assistant directress is outside with my crew. I am suddenly alone in the room.

I kneel down on the floor. I touch my hand to the terrazzo. It is so cool to the touch, even in the sweltering heat of mid day.

I have been where Merton had been throughout America, at his hermitage at Gethsemani, the places he visited or where he lived in Europe and now, Asia. But in that moment, my hand pressed to the spot where he fell, I feel as close to him as I know I may ever be in this life.

He is still here. Unlike the room in Prades where he was born, he lives in the place where he died. And once knowing that, I will carry him with me in a special way forever.

Gilbertville, Massachusetts

Appendix

Centering Prayer

A BOUT A DECADE AGO a simple method of prayer which comes from our oldest Christian traditions found a new life and popularity within the American Church and especially among religious. Workshops were jointly sponsored by the Leadership Conference of Women Religious and the Conference of Major Superiors of Men in various parts of the country. Religious brought the method to prayer centers, retreat houses, campuses and other areas of ministry. This method was first taught in the west by Saint John Cassian who wrote of it in his *Conferences* early in the fifth century. He was reporting what he had learned from 'one of the oldest and holiest Fathers' of Scete who, in his turn, had taught the young Cassian what he had learned when he was young from one of the 'oldest and holiest Fathers'.

This ancient Christian method, as it was taught and shared in this renewal, received a new packaging and a new name. The name given it was 'Centering Prayer', a name inspired by Father

Louis' teaching. In speaking about this kind of prayer, he would say things like this:

> The fact is, however, that if you descend into the depths of your own spirit . . . and arrive somewhere near the center of what you are, you are confronted with the inescapable truth, at the very root of your existence, you.are in constant and immediate and inescapable contact with the infinite power of God.

And like this:

> A man cannot enter into the deepest center of himself and pass through the center into God unless he is able to pass entirely out of himself and empty himself and give himself to other people in the purity of selfless love.

  In a letter to a Sufi scholar, Aziz Ch. Abdul, Father Louis gives a rather long and clear description of his ordinary way of praying. It is quite simply Centering Prayer:

> Now you ask about my method of meditation. Strictly speaking I have a very simple way of prayer. It is centered entirely on attention to the presence of God and to His will and His love. That is to say that it is centered on *faith* by which alone we can know the presence of God. One might say this gives my meditation the character described by the Prophet as 'being before God as if you saw Him'. Yet it does not mean imagining anything or conceiving a precise image of God, for to my mind this would be a kind of idolatry. On the contrary, it is a matter of adoring Him as all. . . . There is in my heart this great thirst to recognize totally the nothingness of all that is not God. My prayer is then a kind of praise rising up out of the center of Nothingness and Silence. If I am still present 'myself' this I recognize as an obstacle. If He wills He can then make the Nothingness into a total clarity. If He does not will, then the Nothingness

actually seems to itself to be an object and remains an obstacle. Such is my ordinary way of prayer, or meditation. It is not 'thinking about' anything, but a direct seeking of the Face of the Invisible. Which cannot be found unless we become lost in Him who is Invisible.

Among Merton's literary legacy there is a manuscript marked, 'Not for publication'. It is entitled 'School of the Spirit'. Much of it has been incorporated into later works. In this incomplete manuscript Tom tells us that 'to live in the fullest sense is to know and to love God the author of life in the center of our soul'. Withdrawing from the multiplicity of objects outside ourselves, rising above the level of argumentation and discourse which can only attain to a remote reflection of God's truth, we seek by the act of living faith to find God present within ourselves.

It is a matter of faith and communion. As Toms tells us in *New Seeds of Contemplation,* if we succeed in emptying our minds of every thought and every desire, we may indeed withdraw into the center of ourselves and concentrate everything within us upon the center where our life springs out of God. Yet we will not by this purely human effort find God. No natural exercise can bring us into personal contact with him. Unless he utters himself within us, speaks his own name in the center of our souls, we will no more know him than a stone knows the ground upon which it rests in its inertia. But when we enter within in faith and love, the point of our contact with him opens and we pass through the center of our nothingness and enter into the infinite reality at the center of his Being where we awaken as our true selves. 'Draw all the powers of the soul', Tom tells us, 'down from its deepest center to rest in silent expectancy for the coming of God', poised in tranquil and effortless concentration upon the point of our dependency on him.

What we are grasping for is a rediscovery of the immanence of our God. But 'the immanentism of Asian religions, fixed and static in exstasis, will not quite do'. We want to recover the New Testament awareness that our God has one indestructible temple here on earth: the human person, where he dwells as a living God. Although the word 'center' seems to express something static, it is truly understood only when we see it dynamically. It is grace and presence. According to 'A New Christian Consciousness', it is an encounter with God 'not as Being but as Freedom and Love'. In *New Seeds of Contemplation,* Tom describes it quite dynamically: 'A door opens in the center of our being and we seem to fall through it into immense depths which although they are infinite are all accessible to us; all eternity seems to have become ours in this one placid and breathless contact.' We have sunk into the center of our own poverty and there we have felt the doors fly open into infinite Freedom. Then we simply abide there, rest there in the Reality: 'In silence, hope, expectation, and unknowing, the man of faith abandons himself to the divine will not as to an arbitrary and magic power whose decrees must be spelt out from cryptic ciphers but as to the stream of reality and of life itself. The sacred attitude is then one of deep and fundamental respect for the real in whatever form it may present itself.'

Centering Prayer is a very simple way of prayer which can be used by anyone who wants to be with God, to experience his love and presence. It is a prayer of longing that leads into a prayer of Presence.

First of all, we settle ourselves down quietly. Most of us pray best sitting down, but we can take any posture that works well for us. It is best if the back is fairly straight and well-supported. If we gently close our eyes, we immediately begin to quiet down, for we use a lot of our psychic energy in seeing.

Once we are settled, we turn our attention to the Lord present within us. We know he is there by faith, that is, we know he is there because he said so. In love we turn ourselves over to him. For these twenty minutes we are all his. He can do with us whatever he wants. This prayer is a pure gift, a gift of self in love.

In order to be able to abide quietly and attentively with our Beloved, we use a love word, a prayer word — a simple word that expresses our being to the Lord in love. It might well be our favorite name for him: Lord, Jesus, Father, Love . . . whatever is meaningful for us. We just let that word be there, to keep us attentive to him. It is not an effortful ejaculation or a constantly repeated *mantra,* but rather a sigh of love, a murmur of love, a 'being to'.

Whenever, during the time of our prayer, we become aware of anything else, we simply use our love word to return to the Lord. Some days we will have to use the word a great deal: there may be a lot of commotion around us or in us. No matter. Each time we use it, each time we return to him, it is a perfect gift of self to him in love. Other days we may not need to use our word much at all. Fine! It really makes no difference. Simply, these twenty minutes are all his to do with as he likes. We do not seek anything for ourselves. It is pure gift. It is not in the twenty minutes we will be aware of things. All our attention is on him. It is outside the time of prayer that we will begin to see the difference, as the fruits of the Spirit—love, peace, joy, kindness . . .—begin to flourish in our lives.

At the end of our twenty minutes, we do not want to jump right back into activity. We have gone very deep, even if we do not seem to sense it. So we want to end our prayer very gently. I suggest praying interiorly, very slowly, the Our Father. Let each phrase come forth with all its meaning. In this the Lord will teach us much. And the deep peace of our contemplative prayer will flow into our active lives.

It is a prayer of experience, so we can only know it by experience. We always urge people learning this prayer to make a commitment to themselves to practice the prayer faithfully, twice a day, for thirty days. Then, perhaps with a close friend for some one else can usually see better than we, look and see what has been the fruit of the prayer in our lives. If the way we were praying before was producing better fruit, don't hesitate to return to it. But if this simple prayer of listening, attentive love has been good for us, then by all means continue it. The important thing is that we do pray regularly and allow God to be to us the source of love, life, peace and happiness that he wants to be.

A Summary

To sum up this simple traditional method of being to the Lord:

Centering Prayer

+ + Sit relaxed and quiet + +

1. Be in faith and love to God who dwells in the center of your being.

2. Take up a love word and let it be gently present, supporting your being to God in faith-filled love.

3. Whenever you become aware of anything else, simply, gently return to the Lord with the use of your prayer word.

+ + Let the Our Father (or some other prayer) pray itself.

Centering Prayer is not an end in itself; no prayer is. Prayer is a moment in life, it is life. We want all life to be prayer, that is, to be a living communion with God and a living out of that communion, a living out of our true oneness with God. That is the center which we first seek to open ourselves to through the practice of Centering Prayer. On the Sunday before Christmas in 1965 Tom came down from the hermitage to speak to the community and he spoke of this:

> What matters is the freedom to be in contact with the center. It is from this center that all comes. We have to be in contact with that deep inner center; we have to face the possibility of the destruction of all else to know that this can never be destroyed. We can't get there by study, analysis, digging. Psychiatrists can't get to it. Not even the devil. Only God. It is the real you. This is where all freedom comes from, the source of all freedom. You can't find it by hunting for it. Leave it be and it will be. You have to school yourself to choose what lets this be; this is what the life of prayer is. Learn never to choose things that throw lots of static in this center. Choose to handle things in a way that remains open to this center.

Freedom lies, then, in our capacity to choose what really is. And this comes out of being centered, in touch with ourselves. If we are manipulating life, trying to correspond to some image or ideal or concept of ourselves, we are not open to the center, to our true self, to things being what they are. Choosing always as best we can the will of God — what is — keeps us in contact with the center.

One of Father Louis' great contributions was his insistence that the contemplative experience both as a way of praying and as a dimension of life, is meant for all:

> I have not only repeated the affirmation that contemplation is real, but I have insisted on its simplicity, sobriety, humility and its integration in *normal Christian life*. This is what needs to be stressed. . . . it is surely legitimate for anyone to desire and to seek this fulfillment, this experience of reality, this entrance into truth.

M.B.P

Assumption Abbey
Ava, Missouri

CISTERCIAN PUBLICATIONS INC.

Kalamazoo, Michigan

TITLES LISTING

THE CISTERCIAN FATHERS SERIES

Texts and Studies
in the
Monastic Tradition

* Temporarily out of print   *† Forthcoming*

THE CISTERCIAN STUDIES SERIES

* Temporarily out of print   *† Forthcoming*

Eight Chapters on Perfection and Angel's Song
(Walter Hilton)

Creative Suffering (Iulia de Beausobre)

Bringing Forth Christ. Five Feasts of the Child
Jesus (St Bonaventure)

Gentleness in St John of the Cross

Distributed in North America only for Fairacres Press.

DISTRIBUTED BOOKS

St Benedict: Man with An Idea (Melbourne Studies)

The Spirit of Simplicity

Benedict's Disciples (David Hugh Farmer)

The Emperor's Monk: A Contemporary Life of
Benedict of Aniane

A Guide to Cistercian Scholarship (2nd ed.)

*North American customers may order
through booksellers or directly
from the publisher:*

Cistercian Publications
WMU Station
Kalamazoo, Michigan 49008
(616) 383-4985

*Cistercian Publications are available in
Britain, Europe and the Common-
wealth through A. R. Mowbray &
Co Ltd   St Thomas House   Oxford
OX1 1SJ.
For a sterling price list, please consult
Mowbray's General Catalogue.*

*Cistercian monks and nuns have been
living lives of prayer & praise, meditation &
manual labor since the twelfth century.
They are part of an unbroken tradition
which extends back to the fourth century
and which continues today in the Catholic
church, the Orthodox churches, the
Anglican communion, and, most recently,
in the Protestant churches.*

*Share their way of life and their search for
God by reading Cistercian Publications.*

*A complete catalogue of texts-in-
translation and studies on early,
medieval, and modern Christian
monasticism is available at no cost
from Cistercian Publications.*